Kant's Transcendental Deduction

STANFORD SERIES IN PHILOSOPHY

Studies in Kant and German Idealism

Eckart Förster, Editor

Kant's Transcendental Deductions

The Three *Critiques* and the *Opus postumum*

ECKART FÖRSTER

Editor

STANFORD UNIVERSITY PRESS
Stanford, California

Stanford University Press
Stanford, California
© 1989 by the Board of Trustees of the
Leland Stanford Junior University
Printed in the United States of America

CIP data appear at the end of the book

Preface

In the Preface to his *Critique of Pure Reason* (1781) Kant wrote: "I know no inquiries which are more important for exploring the faculty which we entitle understanding, and for determining the rules and limits of its employment, than those which I have instituted . . . under the title *Deduction of the Pure Concepts of Understanding*. They are also those which have cost me the greatest labor—labor, as I hope, not unrewarded."

Kant's expectations were at first disappointed; the reception of the deduction fell short of what he had hoped for. Early reviewers of the *Critique* failed to penetrate the complexities of the difficult argument with which Kant tried to prove that the pure concepts of the understanding relate a priori to objects. As one of them put it succinctly, the part of the *Critique* that, in view of its importance, should be the clearest is in fact the most obscure.

Kant acknowledged this obscurity in a long footnote to the Preface of the *Metaphysical Foundations of Natural Science* (1786), pointing out that the shortest way is hardly ever the first the understanding becomes aware of in its inquiries. Confident that a more perspicuous presentation of the deduction was now within his reach, he promised to take the earliest opportunity to clarify his argument.

Such an opportunity presented itself to Kant only one year later, when a second edition of the *Critique of Pure Reason* was called for.

Preface

For this edition, Kant completely rewrote the chapter on the transcendental deduction of the categories. Perhaps even more than its predecessor in the first edition, this argument has fascinated philosophers ever since. But, as 200 years of scholarship suggest, the perspicuity that Kant foresaw for the new version is not one of its many merits. Questions about the details and structure of this argument, and about how the two versions compare, continue to preoccupy Kant's readers. When facing the many problems posed by the transcendental deduction of the categories, the reader may find little consolation in the fact that Kant himself, long after the second edition of the *Critique,* continued to struggle with this argument (C 12 : 222–25).

There is another dimension to the problem of understanding Kant's deduction of the categories that must be mentioned. Kant's aim in writing the *Critique* was to establish the possibility of metaphysics as a science, by determining the origin, limit, and extent of possible a priori knowledge. The *Critique* is designed as the propaedeutics for the entire system of pure reason—the metaphysics of nature as well as of morals. That another critique might be required to secure metaphysics, or one of its branches, in its proper employment is a thought entirely foreign to the *Critique* of 1781.

Yet shortly after, even before the second edition of the *Critique of Pure Reason,* Kant began to realize that the metaphysics of morals requires a separate propaedeutic study, and with it a transcendental deduction of its own. The *Groundwork of the Metaphysics of Morals* (1785), which culminates in a deduction of the moral law, was designed to fill this lacuna. Three years later, however, Kant followed this with a *Critique of Practical Reason,* in which the moral law is presented as a fact of reason, in no need of special justification; instead, Kant here proceeds from the moral law to a deduction of the concept of freedom.

Whether Kant's position in the second *Critique* amounts to a revision of that of the *Groundwork* or merely reflects a shift of emphasis is a question of considerable controversy. However that may be, the question of how any deductions in his moral philosophy relate to, and compare with, Kant's master argument in the *Critique of Pure Reason* suggests itself almost immediately. Any comprehensive interpretation of the transcendental deduction of the categories in the first *Critique* should also elucidate the structure of deductions in Kant's ethics.

Such an interpretation should also be able to accommodate the two transcendental deductions Kant offered two years later when the critical undertaking was further expanded with a *Critique of Judgment* (1790). Here, Kant provides a deduction of the principle of a formal purposiveness of nature, developed in the two versions of the Introduction to this text, and a deduction of pure aesthetic judgments or judgments of taste, to be found in the *Critique of Aesthetic Judgment*.

Finally, we must notice that in the large, unfinished work that has become known as his *Opus postumum*, Kant also speaks, for a while at least, of a deduction of an ether, that is, of the collective whole of the moving forces of matter. In other parts of this text, he develops arguments that have suggested to some commentators that Kant, during the last years of his life, worked on a new transcendental deduction of the categories.

What unity is there in this diversity? Can a better understanding of Kant's strategy in his transcendental deductions result from examining these arguments, not in isolation but in relation to their counterparts in the other domains of Kant's philosophizing?

To explore this possibility, and to commemorate the bicentennial of the second edition of the *Critique of Pure Reason*, the Stanford Philosophy Department invited some of today's leading Kant scholars to discuss their research on the various forms transcendental deductions take in Kant's work. With two exceptions, the papers collected in this volume were presented at the resulting conference, held at Stanford University in April 1987. Wolfgang Carl read his paper the day before the conference at a colloquium of the Stanford Philosophy Department. Lewis White Beck, although unable to be present at the time, kindly agreed to write a commentary on Carl's paper. All papers are published here for the first time.

The conference was made possible by generous grants from the Division of Research Programs of the National Endowment for the Humanities, the Goethe Institute of San Francisco, the Provost of Stanford University, its Dean of Humanities and Sciences, and the Stanford Humanities Center. I record their support with gratitude. I was also fortunate to enjoy a Fellowship at the Stanford Humanities Center, and the intellectual stimulation and freedom from other responsibilities that come with it, during the time when this volume was in its various stages of preparation.

In addition, I owe special thanks to three friends: to my colleague John Perry, without whose unflagging encouragement and good

Preface

advice the conference would hardly have been a success; to Helen
Tartar, humanities editor at Stanford University Press, who with pa-
tience and superior skill transformed some rough manuscripts into
potential chapters of a book; and to Ingrid Deiwiks, my wife, whose
continuous enthusiasm and impeccable copy-editing carried the
project through all the inevitable moments of crisis.

E.F.

Stanford, California
July 1988

Contents

Contents

Contributors

H E N R Y E. A L L I S O N is Professor of Philosophy at the University of California, San Diego. He has written on a variety of topics in the history of modern philosophy and the philosophy of religion. He is the author of *Lessing and the Enlightenment* (1966), *Benedict de Spinoza* (2d ed. 1987), and *Kant's Transcendental Idealism* (1983). He has also edited and translated *The Kant – Eberhard Controversy* (1973).

L E W I S W H I T E B E C K is Burbank Professor of Intellectual and Moral Philosophy Emeritus, University of Rochester. He has edited and translated many of Kant's writings and has written extensively in the history of modern philosophy. Among his many publications are *A Commentary on Kant's Critique of Practical Reason* (1960), *Early German Philosophy* (1969), and *The Actor and the Spectator* (1975).

R E I N H A R D B R A N D T is Professor of Philosophy at the University of Marburg and Director of the Kant Archiv, Marburg. He has edited, among other things, a volume on *Rechtstheorien der Aufklärung* (1981) and is coeditor of *Kant-Forschungen*. His books include *Eigentumstheorien von Grotius bis Kant* (1974) and *Die Interpretation philosophischer Werke* (1984).

W O L F G A N G C A R L is Professor of Philosophy at the University of Göttingen. He is the author of *Existenz und Predikation* (1976) and

Contributors

Sinn und Bedeutung (1982) and has recently completed a book on *Kants Deduktion der Kategorien vor 1781.*

ECKART FÖRSTER is Assistant Professor of Philosophy at Stanford University. He is the editor and translator (with Michael Rosen) of Kant's *Opus postumum*, to be published next year.

PAUL GUYER is Professor of Philosophy at the University of Pennsylvania, Philadelphia, and chairman of his department. In addition to many journal articles he has authored two books, *Kant and the Claims of Taste* (1979) and *Kant and the Claims of Knowledge* (1987). He has also coedited a volume of *Essays in Kant's Aesthetics* (1982).

SIR STUART HAMPSHIRE is Bonsall Professor of Philosophy at Stanford University and formerly Warden of Wadham College, Oxford. He has published widely in philosophy and related areas, especially on literature. His many books include *Spinoza* (2d ed. 1987), *Thought and Action* (2d ed. 1982), *Public and Private Morality* (1978), and *Morality and Conflict* (1983).

DIETER HENRICH is Professor of Philosophy at the University of Munich. He has published studies in a number of philosophical areas, most notably on Kant, Fichte, Hegel, and Hölderlin. Among his many books are *Der ontologische Gottesbeweis* (1960), *Hegel im Kontext* (1967), *Identität und Objektivität* (1976), *Fluchtlinien* (1982), and *Der Gang des Andenkens* (1987).

BARBARA HERMAN is Associate Professor of Philosophy at the University of Southern California, Los Angeles. She has published many articles in moral and political philosophy and is currently working on a book on Kant's moral philosophy.

ROLF-PETER HORSTMANN is Professor of Philosophy at the University of Munich. The author of many articles on topics in Kant and German Idealism, he has also edited several books, among them two volumes of the *Historisch-kritische Hegel Ausgabe*. His book *Ontologie und Relationen* appeared in 1984.

JOHN RAWLS is James Bryant Conant University Professor, Harvard University. He has published many influential articles in moral and political theory. His book *A Theory of Justice* (1971) has been translated into eight languages.

Contributors

SIR PETER F. STRAWSON is Waynflete Professor of Metaphysical Philosophy Emeritus in the University of Oxford and a former fellow of Magdalen College. He has published widely in philosophy of language, logic, epistemology, metaphysics, and other areas. His books include *Individuals* (1959), *The Bounds of Sense* (1966), *Freedom and Resentment* (1974), *Skepticism and Naturalism* (1985), and *Analyse et métaphysique* (1985).

BURKHARD TUSCHLING is Professor of Philosophy at the University of Marburg. He has edited *Probleme der "Kritik der reinen Vernunft"* (1984) and is the author of several books, including *Metaphysische und transzendental Dynamik in Kants Opus postumum* (1971) and *Rechtsform und Produktionsverhältnisse* (1976).

JULES VUILLEMIN is Professor of Philosophy at the Collège de France. He is the author of a variety of studies on topics especially in the history of philosophy and philosophy of science. His books include *L'héritage kantien et la révolution copernicienne* (1954), *Physique et métaphysique kantiennes* (1955), and *What Are Philosophical Systems?* (1986).

Abbreviations and Translations

All references to Kant's works are given in the text, using an abbreviation for the work cited, followed by volume and page number (and, in some cases, line number) of the *Akademie* edition of *Kants gesammelte Schriften*, Berlin and Leipzig, 1900–. Since the translations of Kant's texts usually give the *Akademie* pagination in the form of marginal numbers, page numbers of the English editions have been omitted. References to the *Critique of Pure Reason* are to the standard pagination of the first and second editions, indicated as "A" and "B" respectively.

The authors in this volume have frequently amended the existing translations, without explicitly indicating so, to gain a more exact or felicitous phrasing. Abbreviations and translations used are as follows.

A/B   *Critique of Pure Reason*. Translated by Norman Kemp Smith. London and Basingstoke, 1973.

Anthr   *Anthropology from a Pragmatic Point of View*. Translated by Mary J. Gregor. The Hague, 1974.

C   Kant's correspondence. Partly translated by Arnulf Zweig. In *Kant: Philosophical Correspondence 1759–99*. Chicago, 1967.

Abbreviations and Translations

CJ   *Critique of Judgment.* Translated by James Meredith. Oxford, 1952.

CP   *Critique of Practical Reason.* Translated by Lewis White Beck. Indianapolis, 1956.

DSS *Dreams of a Spirit Seer.* Translated by John Manolesco. New York, 1969.

E   *The Kant-Eberhard Controversy: On the Discovery According to Which Any New Critique of Pure Reason Has Been Made Superfluous by an Earlier One.* Translated by Henry E. Allison. Baltimore, 1973.

FI   *First Introduction to the Critique of Judgment.* Translated by James Haden. Indianapolis, 1965.

Gr   *Groundwork of the Metaphysics of Morals.* Translated by H. J. Paton. London, 1948.

ID   *On the Form and Principles of the Sensible and the Intelligible World (Inaugural Dissertation).* Translated by John Handyside and Lewis White Beck. In *Kant's Latin Writings.* Edited by Lewis White Beck. New York, 1986.

MFNS *Metaphysical Foundations of Natural Science.* Translated by James Ellington. Indianapolis, 1970.

MM   *The Metaphysics of Morals, Part II: The Doctrine of Virtue.* Translated by Mary J. Gregor. New York, 1964.

Mp   *The Use in Natural Philosophy of Metaphysics Combined with Geometry. Part I: Physical Monadology (Monadologia physica).* Translated by Lewis White Beck. In *Kant's Latin Writings.*

Nd   *A New Exposition of the First Principles of Metaphysical Knowledge (Nova dilucidatio).* Translated by John A. Reuscher. In *Kant's Latin Writings.*

NM   *Versuch, den Begriff der negativen Größen in die Weltweisheit einzuführen* (Attempt to Introduce the Concept of Negative Magnitudes into Philosophy). No translation available.

Op   *Opus postumum.* Partly translated by Eckart Förster and Michael Rosen. In *Kant's Opus postumum: A Selection.* Cambridge, forthcoming.

OPB *The One Possible Basis For a Demonstration of the Existence of God.* Translated by Gordon Treash. New York, 1979.

OS   *On the Old Saw: "That May Be Right in Theory, but It Won't Hold in Practice."* Translated by E. B. Ashton. Philadelphia, 1974.

OT   *What Is Orientation in Thinking?* Translated by Lewis White Beck. In *Kant's Critique of Practical Reason and Other Writings on Moral Philosophy.* Chicago, 1949.

Prol   *Prolegomena to Any Future Metaphysics.* Translated by Paul Carus and Lewis White Beck. In *Kant Selections.* Edited by Lewis White Beck. New York, 1988.

R   Kant's *Reflexionen.* No translation available.

Rel   *Religion Within the Limits of Reason Alone.* Translated by Theodore M. Green and Hoyt H. Hudson. New York, 1960.

The Precritical Beginnings

Kant's First Drafts of the Deduction of the Categories

WOLFGANG CARL

Kant's *Nachlaß* contains several drafts of a deduction of the categories, written both before and after the publication of the *Critique of Pure Reason*. Although Kant himself published two versions of this central piece of his theoretical philosophy, there are at least two reasons to study these drafts more closely, apart from an interest in Kant's intellectual biography. First, the deduction of the categories is one of the most difficult parts of the *Critique*. Modern commentators have referred to it as "the mystery" or as "the jungle."[1] By taking account of the drafts, one can see more clearly Kant's central aims and the possible arguments available to him. Second, the first edition of the *Critique of Pure Reason* leaves us very good reason to take account of earlier drafts. We know that the final version of the *Critique* was written within four or five months, but Kant had been working on it, and especially on the deduction of the categories, for almost ten years. Kant himself admitted that, because of the manner of its final production, the *Critique* "contains a certain carelessness or precipitance in the way of writing, and certain obscurities as well" (C 10:272). By looking at the material left over from his work during those ten years, one might be able to correct the defects of the published version, which Kant himself mentions. The attempt is at least worth making, and it is a new attempt in a field that has been treated in many ways by many interpreters, who have considered only the published versions.

After the publication of the Inaugural Dissertation in 1770, Kant did not publish anything at all in theoretical philosophy for over ten years. But documents have been preserved that show clearly that he worked very hard on the problems of the *Critique*. These documents are of three kinds. First, there are letters, mainly addressed to his former pupil Marcus Herz, in which he reports his work. Second, there are notes, called *Reflexionen*, which he made in his copies of A. G. Baumgarten's *Metaphysica* and G. F. Meier's *Auszug aus der Vernunftlehre*; these were the textbooks for his lectures on metaphysics and logic. The editor of these notes has included some *Lose Blätter*— *Zettel*, so to speak—that reflect Kant's thinking on various topics independent of the textbooks. Third, there are copies of his lectures made by students. This material is relevant in different ways to reconstructing the development of Kant's thought in the 1770's. For the prehistory of the deduction of the categories, in particular, it is especially important that we have three drafts for such a deduction in the *Nachlaß*, which differ from each other in important ways.

The first draft comes from the early 1770's and explains the relation between categories and objects by pointing out that the categories are conditions of the possibility of experience (R4629–34, 17:614–19). The argument is based on the thesis that such conditions are conditions of the objects of experience. A second draft is written partly on the back of a letter to Kant from May 1775 belonging to the *Zettel* of the so-called *Duisburg'sche Nachlaß* (R4674–84, 17:643–73). Kant starts with the notion of apperception and tries to discover a connection between the fact that different representations belong to one consciousness and the use of the categories in certain judgments. In a third draft, also written on the back of a letter to Kant from January 1780, the notion of apperception belongs to a transcendental theory of our cognitive faculties, and the relation between categories and objects is explained by the operations of the so-called transcendental faculty of imagination (23:18–20). This draft will not be discussed here.

The sequence of these drafts gives rise to at least three questions. First, the connection between apperception and judgment, which is strongly emphasized in the deduction of the categories of the second edition of the *Critique*, is earlier than the first edition's account in terms of a transcendental theory of our cognitive faculties. Why did Kant pick up his earlier draft for the second edition? To answer this question would require a comparative study of the two published versions of the deduction, which is beyond the scope of this essay.

The second question concerns the relation between the first draft, which argues from the conditions of the possibility of experience, and the other two, which are based on the notion of apperception. Why did Kant move from an argument that, as we shall see, is more or less similar to what is called "objective deduction" in the first edition to an argument that makes the notion of apperception the cornerstone of his reasoning? In the first part of my paper I will explain this switch by pointing out two different claims Kant made about his project for a deduction of the categories.

The last question concerns the two versions of a deduction starting from the notion of apperception. Why did Kant finally come up with an argument given in terms of a transcendental theory of cognitive psychology—a theory that he invented and that invites so many psychological misunderstandings? In the second part of my paper I will show the reasons for this development, which are mainly connected with deficiencies in his notion of apperception in 1775.

So far as we know, Kant first defines the task of the deduction of the categories in his famous letter to Marcus Herz of February 21, 1772. There he states the question that gives the "key to the whole secret of hitherto still obscure metaphysics"—namely, "what is the ground of the relation of that in us which we call 'representation' to the object?" (C 10:130). Greater precision on three points can suggest why a deduction of the categories is supposed to answer that question. First, in this letter Kant distinguishes between two different classes of representations. On the one hand are representations that are causally related to their objects: either the effects of their objects (empirical representations) or the causes of their objects (like the representation of a moral end). On the other hand are representations that are not causally related to their objects. The key question concerns only the latter. Thus, the deduction must explain a noncausal relation between representations and their objects. Second, Kant is not interested in explaining just any kind of relation between representations and their objects, but the special case in which the "understanding may form for itself concepts of things completely a priori, with which concepts the things must necessarily agree" (C 10:131). In other words, these concepts must be related to things in such a way that things will *necessarily* correspond to them. Finally, one must mention that Kant considers only representations of things that affect us in some way or other, that are accessible only by way of experience. The "intellectual representations" of the *Dissertatio* are explicitly excluded. The key question of the Herz letter thus concerns an explanation of how certain concepts a priori, which are not causally related to their objects, can refer to things accessible by experience in such a way that these things correspond necessarily to those concepts. This is the question that a deduction of the categories is supposed to answer.

But even in this more explicit and more precise formulation the term "thing" is ambiguous. Kant uses the expressions *Sachen*, *Dinge*, or *Gegenstände*, which may be interpreted in two different ways. Referring to his earlier Dissertation, he says: "I silently passed over the further question of how a representation that refers to an object without being in any way affected by it can be possible. . . . But by what means are these things given to us, if not by the way in which they affect us?" (C 10 : 130). In the *Critique of Pure Reason* the representations that are related to their objects by being affected by them are called "empirical intuitions," and their objects are called "appearances" (A20/ B34). According to this interpretation, the correspondence to be explained by a deduction is a relation between categories and appearances. But in the same letter to Herz, Kant is discussing the correspondence between the categories and the objects of experience.[2] These objects, here called *Sachen*, are given through sensations as well as thought through a concept. In a remark of the early 1770's, we read: "In every experience there is something through which an object is given to us, and something through which it is thought" (R4634, 17 : 618.17–18). The object of experience, therefore, is something that is given through sensations as well as thought through concepts. According to this interpretation, the relation to be explained by a deduction of the categories concerns their relation to objects of experience.

These two explanations saying to what the categories are supposed to correspond give rise to different determinations of what a deduction of the categories must explain. According to the first, one must prove that whatever is given in empirical intuition must correspond to the categories. According to the second, one must conclude that whatever is accessible to experience must correspond to the categories. Because every experience is based on empirical intuition and what is experienced must be something given by empirical intuition, the conclusion of the deduction according to the first explanation entails the conclusion of the deduction according to the second explanation. But the converse does not hold: that all objects of experience must correspond to the categories does not imply that whatever is given by the senses corresponds to them. Conceivably, we may have empirical intuitions to which the categories cannot be applied, that is, which cannot be organized to make up an experience. As Kant himself points out in the *Critique*: "Appearances might very well be so constituted that the understanding should not find them to be in accordance with the conditions of its unity. Everything might be in such confusion that, for instance, in the series of appearances nothing presented itself which might yield a rule of synthesis and so answer to the concept of cause and effect" (A90/B123).

In the letter to Herz, Kant doesn't seem to be aware of these differences, and this provides a clue for understanding why he first tried to solve the problem of the deduction of the categories without using the notion of apperception, whereas after 1775 this notion became the cornerstone of his further attempts. I believe that this change must be interpreted as a shift from one to the other of the two different conceptions of what is proved by such a deduction. It is important to recognize this shift for two reasons. First, the shift makes clear why Kant introduced the notion of apperception at all. He wanted to use this notion to establish the more far-reaching conclusion that whatever is given by an empirical intuition must correspond to the categories. Second, the shift can explain the much-discussed distinction between an objective and a subjective deduction drawn by Kant in the first edition of the *Critique*.

In the letter to Herz, Kant announced that he would publish "within three months" a *Critique of Pure Reason* (C 10 : 132). The kind of answer he might have given to the "key question" of the letter can be seen from *Reflexionen*, which were written, according to Erich Adickes, around 1772 and which contain the first draft of a deduction of the categories. The question of how to explain the relation of concepts a priori to objects is called "the first and most important question," and "even to raise this question is meritorious" (R4633, 17 : 616.4–6; cf. R4470). His attempt to answer this question can be found in R4634:

If certain of our concepts contain only what makes experience possible for us, then they can be specified prior to experience; indeed, they can be specified a priori and with complete validity for everything we can ever encounter. In that case, although they are not valid of objects in general, they are valid of anything that can ever be given to us by experience, because they contain the conditions under which experience is possible. These propositions will, therefore, contain the conditions of possibility—not of things, but of experience. Things that cannot be given to us by any experience, however, are nothing for us (R4634, 17:618.1–10).

If we suppose that there are concepts that contain the conditions of the possibility of experience, then an argument from such conditions would answer the question of the Herz letter. These concepts should be valid for all experience as well as for whatever may be accessible through experience. That they are valid for all experience follows from the fact that these concepts contain the conditions under which experience is possible. If there is to be any experience at all, these conditions must be satisfied. By why should the concepts hold of whatever we may experience? The question asked in the Herz letter concerns the relation of the categories to objects, not their validity vis-à-vis a certain kind of knowledge, called "experience." Kant explicitly restricts the realm of objects to whatever can be given to us by experience. But even then it is far from evident that the concepts that are conditions of the possibility of experience are concepts that are related to the objects of experience. The fact that Kant was nevertheless convinced that this relation holds must be explained by his interpretation of the notion "object of experience." He says: "Things, however, which cannot be given to us by any experience, are nothing for us." That things are something "for us" implies, therefore, that they can be given to us by some experience. It is essential for the things that are something "for us" that they can be given in this way, that they cannot be conceived without this possibility. So things of the kind referred to must satisfy the conditions of the possibility of their experience. This epistemological specification of the notion of an object is the foundation of Kant's well-known and often-stated thesis that the conditions of the possibility of experience are the conditions of the possibility of objects of experience. I don't want to enter into a more detailed discussion of that thesis, but will confine myself to a consideration of what is relevant for answering the question of the Herz letter. Within the framework just outlined, this answer can be stated as follows: if the categories can be interpreted as concepts stating or containing conditions for the possibility of experience, and given the thesis mentioned above, then the categories will be related to objects. If they are related to objects at all, they will be related to objects of possible experience.

This argument is Kant's first attempt to solve the problem of the deduction of the categories. Two peculiarities of this argument become obvious as soon as Kant specifies which concepts contain conditions of the possibility of experience: "In every experience there is something through which an object is given to us, and there is something through which it is thought. If we take the conditions that lie in the activities of our mind, through which alone an object can be given, we can know something a priori about the objects. If we take the conditions through which alone an object can be thought, we can also know something a priori of all possible objects" (R4634, 17:618.17–23).

Kant starts from experience as a kind of knowledge that, insofar as its subject matter is concerned, is to be characterized in a complex way. Experience is knowledge of something that is given as well as thought. The conditions of the possibility of experience, therefore, can be divided into those that concern the fact that objects have to be given, and into those that are related to objects being thought. Space and time are conditions of the first kind, whereas the categories are conditions of the second kind. Both are related in the same way to objects—as conditions of the possibility of those objects' experience. Within the framework of the argument under consideration, it is essential that space and time on the one hand and the categories on the other be related in the same way to objects. The notion of conditions of the possibility of experience does not mark any difference between them.

A further peculiarity of this argument consists in a common presupposition for the relationship between objects and the conditions of the possibility of experience. As conditions of the possibility of experience, space and time as well as the categories are only related to objects if this possibility is realized, that is, if there are any objects of experience. The claim that they are related to objects if and only if they are conditions of the possibility of experience does not prove that they are in fact related to objects. We need the further premise that the concept of experience is not empty, that we have experience and that there are objects of experience. Without that premise the argument from the possibility of experience does not show that the categories are related to objects and, therefore, does not give an answer to the question asked in the Herz letter. Some interpreters of

Kant are convinced that the deduction of the categories in general relies on that premise, and that without the so-called *Faktum der Erfahrung* no transcendental argument will prove anything.[3] These commentators ignore the fact that in the *Critique*, in the section "Principles of Any Transcendental Deduction," Kant strongly criticizes the argument I have been considering up to now (A88–90/ B120–23) and gives the reasons why, after 1775, he came up with an argument that is based on the notion of apperception.

In his first draft of a deduction, the proof that the categories are related to objects of experience is given in direct analogy to the corresponding proof for space and time. In the *Critique*, however, Kant points to an important difference between space and time on the one hand and the categories on the other. The difference concerns the relevance of a deduction for them. If they are related to objects at all, this relation must be a priori. An explanation of "the manner in which concepts can relate a priori to objects" is called "a transcendental deduction" (A85/B117). Now, the difference between space and time on the one hand and the categories on the other hand consists in the fact that for the latter a transcendental deduction is "indispensably necessary," whereas it is necessary that if you give a deduction of space and time at all, it must be a transcendental deduction (A88/B121). Space and time permit such a deduction, but the categories require it.

Kant explains the differences as follows: "We have already been able with but little difficulty to explain how the concepts of space and time . . . must necessarily relate to objects. . . . For since only by means of such pure forms of sensibility can an object appear to us, and so be an object of empirical intuition, space and time are pure intuitions which contain a priori the condition of the possibility of objects as appearances" (A89/B121). Whatever may be an object of an empirical intuition fulfills these conditions because what is given by the senses is in time or space. They are the forms of our intuition and are formal conditions of whatever may be an object of our empirical intuition. But with the categories it is otherwise. They "do not represent the conditions under which objects are given in intuition" (A89/ B122). This is important not for the reason that the categories are not forms of intuition but because they are not, like the forms of intuition, formal conditions of the objects of empirical intuition. As Kant explicitly states, "objects may, therefore, appear to us without being necessarily related to the functions of understanding" (A89/B122).

That categories are not formal conditions of objects of empirical intuition makes room for the possibility that we have a manifold of sensuous data without being able to organize them according to the categories. Kant describes this possibility as the case that we might have "intuition without thought [*gedankenlose Anschauung*], but not knowledge," or "that appearances would crowd in upon the soul, and yet be such as would never allow of experience" (A111). Kant wants to exclude this possibility by showing that the categories have "objective validity," and to show this is nothing other than to give a transcendental deduction of them. So the deduction of the categories—in this new version—must prove that there can be no objects of empirical intuition, that is, appearances that cannot be organized according to the categories. In other words, it must prove the validity of the categories for all possible appearances.

This project differs substantially from the one in the first draft. In the first place, it concerns a relation between the categories and appearances according to the first explanation in the Herz letter of what has to be shown by a deduction of the categories—as opposed to the objects of experience that are given through intuition as well as thought through a concept. This project, second, is based on a fundamental difference between the relations of space and time to appearances and the relations of the categories to them. The proof that relations of the former kind hold can be given by reflecting on the formal conditions of appearances; but, because "intuition stands in no need whatsoever of the functions of thought" (A91/B123), the second proof must proceed in a very different way. It has to be shown that appearances must exhibit a certain order or structure that is not due to our forms of intuition. And third, this project cannot take for granted what is called *das Faktum der Erfahrung*. It is experience itself, as a synthesis of empirical intuitions and concepts, that has to be proved. To prove the validity of the categories for all appearances is to show that experience as a certain form of organizing our sensory data is the only form in which we can have such data. That we have experience cannot any longer be presupposed; rather the necessity of experience must be proved. This is the aim of a subjective deduction, and because of this aim the notion of apperception is introduced within the framework of a deduction of the categories.[4]

The first draft of a subjective deduction is to be found in a series of *Zettel* that belong to the so-called *Duisburg'sche Nachlaß*, one of which is written on the back of a letter addressed to Kant on May 20,

1775. So this date may be used as a *terminus post quem*.[5] The notion of apperception appears for the first time within his theoretical philosophy in these notes. The object of an empirical intuition is called "appearance," and an "appearance of which we are conscious is perception" (R4679, 17:664.1). Perception is a conscious representation, and having such a representation includes knowing what the representation is a representation of. But, being a *conscious* representation, perception is also a representation belonging to somebody who knows that it is his representation. This knowledge is described by Kant as a consciousness of our "existence in our inner sense" (R4681, 17:667.28). What that means will become clearer with the following distinction: "Intuition is either of the object (*apprehensio*) or of ourselves; the latter (*apperceptio*) concerns all our cognitions" (R4575, 17:651.6–8). The intuition of ourselves is our consciousness of "our existence in our inner sense." The inner sense or apperception is the way in which we are conscious of ourselves. But Kant was well aware of the fact that it is misleading to describe apperception as a special kind of intuition that differs from the outer senses only by its object. In a later note he says: "Sense is either inner or outer; only one sense will be called inner, and we mean by that apperception. But this is no sense at all, we are rather conscious by that of the representations of outer sense as well as of those of inner sense. Apperception is only the relation of all representations to their common subject" (R224, 15:85). Thus, to understand apperception by analogy with any kind of perception is quite misleading, because it concerns all kinds of perception and representation and connects them with their "common subject." Apperception doesn't give us any special kind of perception, but it defines a certain manner of having them—namely, as perceptions of which we are conscious and which all belong to one common subject. Therefore, Kant describes apperception more correctly as a "perception of oneself as a thinking subject in general" (R4674, 17:647.14–15). This subject is essentially a "unitary subject" (*einiges Subjekt*) (R4673, 17:641.17). Its unity is "the condition of all apperception" (R4675, 17:651.13–14).

Given these explanations, we can define Kant's notion of apperception as the notion of a subject's consciousness of his unity, however different what he is thinking about and however different the kinds of his thinking may be. This subject is related to a manifold of representations, and apperception, being the consciousness of the unity of this subject, is a knowledge of something identical with regard to a manifold of different representations.

The reason Kant introduced this notion of apperception within the framework of a deduction of the categories becomes obvious from his claim about the relation between the unity of a thinking subject and the connection of its representations: "The condition of any apperception is the unity of a thinking subject. From that comes the connection (of the manifold) according to a rule" (R4675, 17 : 651.13–15). This can be interpreted in two ways, depending on the reference of "from that." The phrase can refer to the entire preceding sentence. In that case Kant claims that the unity of the subject as the condition of apperception allows the connection of the manifold according to a rule. Because of that condition, apperception is consciousness of an identical self, and the thesis Kant wanted to put forward would amount to something like this: consciousness of an identical self implies the connection of representations according to a rule. Let's call that thesis "the epistemological foundation of such a connection."

But one can also read the sentence in another way: "from that" may refer to the unity of the subject. In that case the connection of the manifold according to a rule would be founded on the unity of the thinking subject. Because of that unity, the representations must be connected in a certain way. I call this the "ontological foundation of the rule-connectedness of our representations," because the unity of the thinking subject itself is taken as the basis for the connection. Kant, in this context, makes only a claim for an argument; he doesn't give it, nor is it possible to decide on the basis of the text which kind of foundation he had in mind. But this question can be decided by looking more closely at the notion "function of apperception."

He claims that whatever is perceived "will be taken into the function of apperception" (R4676, 17 : 656.2–3). So, perceptions as conscious representations do not just belong to one consciousness; they belong to it in a certain way. To be more precise on that point, one must explain what is meant by "function." Kant speaks of "three functions of apperception which can be found in thinking of our own state" (R4674, 17–646.29–30). What are these three functions? In R4674 we read: "Apperception is the consciousness of thinking, i.e., of representations as they are posited in the mind. Here we find three exponents: (1) the relation to a subject, (2) the relation of subordination, (3) and of coordination" (17:647.16–19). These exponents or functions are without doubt the categories of relation. Thinking of our own state is for Kant being conscious of our representations; whenever we think of that state, we find these functions. Thus, our representations must be ordered according to them. They determine the relations between the subject of thinking and its various perceptions. This becomes clear from what follows the thesis that whatever is perceived will be taken into the function of apperception: "I am, I am thinking, thoughts are in me." These functions of apperception can be identified with the three categories of relation. They are the different ways in which a self is related to its representations. The sentence "I am" describes the relation of the I as a substance to its representations as accidents; the sentence "I am thinking" gives the relation of the I as a cause of its representations; and the last sentence, "Thoughts are in me," mentions the relation in which the I as a whole is related to its parts.[6] The functions of apperception, therefore, are the relations between the self and its representations.

To claim, as Kant does, that whatever is perceived will be taken into the function of apperception is to claim that all our perceptions are related to a thinking subject according to the categories of relation. Now, returning to the problem of how to read his argument for the "connection of the manifold according to a rule," one must say that he favored what I have called "the ontological foundation." If we assume that being connected in that way means the same as being taken into the function of apperception, then it is not the consciousness of our own identity, but the unity of the thinking subject that is the foundation of the connection of the manifold according to a rule. We shall soon see that for Kant at that time this unity is the unity of a mental substance, of a *res cogitans* in the sense of Rational Psychology.

To describe Kant's first "subjective deduction," then, one must start with his notion of an objective representation, or representation of an object. Kant claims that "an appearance is related to an object only because the relation, which is posited according to the conditions of intuition, is assumed to be determinable according to a rule" (R4676, 17:657.25–28). What he must prove is that the rules governing our representations of objects are connected with the functions of apperception in such a way that all perceptions belonging to the unity of apperception are representations of objects. Thus Kant wants to show that whatever will be taken into the function of apperception is necessarily a manifold of representations ordered according to rules or governed by the categories. How does he do this?

Kant takes for granted that we have perceptions. Perceptions are conscious representations that refer to appearances. Perceptions, as conscious representations, belong to the unity of a thinking subject and are related to that subject according to the functions of apperception. What follows from the fact that my perceptions are related in this way to my thinking self? It does *not* follow that the perceptions and their objects, the appearances, are related to each other in a certain way. The unity of the subject to which all perceptions belong does not give any unity to the perceptions themselves or to their objects. They may be totally unrelated to each other, although they all belong to one thinking subject. Kant was well aware of this: "The three relations in the mind require three analogies of appearance in order to change the subjective functions of the mind into objective ones and to make them into concepts of the understanding which give reality to the appearances" (R4675, 17:648.23–27). How can we effect this change?

Roughly speaking, Kant effects this change by moving from a necessary condition to a necessary and sufficient condition. He first claims that all appearances, being objects of perceptions, presuppose a unity of the mind—a unity that, according to his notion of apperception, is a necessary condition of perceptions as conscious representations. He then concludes that this is sufficient for a unity of these representations themselves (cf. R4678, 17:660.10–12). They have a unity just by belonging to a "unitary" subject. In Kant's words: "An appearance will be made objective by bringing it about that it is contained under a title of self-perception" (R4677, 17:658.4–5). The "titles of self-perception" are nothing but the functions of apperception, which govern the relations between perceptions and the thinking subject. If perceptions become representations of objects just by the fact that they are related to a thinking subject according to the functions of apperception, then all conscious representations must be representations of objects. The unity exhibited by representations of objects is just the unity of perceptions, which consists in belonging to one thinking subject.

Kant's precritical assignment of a special status to the unity of the thinking subject accounts for this identification of the unity of representations of an object with that of the perceptions that belong to one thinking subject. He writes: "The conditions a priori under which *a* (scil. a given representation) can refer to an object . . . can be discovered in the subject. This object can only be represented according to the relations (scil. of the subject) and is nothing but the subjective representation (of the subject) itself, but generalized, because I am the original of all objects" (R4674, 17:646.7–13). We are to understand quite literally this assertion that the conditions for relating given representations to objects can be discovered in the subject: these conditions are given by the subject because the representation of an object is nothing other than the representation of the subject. The self is the original of all objects—both the origin and the paradigmatic instance of them. Kant's favorite example is substance: the self is a substance, more precisely, the paradigmatic instance of a substance. As he says quite early: "The idea of substance comes really from the *representatione sui ipsius*" (R3921, 17:346.7–8; cf. R5294, R5295, R5297, 18:145–46).

In the Herz letter, as we saw, Kant asked how we can explain the fact that appearances are ordered according to the categories. The first draft of a subjective deduction gives the following answer. Appearances are objects of given perceptions. The conditions a priori of perceptions are also conditions a priori of the objects of perceptions. Perceptions are conscious representations and belong to the unity of a thinking subject. This implies that they are related to that subject according to the functions of apperception. But these functions are identical with the categories. Therefore, all appearances are ordered according to the categories.

I want to comment here on two points of this argument. First, when Kant for the first time introduces the notion of apperception within the framework of his theoretical philosophy, he combines the idea of the unity of apperception with the assumption of certain relations between our perceptions. In 1775 the basis for this connection is the unity of a thinking subject. After the discovery of the paralogisms he has to change his argument, but he never gives up the idea of such a combination.

Second is the remarkably straightforward identification of the functions of apperception with the categories. The claim that the "titles of self-perception" are identical with the categories is not convincing at all. There is no space here to sketch Kant's theory of the categories in 1775, but much earlier even than the Herz letter we find the categories connected with the forms of certain judgments. Because the functions of apperception are relations between the self as a mental substance and its perceptions, this identification with the categories is more a fancy than a well-founded suggestion. Kant gives no reason at all for correlating these relations with something based on judgments. But even if one could find an argument for the identification, it would not follow that our perceptions are representations of objects that are governed by rules and so exhibit a certain unity. T. Haering aptly states Kant's error: "Every act of apprehension relates the appearances to the unity of self-consciousness, and by that to a unity of themselves."[7] The error is that one takes a unity that consists in representations, belonging to a unitary subject, to be a unity exhibited by the representations themselves. Whereas the first unity is based on the unity of the thinking subject, the second unity concerns the representation's interconnectedness, which must be specified by reference not to the subject but to the content of the representations. The first kind of unity can be realized without the second one.

I want to return now to the questions with which I began. I observed that the drafts for a deduction of the categories before 1781 can be divided into two sets: an argument that the categories are conditions of the possibility of experience versus two arguments based entirely on the notion of apperception. These two sets correlate with two different possible aims for the deduction, which Kant identified in his letter to Herz in 1772: the validity of the categories for all objects of experience, or their validity for whatever may be given by the senses. Given his remarks in the *Critique*, in the chapter "The Principles of Any Transcendental Deduction," it is easy to understand why he didn't content himself with the deduction outlined in the first draft and went on to an argument based on apperception. These remarks can be read as a critical analysis of that draft, and they make explicit the reasons for the development of his thought in the so-called silent decade.

Closely related to the difference between the two sets of drafts is Kant's distinction in the Preface to the first edition of the *Critique* between an objective and a subjective deduction.[8] There he identifies as essential to his purposes the demonstration that the categories are conditions of the possibility of experience. He is referring to A93, where he attempts to prove that the categories are related "necessarily and a priori to objects of experience." The argument, the so-called objective deduction, is based on the premise that by means of the categories only "an object of experience can be thought." This argument is essentially similar to the one we know from the first draft. It is difficult to see how such an argument can cope with the problem stated by Kant himself three pages earlier: that there might be appearances to which we cannot apply the categories. I believe this problem forced him to change the argument and to base the deduction of the categories upon his theory of apperception. Kant's contemporaries, at least, followed the indications in the Preface and interpreted the deductions of the categories as proving that "experience is made possible by them," in the words of Johann Schultz—court preacher, professor of mathematics, and, according to Kant's own public declaration, the one "who understands my writings, at least the main points, in the way I want them to be understood" (C 12:367). For Schultz, the central piece of the deduction—the second and third sections of the second chapter of the Analytic—is only an appendix on the "subjective sources of the soul."[9] How could Kant acclaim such a misunderstanding, let alone induce it by his own remarks?

The first reactions to the *Critique* concentrate on the Transcendental Aesthetic and Transcendental Dialectic and more or less leave out the deduction of the categories. J. A. H. Ulrich, in his book *Institutiones Logicae et Metaphysicae*, is not interested in it,[10] nor is Dietrich Tiedemann in his rather critical review.[11] In an anonymous review of Ulrich's book—praised by Kant as "profound" (MFNS 4:474n)—Schultz declares that the objective reality of the categories is proved by their being necessary conditions of experience.[12] An exception is the review by Christian Gottfried Schütz, who gives an abstract of the second and third sections of the second chapter of the Analytic by interpreting them in terms of an "objective deduction."[13]

So, if Kant's contemporaries appreciate the deduction at all, they focus on the so-called objective deduction. By contrast, I believe that the subjective deduction is the most important and ambitious project for a deduction of the categories. But this project cannot be identified by reference to arguments that concern certain cognitive faculties, as H. J. Paton believed, nor can it be in general characterized as the "psychological part" of the deduction, one that Kant, fortunately, removed from the second edition, as A. Riehl and so many others hold. What is essential to a subjective deduction is its aim: to explain a connection between representations that belong to one consciousness and the application of the categories to them. The central task of a subjective deduction must be to show that there is some relation between the unity of apperception and a certain kind of conceptualization of what is given by the senses. Unlike an objective deduction, such an explanation cannot take for granted the fact that we have experience. "The task," as Kant remarked in a note in his copy of the *Critique*, is to explain "How is experience possible?" (23:25; cf. A128). C. F. von Weizsäcker and others have claimed that "one cannot deduce a priori that there is experience at all."[14] But that was what Kant aimed to do. The "analytic" strategy, as it is called in the *Prolegomena*—that is, to start from the fact that we have experience and then ask for the conditions of the possibility of experience (Prol §4, 4:274–75)—was Kant's first idea for a deduction of the categories, but not his last word on the matter.

Now, turning to the two drafts for a subjective deduction, I have given a rough sketch of the earlier one, which stems from 1775. We have seen that the apperception is based on the unity of the subject understood as a *res cogitans*. At that time the paralogisms were yet to be discovered; their discovery is to be dated rather late. Even in his lecture on metaphysics given about 1777 or later, Kant adopted the dogmatic position of Rational Psychology (28:224–27, 265–69). When he gave up this position, he radically changed his notion of apperception and its role within the framework of a deduction of the categories, as we can see from the third draft, written after January 1780 (23:18–20). Instead of founding apperception on the unity of a self taken as a mental substance, he developed the theory of synthetic unity of apperception, which takes account of the cooperation of basic cognitive faculties. The theory of cognitive faculties and the notion of synthesis, closely related to this theory, is often taken as a deplorable turn to psychologism in epistemology. But seen from his position in 1775, it is rather an attempt to explain the rule-connectedness of our representations by reference to the conditions under which representations belong to one consciousness, instead of by reference to the unity of the subject. An epistemological analysis of three basic features of knowledge, not an ontology of the thinking subject, becomes basic to the whole enterprise.

But one must see the point of this move within the overall development of Kant's thought. His notion of the synthetic unity of apperception has been criticized by Paul Guyer, who states that the connection between apperception and synthesis is based on the supposition of a Cartesian evidence of our self-identity.[15] But Kant makes no claim for such evidence, and such a claim would be of no help for the purpose for which the notion was introduced. P. F. Strawson wonders how a theory of synthesizing activities of the understanding is supposed to elucidate the conditions under which self-consciousness is possible, and he states disappointedly that Kant "does not really make it clear in the deduction how the doctrine of the mind's activity explains the possibility of ascribing experience to the one self." [16] Looking at the development of his thought, one immediately realizes that such an explanation was not what Kant was aiming at. The point of his notion of the synthetic unity of apperception was *not* to explain the possibility of self-ascription of experiences; this possibility was taken for granted and should be used, with the help of further assumptions about some basic features of our knowledge, to explain that representations could belong to one consciousness only if they would be combined according to certain rules. Strawson adopts the general strategy of by-passing the doctrine of synthesis altogether as being a piece of "transcendental psychology." But the so-called transcendental psychology of the first edition of the *Critique* can and should be understood in a new way, if one has a clearer view of the development of Kant's thought.

Two Ways of Reading Kant's Letter to Herz: Comments on Carl

LEWIS WHITE BECK

Professor Wolfgang Carl has made an important contribution to our understanding of the complexities of the transcendental deduction of the categories. Unlike those who embraced the "patchwork theory," he does not think (at least he does not assert) that the A-deduction is made up of actual (even if irrecoverable) writings of the 1770's; nor does he, like them, cut the deduction into small pieces, cutting across the bones instead of dissecting the joints of the argument (as Plato says). Rather, he sees only two major lines of division in the deductions of both A and B. Each is divided into an objective and a subjective deduction, the former working mostly without, the latter mostly within, the context of the transcendental unity of apperception. For these fairly easily distinguished parts of A, as well as for the more difficult distinction in B, Carl has found distinctive *Reflexionen* and other *Nachlaß*-passages that show Kant's earlier efforts to establish one or the other of these deductions without aid from the other. That the various stages in the arguments were temporally successive is perhaps not easy to show; but with short passages, there is unlikely to be dispute about which deduction encompasses a specific passage. Knowledge of these two competing efforts at a single deduction and their coexistence in both editions of the *Critique* makes for a welcome clarification of the proof-structure in both A and B. Unlike the classical patchwork theory, Carl's interpretation of the provenance of the different phases of the deduction simplifies the task of understanding the *Critique of Pure Reason*.

Professor Carl also contributes important information about, and a vivid interpretation of, what went on during the so-called silent decade. Because of the collection, collation, and publication of the lectures and a growing mastery of the *Reflexionen* of that period, I think it not too venturesome to hope that by the end of this century we may expect to have gained as good an understanding of the silent decade as we now have of earlier and later periods in Kant's career. Toward this goal, Professor Carl's paper and his projected book will be important *bahnbrechende* steps.

My only hesitation in accepting Carl's narrative of the silent decade arises from his understanding of the letter to Marcus Herz of February 21, 1772. Since I have already dealt extensively with this letter,[1] I can be brief. I see the letter as Kant's report of his last effort to answer some questions he should have raised in the Inaugural Dissertation, questions which in 1772 he did not yet see cannot be answered at all. This is to read the letter as backward looking, and I agree with H. J. De Vleeschauwer when he writes "la lettre de 1772 est plutôt un bilan que l'ebouche d'un programme futur."[2]

Professor Carl, on the contrary, reads the letter as a harbinger of the problem Kant faced in the A-deduction nine years later, viz., the problem of how there can be a priori concepts that necessarily apply to objects sensibly given to us. Knowing the *Critique of Pure Reason* and, even more, knowing the *Reflexionen* of the 1770's incline one to see the letter, as Carl does, as an anticipation of the *problem* of the *Critique* and the *Reflexionen* as anticipations of the *Critique*'s solution to these problems. But without the benefit of hindsight (a benefit Kant regrettably lacked when writing to his pupil), *I* cannot see any clear evidence that in 1772 Kant's problem was how a priori concepts must be applicable to sensible objects (the problem of the *Critique*) rather than the problem of how there can be a priori knowledge of *intelligibilia* without intellectual intuition (the problem Kant now discovers he had overlooked in the Inaugural Dissertation).

Any reader of the Inaugural Dissertation must have faced this question when Kant asserts that we human beings have no intellectual intuition (ID §10, 2:396) and that sensible intuition leads only to subreptive concepts of the intelligible world (ID §25, 2:412–13). Something important was missing from Kant's account of knowledge of noumena. When Kant tells Marcus Herz that "I noticed that

I still lacked something essential" and "I asked myself: What is the ground of the relation of that in us which we call 'representation' to the object?" (C 10:130), he quickly disposes of the relation of representations to empirical objects, where the representation is caused by the object, and the relation of representations to objects of the will, where the representation causes the object. All these representations are sensible, and their objects are empirical. But Kant's use of the words "intellectual representations" (*intellectuale Vorstellungen* in the letter, corresponding to *intellectualia* in the Dissertation) in the remainder of the paragraph[3] convinces me that he was still thinking that there can be pure conceptual a priori knowledge of noumena; I do not think he is dealing with the problem of how an a priori representation can represent an empirical object that causes the content but not the conceptual function of the representation. He may even have believed that intellectual concepts do *not* apply to objects of experience, as he did when in §5 of the Inaugural Dissertation he denied that there is a real use (*usus realis*) of reason in our observational knowledge.

Assuming that the book Kant was writing in 1772 and expecting to finish within three months was a revision of the Dissertation—a likely assumption in the light of the history of Kant's relations with Herz—it is plausible to conclude that he was filling in lacuna in its argumentation, not radically giving up his segregation of intellectual concepts from objects of experience. As I have argued elsewhere, the Inaugural Dissertation contains the first stage of the Copernican Revolution: objects appear to us by conforming to the sensible conditions of our experience of them.[4] But Kant was not yet prepared to go the whole way with this revolution and withdraw his claim that intellectual concepts give us direct knowledge of things *as they are*. It is only when he realizes that the "something essential" missing from the pre-Copernican half of his Dissertation cannot be supplied that he gave up claims to purely conceptual knowledge of transcendent objects as they are, and thus completed the Copernican Revolution. This recognition, however, came after the letter to Herz, and not merely from his meditations on the inadequacy of the Dissertation.

Professor Carl is able to document Kant's slow recognition of the inadequacy of the Dissertation on the a priori knowledge of objects of sense. He does so in an illuminating fashion by the writings after the letter, but I do not believe he can do so by citing the letter itself. Had Kant been aware that the "something essential" to knowledge of noumena could not be supplied but could be supplied if the function of intellectual representations lay in their constituting empirical objects by giving them an a priori structure—in other words, if the whole of metaphysics as a system of the forms and principles of the intelligible world had to be given up and replaced by an immanent metaphysics of experience—no doubt the conclusion of this part of his letter would have been quite different. Kant quickly surveys and rejects the answers to the problem (to the problem as I see it, not I think, to the problem as Carl sees it) without supplying any clue to anything better; he then describes his effort to establish a system of categories (no doubt an anticipation of the metaphysical deduction). Presumably thinking that the task we know as that of a transcendental deduction could be accomplished by performing what he later was to call a metaphysical deduction, Kant optimistically promises the finished book within three months. If his problem was supplying "something essential" to the Inaugural Dissertation (and if this could in any way be supplied!) three months do not seem unduly optimistic on his part.

Professor Carl bases his revisionist reading of the letter mostly on the last sentence of the very long first paragraph. The sentence states that three overlapping problems "are still left in a state of obscurity," as well they might be whether they are problems involving a not-yet-performed transcendental deduction of the categories, as Carl believes, or (as in my view) because purely conceptual knowledge of noumena is in principle impossible. The wording of the problems fits either interpretation; as is so often the case with Kant, a crucial sentence that might be decisive for or against some interpretative hypothesis is itself fatally ambiguous.

The three overlapping problems are: (1) how my understanding may form for itself concepts of things (*Dinge*) completely a priori, with which concepts the things (*Sachen*) must necessarily agree; (2) how my understanding may formulate *real* principles concerning the possibility of such concepts, with which principles experience must be in exact agreement, and which nevertheless are independent of experience; (3) how our faculty of understanding achieves this conformity with things (*Dinge*) themselves (C 10:131).

Some of the obscurity of which we might complain may arise from Kant's apparently indiscriminate use of *Ding* and *Sache*.[5] If *Ding* and *Sache* mean the same and refer to ordinary objects of experience, we can say: these are the questions that were answered a decade later in the *Critique*; if, on the other hand, they refer to noumenal objects, these problems are going to remain forever unsolved. But there is no reason to suppose, in the light of Kant's optimism in the next paragraph but one, that he had seen the irretrievable failure of the Dissertation and the inexorable demand for a *Critique of Pure Reason* and its transcendental deduction of the categories.

I must admit, however, that the problem in its second formulation strongly suggests that Kant is, as Carl insists he is, concerned with the application of concepts to objects of experience. Here the objects cause the content of our representations, but (we now know) there are also a priori concepts that necessarily apply to objects of sense but are not caused by them. I refer to the words: "with which principles experience must be in exact agreement." Almost the entire case for Carl's interpretation rests on the foundation of the most facile reading of this sentence. I cannot be sure that this is not a prescient insight of Kant's into his future work, but I am prepared to argue that in speaking of "principles" here Kant is not speaking of intellectual concepts in the manner of 1770 as if they were to do the work of the categories in the manner of 1781.[6] In my opinion he is, rather, espousing an essentially Leibnizian view of the relation of ontology to phenomenology, of reality to appearance. This was a view characteristic of the precritical Kant and dominant in the transitional Inaugural Dissertation; if we are willing to follow Norman Kemp Smith in one of the more egregious stratifications of the transcendental deduction, it can be found even in the first stage of the deduction, a stage in which the categories apply to things in themselves, and if they apply to phenomena at all it is only because "the entire empirical world is still to be conceived as grounded in the nonempirical."[7] However debatable it may be whether this view is actually to be found in the *Critique*, there can be no doubt that it was an intrinsic part of the ontology if not the epistemology of the Dissertation of 1770.

Hume's attack on the notion that we have an a priori concept of the causal connection (in metaphysics) of which the temporal sequences of impressions are derivative phenomena, so that an a priori concept applicable to things as they are derivatively applies to the appearances of things, awoke Kant from his dogmatic slumber. Quite suddenly an unanticipated demand for a transcendental deduction that would show that a priori concepts necessarily apply to empirical objects arose before Kant's mind, and the work of "three months" took nine years to perform. In my opinion this awakening occurred after Kant had written to Herz, and the fragments that Professor Carl so skillfully mustered for our inspection are attempts to answer the doubts raised by Hume, not to supply "something essential" to the Inaugural Dissertation. I am arguing, in other words, that the discontinuity between the Dissertation and the *Critique* occurred after the letter to Herz, not before it.

PART I

The *Critique of Pure Reason*

Kant's Notion of a Deduction and the Methodological Background of the First *Critique*

DIETER HENRICH

How did Kant conceive the program and the method of the transcendental deduction in the first *Critique*? In trying to provide an answer to this question, I shall draw on sources that have been hitherto unused or unknown. At the same time, I shall point toward a framework that could accommodate and account for all deductions in Kant's work.

The range of problems and sources implicated is too extensive, however, to be covered adequately within a single paper. Thus my remarks will take the modest form of a research report. But as I progress I hope it will become apparent that a survey of the assumptions and the context within which Kant's program of philosophical deductions unfolds has a greater interest than the careful elaboration of one of its facets. I shall, however, clarify Kant's notion of a philosophical deduction in a more detailed fashion, and then turn to a more summary treatment of further aspects of, and perspectives on, Kant's philosophical methodology.

In spite of long-lasting efforts, the key chapter of the first *Critique* resists penetration. We have no commentary that explains, in terms of shared principles and intentions, the argumentative strategy Kant employs—both in detail and as a whole, and for both editions jointly. Furthermore, attempts to reconstruct or to extend Kant's way of reasoning by means of similar but independent philosophical theories or forms of analysis cannot yet account convincingly for the nature and the source of the similarities and differences between their own projects and Kant's. This situation appears not to be accidental. To understand it, we must clarify the background against which Kant's reasoning in the deductions unfolds. We have reason to believe features of this background that Kant could take for granted have escaped us thus far.

Any successful interpretation of Kant's deductions must meet a number of criteria, of which I shall mention only three.

First, an interpretation should be capable of comprehensively explaining the vocabulary that Kant employs when he comments on the program of his deductions, in a way that exhibits the unity and the internal connectedness of its various terms.

Second, an interpretation should provide means for understanding the way in which Kant composed the texts of his deductions— not only the two deductions of the first *Critique*, but also the deductions in Kant's work in general. The deduction of the first *Critique*, to be sure, deserves special attention, for it was within the context of this deduction that Kant became convinced that the program he carried out under the name "deduction" is indispensable and is best characterized by the term "deduction." Furthermore, the deductions of the first *Critique* are by far the most extensive ones, and they stand out clearly against the rest of the corpus of the first *Critique* because of their style and the condensed and intense reasoning in which they engage.

Third, an interpretation of Kant's deductive strategy must be able to apply to the deduction of the second *Critique*. There the deduction depends upon a so-called fact of reason (which Hegel derided as "the undigested log in the stomach, a revelation given to reason"). We are inclined to adopt, almost automatically, an understanding of the term "deduction" that immediately creates a tension between a deduction and reference to a fact. This results in misunderstanding of Kant's argument in the second *Critique*—misunderstanding also of the way in which it is sytematically related to the deduction of the first *Critique*.

I

In Kant's philosophical language, the meaning of the term "deduction" is different from what we almost irresistibly expect, and this largely accounts for a persistent failure to understand Kant's deductions as a unitary and (within its unity) well-structured program. For "deduction" is a term that is quite familiar to us. It refers to the logical procedure by means of which a proposition—namely, the conclusion—is established through the formal relationship of other propositions, its premises. Thus we take a deduction to be a syllogistic proof. Kant was familiar with this usage of the term "deduction." Yet, unlike now, this was not the only, and not the most common, usage in eighteenth-century academic language. Indeed, if we assume that Kant announces under the heading of "deduction" a well-formed chain of syllogisms, we must arrive at a very unfavorable conclusion about his capability of carrying out such a program. The deduction of the first *Critique*, to be sure, does claim to be a proof. But if it is to be defined as a deduction on the basis of its correctness and, above all, its perspicuity as a chain of syllogisms, its failure to meet its own standards would be completely obvious. We know, however, that within the first *Critique* Kant repeatedly showed his ability to design accurate syllogistic proofs—for instance, in the Refutation of Idealism and in the Antinomies. We have, consequently, good reason to look for a reading of the term "deduction" in Kant's sense, one that does not make the meaning of his very program entirely dependent upon the design of a chain of syllogisms.

The literal meaning of "to deduce" (in Latin) is: "to carry something forth to something else." In this very general sense it is not restricted to derivations within a discourse, for one "deduces" a river by digging a new riverbed. Within the range of the methods of discourse, "deduction" can have a variety of applications. A "deduction" in the original (Latin) sense can take place wherever something results from a methodological derivation from something else.[1] Relics of this very widespread usage are preserved in the European languages in various ways: in English, for instance, in "tax deduction."

Everybody who is familiar with the first *Critique* will remember the first sentence under the heading "The Principles of Any Transcendental Deduction": "Jurists, when speaking of rights and claims, distinguish in a legal action the question of right (*quid juris*) from the question of fact (*quid facti*); and they demand that both be proved. Proof of the former, which has to state the right or the legal claim, they entitle the *deduction*" (A84/B116). Since here Kant apparently wants primarily to distinguish the two questions, one can easily be led to the opinion that he employs "deduction" in the ordinary logical sense, with the further qualification that the premises of the syllogism should be capable of justifying legal claims—thus, presumably, normative propositions.

But by adopting this seemingly natural and almost irresistible reading one has already missed what is distinctive to the methodological idea that gives to Kant's deductions a unitary structure. One also misses the reasons for which Kant refers to the juridical paradigm, and why he could and did structure the first *Critique* in its entirety around constant reference to juridical procedures. In four steps I shall try to elucidate the background of Kant's adoption of the term "deduction" from its juridical context and set out the reasons why he transferred it to his philosophical program.

1. By the end of the fourteenth century, there had come into being a type of publication that by the beginning of the eighteenth century (when it had come into widespread use) was known as *Deduktionsschriften* ("deduction writings"). Their aim was to justify controversial legal claims between the numerous rulers of the independent territories, city republics, and other constituents of the Holy Roman Empire. They presupposed both the invention of printing and the establishment and universal recognition of the Imperial Courts as an authority above the otherwise largely independent members of the Empire. These deduction writings were not sold by publishing houses but were distributed by governments, with the intention of convincing other governments of the rightfulness of their own positions in controversies that might eventually lead to military force and thus to the need of finding support from other rulers. Before the final decisions of one of the Imperial Courts (which were by no means always respected), legal proceedings also required that a deduction had to be submitted by both parties. Most of the legal controversies concerned inheritance of territories, the legal succession in reigns, and so forth. In all the cases extensive arguments about the way in which a claim had originated and had been maintained over generations had to be given.

The size of the deduction writings varied, from brochures to folio volumes of up to three thousand pages. Governments preserved deductions in special libraries so that they could be drawn upon in unforeseeable future conflicts. Since their printing was often very fine and elaborate, deductions were also collected—for instance, by former diplomats, who had access to them. Thus, after centuries, auctions of special deduction collections could bring considerable

Kant's Notion of a Deduction

amounts of money. Approximately twelve thousand deductions were published from the fifteenth century to the eighteenth century. At the beginning of the eighteenth century, it proved profitable to publish bibliographies of the deductions. Writing deductions was a juridical specialty, and a famous deduction writer could easily become rich. The most admired deduction writer of Kant's time was J. S. Pütter, professor of law at Göttingen and coauthor of the textbook that Kant used in his frequent lectures on natural law.[2]

It can be shown that Kant was familiar with the practice of deduction writing. He was for six years a librarian of the royal library in Königsberg and had to check its stock when he assumed his office. He uses the terminology of the deductions in his own little juridical quarrels (C 12:380, 421). And he speaks occasionally about deductions in the archives that had been ignored by rulers who preferred to use violence (MM §61, 6:350). Kant also had very good reasons to assume—given the widespread practice of arguing through deduction writings—that his audience would understand him when he transferred the term "deduction" from its juridical usage to a new, philosophical one. What he could not foresee was that such a widespread usage would very soon become obsolete, when the Holy Roman Empire was abolished under pressure from Napoleon. With this, the Imperial Courts and the practice of writing deductions disappeared forever, and the term "deduction" became extinct and almost incomprehensible. With regard to the *Critique* and its deductions, we can thus understand in a new light the old saying that books, too, have their destiny.

2. The practice of deductions reaches back to a time when the tradition of Roman law was not yet revitalized and the modern theory of law had not yet been founded. These two processes resulted in a need to refine and regulate the practice of the writing of deductions, and this affected Kant's way of conceiving their philosophical correlate in the first *Critique*. The old deductions were perceived by the new generations of jurists as clumsy and largely unfit for the purposes for which they were written. Thus, within the fast-growing methodological literature on law, academic jurists provided analyses of what a deduction was and guidelines for a deduction's author. This literature provides clues for reading the transcendental deduction as well. In 1752, for instance, one of the methodologists produced the following criteria for a good deduction: Since a deduction is not a theory for its own sake, but rather an argumentation in-

tended to justify convincingly a claim about the legitimacy of a possession or a usage, it should refrain from unnecessary digression, generalizations, debates about principles, and so forth, which are of interest only to the theoretician. A deduction should be brief, solid but not subtle, and perspicuous.

The author of this treatise praises highly a practice of Pütter, the famous deduction writer. If Pütter did not succeed in producing a deduction that satisfied these criteria, he would write a second deduction, a brief and elegant text that summarized the main points of his argument. I have checked some of Pütter's deductions, and there is indeed one to which such an additional text is attached, printed in different format and on less expensive paper; it carries the title "Brief Outline [*Kurzer Begriff*] of the Zedwitz Case." Now, if one looks at the text of Kant's transcendental deduction, one finds at the end of it a similar summary, which Kant gives nowhere else. More importantly, the summary carries in the second edition the very same title: "Brief Outline [*Kurzer Begriff*] of this Deduction" (B168).

It does not seem very probable that this is an accident (although the phrase *Kurzer Begriff* as title for an outline was indeed common in eighteenth century scholarly language). It appears that Kant thought his deduction as a text should be modeled on the juridical paradigm and meet its criteria of excellence. Thus we conclude—before analyzing the argumentative form of the deduction—that Kant wrote the text of the deduction of the first *Critique* following the standards of a good juridical deduction, which focuses exclusively upon justifying a claim. Not only is the argumentation of the deduction correlative to the juridical argumentative form (as we shall see shortly), the text of the transcendental deduction is a deduction writing in the technical sense. That explains why Kant could not agree with those who complained that he refrains from extensive theorizing. He deliberately intended to be brief and to focus exclusively upon his crucial points. In the first edition of the deduction he says explicitly that he intends to avoid elaborate theory. Later he recommended the second-edition deduction because it arrived at the intended result by the easiest way.

3. We must now turn to questions about the argumentative form of a juridical deduction. They have been discussed by the theoreticians of natural law, and the first to come up with a definition of what a deduction consists in was Christian Wolff. The basic distinction between types of rights is between innate and acquired rights.

In J. S. Pütter and G. Achenwall (the authors of Kant's textbook), these are called absolute and hypothetical rights, respectively. Hypothetical rights originate in a "fact" (*factum*, meaning both "fact" and "action"), which must exist before the right in question can come into being—mostly from an action by virtue of which the right is "acquired." Innate or absolute rights, conversely, are inseparable from a human being as such. Humans by their very nature possess such rights.

But acquired rights have a particular origin. I have the right, for example, to carry a title of nobility if I am the legitimate child of a particular couple. I have the right to carry an academic title if I have successfully passed the examinations without fraud. I can use a particular good—a house, for instance—if I have purchased it by a valid contract or if I have inherited it by a valid last will.

In order to decide whether an acquired right is real or only presumption, one must legally trace the possession somebody claims back to its origin. The process through which a possession or a usage is accounted for by explaining its origin, such that the rightfulness of the possession or the usage becomes apparent, defines the deduction. Only with regard to acquired rights can a deduction be given. This implies that by definition a deduction must refer to an origin.

We now understand why these two notions, the methodological notion of a deduction and the epistemological notion of an origin of our knowledge, are inseparably linked in the terminology of the first *Critique*. In this context the question that Kant raises constantly in the *Critique* also exhibits its distinctive meaning: "How is it possible . . .?" The question does not ask for one or another sufficient condition for our possession of knowledge. In a state of doubt about the rightfulness of our claim to be in the possession of genuine knowledge, it seeks to discover and to examine the real origin of our claim and with that the source of its legitimacy.

But doesn't this confuse and blur the distinction between explanation and validation, between the question of right and the question of fact, to which Kant assigns such importance throughout the opening paragraphs of his first deduction? In response to this question we can observe that the distinction between the two questions (of right and of fact) cannot be drawn in such a way that only the question of fact remains concerned with the origins of our knowledge. Both questions require an understanding of the origin, but each in its particular way.

Consider the example of a last will: It is possible to tell a story about the way in which the will has been conceived of and arrived at, when it was written and how it has been preserved. This is what the deduction writings call *Geschichtserzählung* ("report of the story"), or *species facti*. Such a *species facti* can be produced in court and can be disputed—for instance, if it becomes doubtful whether a possession or a usage exists at all. But it cannot settle by itself the *quaestio juris*. To answer this question, one has to focus exclusively upon those aspects of the acquisition of an allegedly rightful possession by virtue of which a right has been bestowed, such that the possession has become a property.

It should be mentioned in passing that the idea of an acquisition of legal titles does not necessarily presuppose a particular legal system with reference to which the entitlement becomes decidable. The Natural Right Kant uses as his paradigm recognizes an original acquisition. The conditions of its rightfulness can be determined prior to any particular legal system. The categories of the pure understanding are justified with regard to their "original acquisition" through an operation of the mind by means of Kant's deduction of the categories within the first *Critique*. It is important to realize, furthermore, that the *quaestio juris* can be answered in a satisfactory way even if the *quaestio facti* meets with insurmountable difficulties. Consider again the example of the last will: in many cases we are unable to produce a complete story of the way in which the will has been made. But if it can be determined in court that the will is authentic and valid, by means of only a few but crucial aspects, the question of right can still be answered decisively.

This consideration can be applied to the transcendental deduction of the categories. Kant is of the opinion that it is impossible to produce an adequate *species facti* about the acquisition of our knowledge. The text appears to suggest that the story about acquisition that Locke and others had to tell is possible, albeit irrelevant. However, from other sources we can clearly show that Kant's position was a different one. Within philosophy, to the *species facti* of the jurists— the report of the story—corresponds what Kant calls the "physiology of reason." For a number of reasons he became convinced that such a physiological account is impossible. For Kant, Leibniz as well as Locke is a physiologist of reason. This description implies a twofold criticism on Kant's part. (1) The attempt of these philosophers to give a complete account of the roots and the genesis of our rationality is not a promising undertaking. (2) They also refrain from doing what ultimately matters in philosophy: justifying the claims of reason against skepticism. Critical philosophy thus opens an entirely new pathway, which can be defined in terms of what the notion of a deduction implies, once it is understood in its distinctive sense.

But deductions can never be given without reference to the facts from which our knowledge originates. We cannot arrive at, and don't need a comprehensive understanding of, the genesis and constitution of these facts in themselves. Yet we must arrive at an understanding of the aspects of them that suffice to justify the claims attached to our knowledge. Most of the facts the deductions rely upon are basic operations of our reason. The deductions refer to the intrinsic, quasi-Cartesian forms of these operations: their independence from particular experiences. Yet their status as operations and forms of operations does not exhaustively define their roles as principles upon which a deduction can be built. Operations that are *facta* (therefore actions in the juridical sense) imply factual elements that cannot be explained by virtue of actions we can always perform. Most of the origins from which Kant's deductions are derived exhibit clearly this additional factual element. The features shared by the unity of apperception, the consciousness of space and time as such, and the moral law as a fact of reason illustrate this common feature of the principles according to which Kant's deductions have been designed. Viewed in this light, the deduction of the second *Critique* does not deviate from the general pattern Kantian deductions exhibit, whatever their particular course.

The differences between Kant's deductions can be explained by means of the different ways in which we have access to the origins and the principles of our discourses, and by variants in the notion of an origin itself. These differences result in the distinction between strong and weak versions of philosophical deductions, which I have discussed elsewhere.[3]

4. We don't know just when Kant decided to present his new method of philosophical justification in the form and the terminology of juridical deductions. This probably happened rather late in his long preparations for the publication of the first *Critique*. We do know, however, that the decision concerned more than the chapter that became entitled "Transcendental Deduction of the Pure Concepts of the Understanding." The fact that Kant composed this chapter in the style of a deduction writing largely explains its unique

character, which contrasts markedly with the rest of the first *Critique*. But the entire first *Critique*, and the way in which Kant presents its theory as a whole, was thoroughly affected by the decision to adopt juridical procedures as a methodological paradigm.

The *Critique* is not just permeated by juridical metaphors and terminology. Its major doctrines are related to one another by means of the theory of legal disputes presented by Pütter and Achenwall. A legal dispute originates when a party's claim has been challenged by an opponent, so that a court case must be opened. This happened in philosophy when the skeptic challenged the claim of reason to be in possession of a priori knowledge of objects. The dispute makes indispensable an investigation into the origins of such knowledge. To the extent to which a deduction can be produced, the claim of reason becomes definitely justified and the challenge of the skeptic is rejected. This is the aim of the Transcendental Analytic.

But there is the other possibility, to which the Transcendental Dialectic corresponds: a deduction might turn out to be impossible. If the claim to knowledge that transcends the limits of experience cannot be justified, the challenged party must retract its claim. But that does not necessarily mean that the opposing party wins the court case. For the skeptic—here, in the guise of the empiricist— may in turn be unable to validate his claim that the usage of ideas transcending experience is illegitimate and an empty presumption. In such a situation, where conflicting claims cannot be settled in court in favor of one of the parties, the parties threaten to become engaged in an endless struggle, which would destroy the peace and result in a war within reason itself. The ruling of the court of reason in such a situation consists in an order to keep the peace. The dogmatic philosopher must refrain from claiming that he is in possession of valid knowledge beyond narrow limits. "A complete review of all the powers of reason—and the conviction thereby obtained of the certainty of its claims to a modest territory, as also of the vanity of higher pretensions—puts an end to the conflict, and induces it to rest satisfied with a limited but undisputed territory" (A768/B796). This is, of course, the territory whose borders are drawn by the conditions of possible experience. But the rule of the court to keep the peace does not permit the challenger to deny our right to use ideas of reason that transcend experience. Since neither a deduction nor a proof of the emptiness of these ideas could be produced, and since it has been shown that both proofs are impossible, reason, which is in possession of these ideas, becomes entitled to use them as long as it refrains from claiming that they are used as justifiable knowledge. The court of reason rules on the basis of the juridical principle that applies in such cases: if a dispute about the rightness of a usage cannot be settled, the usage remains with the possessor: "*melior est conditio possedendi*" (A777/B805). Because reason remains in possession of its ideas, though in using them it cannot lay claim to any knowledge, the way to a purely practical philosophy remains open.

This clarification of the precise meaning of the term "deduction" in Kant's work makes possible two conclusions about the argumentative structure of the transcendental deduction of the categories.

First, in its fundamental structure the transcendental deduction is patterned on a deduction that aims to justify an acquired right by appealing to particular features of the origin of the categories and their usage—features that had been challenged. Different parts or steps discernible within the text of the deduction can be explained primarily as partial moves aimed to elucidate the origin of the usage of the categories—and thus as a partial answer to the question about the conditions that would make possible a legitimate usage of the categories. These steps can also function as links within a chain of syllogisms, but such functioning by itself does not make them partial moves within a juridical deduction. This is particularly important to our understanding of the structure of the deduction in the second edition of the *Critique*. The deduction is indeed a proof, and it brings its various partial results together by means of a syllogistic chain, but its being a "deduction" is not defined in terms of a chain of syllogisms. Any relatively independent part of it must also be a relatively independent move in the uncovering of the origins of the usage of the categories. For the purpose of the deduction is to determine, with regard to origin, the domain and the limits of the categories' legitimate usage.[4]

Second, once we have realized that the deduction as such cannot be founded upon a syllogistic structure, we have gained a new flexibility in our understanding of the various kinds of argumentation Kant might employ in the course of the deduction. The very notion of a deduction is compatible with any kind of argumentation suitable for reaching the goal—namely, the justification of our claims to a priori knowledge. As a matter of fact, several types of argument operate within the text of the deduction before it begins to establish its results by means of a syllogistic proof. The task of a philosophical commentary—as yet unwritten—would be to discriminate these types and to assess their respective function and philosophical value. Within such a context, we could reopen the question about whether Kant employs a particular kind of argument (that is, in some sense, distinctly "transcendental").

II

But further problems must first be taken up. Although we now understand the program implied by the notion of a deduction, we don't yet know anything about Kant's ideas concerning how to arrive at a philosophical deduction. We must still explore his views about the methodological foundations on which one might justify acquired rights in philosophy.

In this regard, the first *Critique* remains completely silent. It employs a number of methodological terms: it *examines* origins; it *inspects* reason as such; it *searches* for sources and *explores* how we can proceed from them; it *explains* possibilities; it *investigates* content, usage, and right; and it designs proofs that *indicate* conditions of possibility. But it does not analyze or account for any of these terms.

It is not unusual in philosophy for completely new theories to be unable to explain their own procedures. The terms Kant employs indicate a complex and evasive field of problems, and so he probably had good reason to concentrate on the content rather than on the methodology of his project. It would, however, be disappointing if nothing could be said about Kant's methodological assumptions and about his theory of the foundations underlying the practice of deducing knowledge claims.

To pursue this topic, one must turn to yet another literature. This body of texts—the literature of applied logic—has been forgotten almost as completely as the literature of juridical deductions. Kant covered its problems extensively in his lectures on logic (although he excludes these problems from what belongs to logic proper in a narrow sense). There he sketched his views about philosophical methodology, including the methodology of the *Critique*. I shall present Kant's views in four more steps.

1. The first step in examining Kant's views on methodology is to note a few aspects of his assessment of proofs within philosophy. In assessing the role of syllogisms in philosophy, Kant follows Descartes

and the school of Rüdiger: syllogisms are secondary, merely sub-sequent organizations of knowledge already acquired. What matters most in philosophy is to ascertain the reliability of premises (of *Beweisgründe*, that is, of the notions and reasons that proofs can rely upon).

He also believed that philosophical knowledge cannot be based upon logical possibility. It must find what Kant calls "real reasons" (*rationes verae*). Using them, it must show in what way knowledge issues from its real source. In this sense, philosophy has to provide "genetic" explanations. (This corresponds to what the deduction provides—sources or origins.)

Such explanations, for Kant, could never become "demonstra-tions." They are "probations" (*probationes*). Demonstrations are pos-sible only in mathematics. Mathematical demonstrations provide os-tensive knowledge, but philosophical knowledge cannot become equally secure. It is always possible that in the course of philosophi-cal reasoning one might overlook an important aspect of the prob-lem. For that reason, philosophical argumentation must be holistic in the following sense: any result we arrive at must be checked against results that have been gained in other fields of philosophy. One can-not present philosophical insights without hesitation, and separately from the other proofs we are inclined to accept (see, for example, R2513, 16:400). This stance explains Kant's claim that the *Critique* becomes convincing only by virtue of the totality of its theorems and proofs. It explains, furthermore, why the deduction is not situated at the beginning of the work (where one might expect it). It also ex-plains why Kant does not try to achieve in the deduction the per-spicuity and the rigor distinctive to the kinds of knowledge it is about to justify. Justification as a method cannot excel in the forms of discourse for whose sake the justification is undertaken, and it cannot compete with the clarity and the perspicuity of foundational disciplines as they had frequently been conceived within the tradition founded by Leibniz. But these disciplines cannot really solve—can-not even address—basic philosophical problems, and for that reason they are in a sense unphilosophical.

2. But these three theorems taken together cannot by themselves clarify the epistemic basis upon which a deduction has to rely. For this, we must take a second step and consider a central and basic dis-tinction Kant frequently makes in his lectures beginning in the early 1780's (see 24:161 ("Logik Blomberg"), 424, 547, 641), which is pres-

ent also in the first *Critique* (although there one can hardly grasp its methodological importance). The distinction is between "reflection" (*Überlegen, reflexio*) and "investigation" (*Untersuchen, examinatio*).

The *Critique* is an examination, or investigation. Since Kant claims that reflection precedes investigation, it is plausible to suppose that reflection is the source by means of which an investigation can be undertaken. Kant's theory of reflection (which is utterly different from the meaning of "reflection" that became current in post-Kantian philosophy) is as follows. (a) Our cognitive capacities are a "mingled web." They cannot be reduced to one single form of fundamental intelligent operation. (b) Each of these capacities becomes operative spontaneously and with regard to its appropriate domain. (c) To arrive at genuine knowledge, it is necessary to control and to stabilize these operations and to keep them within the limits of their proper domains. Our mind must regulate when a particular activity comes into play and be sure that it alone remains operative. For that purpose, the mind must implicitly know what is specific to each of its particular activities. This implies, furthermore, that the principles upon which an activity is founded must be known by contrast with the other activities. Reflection consists in precisely this knowledge. Without it we would, for example, confuse counting with calculating, analysis with composition, and so forth. Kant says explicitly that without reflection we could only utter meaningless sequences of words. (d) Therefore, reflection always takes place. Without any effort on our part, we always spontaneously know (albeit, informally and without explicit articulation) about our cognitive activities and about the principles and rules they depend upon. Reflection in this sense is a precondition of rationality.

Reflection is not introspection. It accompanies operations internally. It is not the achievement of a philosopher who, by means of a deliberate effort and within an *intentio obliqua*, turns inward to examine the operations of reason. Thus it is a source, not an achievement, of philosophical insight. Now notice the similarity of and connection between "reflection" on the one hand and the program of a "deduction" on the other:

Deductions are founded upon a partial knowledge of significant features of the origin from which our knowledge arises.

Reflection is not a descriptive, let alone an exhaustive knowledge of the processes and operations of cognition. It is only an awareness of what is specific to them, presumably the general principles and rules upon which they rely.

Thus it appears that deductions can be built upon a reflective knowledge of precisely this kind.

3. We take a third step when we note that the *Critique*—and with it, its deductions—is an investigation by means of which claims about knowledge are examined. Kant defines investigation and examination as correlates of reflection. We reflect always, but investigation is a deliberate activity. It is only undertaken when doubts about and challenges to knowledge claims have arisen. Then we must search for the ground upon which our (real or only presumptive) knowledge is founded—eventually we must try to produce a "deduction." But the investigation cannot depart from the domain within which reflection is operative: it detects connections of which reflection itself is not explicitly aware. And it relates the principles that orient a discourse to fundamental facts and operations that constitute it yet which can also interpret and validate it.

These are the very facts we referred to when we clarified the philosophical correlate of the juridical deduction—notably, the unity of apperception, space and time, and the fact of reason. In exceptional cases deductions might have to transcend the limits of the domain that is disclosed in reflection: for example, in the case of the deduction of the reality of freedom. But even then they rely upon principles and fundamental facts we already know about by reflection, although we understand them and their central position within the discourse in question only by means of an investigation. The systematic interconnectedness of the various forms of discourse can also be understood by means of investigation. But investigation is preceded by, and made possible through, reflection, by which the multidimensional system of our cognitive capacities is accessible to us, persistently and prephilosophically.[5]

Two corollaria can be added to this third step:

(a) Since the deduction, as an investigation, always depends internally on what reflection provides, we can reasonably expect that no deduction can get under way unless it relies primarily on arguments that refer directly to what is revealed by reflection. These arguments constitute the core of every transcendental deduction. And their formal feature is a clarification of the awareness that a particular operation cannot be carried out unless another and more fundamen-

Dieter Henrich

tal operation comes into play. This is the distinctive feature of the arguments that appear within the *Critique* in the grammatical form "not without." To this type belongs the argument in the second-edition deduction that analysis is not fundamental but is always intrinsically accompanied by synthesis on a deeper level, and the argument of the first-edition deduction to the effect that synthesis in turn requires principles of unity that cannot originate within experience. Kant appears to believe that the key argument of the deduction connecting the unity of apperception with the principles of unity that guide all synthesis belongs also entirely to the same type. But in my opinion this is true only with qualifications and must be further explored. But such an exploration presupposes that the methodology of a deduction based upon reflection has been understood.

(b) We can indicate a reason for Kant's reluctance to present explicitly his philosophical methodology. (Almost all of the above has been taken from transcripts of Kant's lectures; very little of it is in his printed texts. He must have had reason for being reticent.) Since reflection is a permanent, albeit implicit, knowledge, and investigation is a deliberate undertaking on the part of the philosopher, there remains a gap between these two cognitive activities, regardless of the essential correlation between them. Thus the question arises as to how an implicit knowledge can be transformed into an explicit one. There must be a device by which the transition can be made in a methodologically safe and respectable way. Kant realized this and was inclined to put the theory of "preliminary judgments" (*judicia praevia*) to work at precisely this place: within reflection a tendency to conceptualize our cognitive faculties in a particular way somehow arises. These "preliminary judgments" are the point of departure for philosophical investigation. The investigation does not have to accept them, but it starts off from them. In his lectures on logic, above all in the Vienna transcript, Kant acknowledges that we have only a rudimentary understanding of this mechanism and that for this reason a satisfactory methodology of philosophical reasoning meets with hitherto insurmountable difficulties.

4. In a fourth and last step we turn to an important and surprising application of Kant's doctrine of the role of reflection within philosophy. The key notion of the deduction in the first *Critique* is, without doubt, the unity of apperception. Much can be said in favor of the view that this principle must be relied on, at least indirectly, in the other transcendental deductions as well. Now, when Kant turns

to discuss this principle, he refers to it constantly as "the I think." Presumably a number of reasons are responsible for the persistent usage of this peculiar phrase. But among them is one that can be directly derived from Kant's theory of reflection: the awareness "I think" is precisely the self-consciousness that can be attached to natural and spontaneous reflection. And it is, in addition, the self-consciousness that can accompany every kind of reflection, regardless of the field of its employment. We can see this if we consider that: (a) It is neither concept nor intuition and does not belong to any of the various cognitive activities. (b) It is established prior to all kinds of theorizing. (c) It emerges from an operation. But this operation is not itself an act of reflection nor does it define reflection as such. (d) Yet it potentially accompanies every case of reflection and is not restricted to a specific area of reflective awareness or a particular discourse whose principles are disclosed by virtue of reflection. It has the same generality and scope as reflection, and can thus be thought together with any act of reflection. It is, as Kant says, "The I as subject of thinking, that is to say the pure apperception, the reflected I" (Anthr §4, 7:134n).[6]

It is impossible to understand these passages without the help of Kant's notion of reflection in its distinctive sense. But once the notion of reflection has been clarified, we can also understand the fundamental role the unity of apperception plays within Kant's system as a whole. The ultimate justification of the principles of our knowledge should depend upon an origin that has a central position within our cognitive system as it is accessible to us by virtue of the implicit knowledge of reflection. This suggests that the principle by which the most fundamental deduction can be carried out will have the generality and unrestricted applicability that is the distinctive feature of the process of reflection upon which the method of philosophical justification or investigation continuously relies.[7] In this manner the key notion of the deduction in the first *Critique* and the methodological principle of all philosophical deductions, the correlation of reflection and investigation, appear to be related to each other.

This leads us to a final point. The unity of apperception has appeared in two very different roles: On the one hand, it is an awareness that can accompany any reflectively accessible knowledge. But this knowledge is manifold and appears to lack systematic unity. On the other hand, the unity of apperception is the origin of the system of the categories and the point of departure for the deduction of the legitimacy of their usage. It is easy to sense the tension between the loose generality of reflection, on the one hand, and the rigidity of the claim that issues from the program of the deduction, on the other. The *Critique* claims that reason as such is a system and, furthermore, that philosophy must provide an exhaustive account of its principles and of the various modes of its usage.

The tension disappears once we consider reflection in a slightly different perspective: Kant's theory of reflection is founded upon the observation that our various discourses would become confused and inconsistent if they were not accompanied and guarded by a constant process of reflected control. But we might wonder whether such a confusion would be likely to occur if the discourses were not systematically related to one another, so that erroneous transitions can suggest themselves. Within a reason that was nothing but a bundle of independent activities, the constant danger of confusion could hardly occur. Such a reason might function properly as a coordinated set of cognitive machines.

But reflection is omnipresent because reason is one, in spite of its comparatively independent operations. The unity of reason, as far as the systematic structure of its principles is concerned, is represented in the most fundamental way by the implications of the thought "I think," the system of the categories. But the very same thought is intimately and universally related to the process of reflection upon which the methodology of philosophical justification must be founded.

Deductions cannot assume the shape of a rigorous and exhaustive reasoning. Yet the philosophical theory of reason whose argumentative core they provide must be systematic and exhaustive. But the discrepancy between loose argumentation on the one hand and a lofty pretension about systematicity on the other turns out to be illusory. The difference between the two programs is to be understood as the difference between two tasks within one single program, which Kant has conceived and designed in a perfectly consistent way.

Psychology and the
Transcendental Deduction

PAUL GUYER

This paper will consider the hoary question whether Kant's transcendental deduction of the pure concepts of the understanding is a psychological argument, or whether it is damagingly psychological—whether any feature that would seem to make it psychological must also keep it from its goal of demonstrating the objective validity of concepts, which, because they are known a priori, must be somehow subjective in origin. This question has been discussed for a century, since the revival of the serious study of Kant, but, it seems to me, to little effect. Perhaps this is because few writers have paused to give both a clear account of what is to be expected as well as feared from a psychological argument and also a sufficiently clear exposition of Kant's deduction to allow adjudication of the issue. In what follows, I will attempt to shed enough light on each of these two issues to suggest a negative answer to the question.

Indisputably Psychological Arguments and Explanations

Since the distinction between a philosophical and a psychological argument or explanation is relatively recent—it can be claimed to have been invented by Kant himself—and since conceptions of the goals and methods of psychology have changed so frequently within

Paul Guyer

the last century, during which the distinction has been generally assumed, it seems reasonable to begin with a historical elucidation of
what Kant himself might have taken to characterize a psychological
approach to questions about the validity of fundamental concepts. A
detailed study would require examination of the empirical psychologies of Christian Wolff and A. G. Baumgarten as well as of Kant's
immediate predecessor J. N. Tetens. But although I will include one
example from the latter, I will devote more attention to the better-
known and more influential—then as well as now—British figures,
whose views on the nature and limits of psychological argument and
explanation were influential in Kant's own time as well as in the subsequent evolution of our issue.

Kant does not use the term "psychology" to characterize that from
which his own transcendental deduction must be distinguished; he
uses the term chiefly in the phrase "rational psychology," which denotes a body of a priori but fallacious arguments for ontological
claims about a *transcendent* self from which his own *transcendental*
claims about the self—claims about the concepts, principles, and capacities of the self that are the necessary conditions of the possibility
of knowledge—must carefully be distinguished. But he does explicitly
contrast his own arguments for these transcendental conclusions to a
"certain *physiology* of the human understanding—that of the celebrated Locke" (Aix).[1] The "illustrious Locke," Kant holds, "meeting
with pure concepts of the understanding in experience," proceeded
"*inconsequently*" in attempting to deduce "them also from experience" (B127); instead, Kant claims, a transcendental deduction of the
categories must be distinguished from any such empirical, physiological deduction of them:

I therefore entitle the explanation of the way in which concepts can relate a
priori to objects the *transcendental* deduction of them, and distinguish this
from the empirical deduction, which indicates the way in which a concept is
acquired through experience and reflection upon it, and which therefore
concerns not the legitimacy [of the concept] but the fact through which possession [of it] arose (A85/B117).

But the contrast with Locke is less helpful than it may seem,
in large part precisely because Locke is primarily concerned with
our *empirical* concepts of substances and virtually concedes that his
method is helpless in the case of the very categorical concepts that so
concern Kant—substance, causation, interaction, and the indepen-

48

Psychology and the Deduction

dence of objective existence itself.² Locke's primary interest is not in explaining or justifying the philosophical concept of *substance*, but in attacking Aristotelian misconceptions about concepts of natural *substances*; so he is really interested in very different issues from Kant, and his "method" is not really an appropriate object for Kant's contrast.

Other British thinkers, however, do provide a more relevant contrast. At the very beginning of modern philosophy, Hobbes clearly explained at least what is to be feared from a psychological rather than philosophical approach to the basic principles of science. This is the point of his distinction between "philosophy" and mere "experience," by which Hobbes makes plain that his decidedly mechanical world-view is most definitely not empiricist. "Philosophy," Hobbes holds, "is such knowledge of effects or appearances, as we acquire by true ratiocination from the knowledge we have first of their causes or generation: And again, of such causes or generations as may be from knowing first their effects." As such it is to be distinguished from "Sense and Memory," which are "given us immediately by nature, and not gotten by ratiocination," as well as from "Experience," which "is nothing but memory; and Prudence, or prospect into the future time," which "is nothing but expectation of such things as we have already had experience of."³ The reason why this distinction must be drawn, in turn, is the inability of mere experience to yield certitude:

This taking of signs by *experience*, is that wherein men do ordinarily think, the difference stands between men and men in *wisdom*, by which they commonly understand a man's whole ability or *power cognitive*; but this is an *error*: for the signs are but *conjectural*; and according as they have often or seldom failed, so their assurance is more or less, but never *full* and *evident*: for though a man have always seen the day and night to follow one another hitherto; yet he can not thence conclude that they shall do so, or that they have done so eternally: *experience concludeth nothing universally*.⁴

Empirical arguments, in other words, can never yield more than probability, and only rational deduction from self-evident first principles can yield truly necessary and universal conclusions with certitude.

Hobbes thus states clearly what Kant feared from a physiological and empirical deduction of key philosophical concepts. But Hobbes did not himself think physiology was limited to an experimental

49

method—what he offers is, after all, not rational psychology in Kant's special sense but, precisely, rationalist physiology. For a clear case of an actual psychological approach to the deduction—or rejection—of a basic philosophical concept or principle, we must of course turn to Hume—whom I find it hard to understand, indeed, except as having concluded that it was only Hobbes's prudence and not his ratiocination that could explain our knowledge of any basic concepts, and of having willingly accepted the epistemological constraint that Hobbes placed on prudence.

I will consider two examples from Hume: his clearly psychological *explanation* of our belief in causal inferences, and his equally clearly psychological *argument* against long chains of reasoning (his notorious scepticism about reason).

1. Hume's treatment of causal belief can be reduced to two steps. Hume first offers a—thoroughly nonpsychological—argument against the Hobbesian supposition that relations between causes and their effects, or vice versa, can be discovered by true ratiocination; this argument turns on the claim that there is neither a direct logical connection between a putative cause and effect sufficient to allow any deductive inference or "*demonstrative* argument" from one to the other, nor any logically necessary intermediate premise, such as that "the course of nature continues always uniformly the same,"[5] which could be added to repeated experience of conjunctions of events of the relevant type to ground such an inference.[6] Using Hobbes's own terms of contrast, Hume then announces that the alternative to such a deductive justification of causal inferences is an empirical, inductive account drawn from the actual observation (presumably but not necessarily exclusively introspective) of human mental behavior: "Since it is not from any knowledge or scientific reasoning, that we derive the opinion of the necessity of a cause to every new production, that opinion must necessarily arise from observation and experience."[7]

Hume next "sinks" the question of why we believe the general principle that every event has some cause into the further question why we believe in particular connections between causes and effects; and for the sake of brevity, we may further treat together two questions that he does keep separate: why we infer the occurrence of an effect given an impression of its cause (or vice versa) and why we include the idea of "necessary connexion" in our idea of causation when the only impressions objects yield in any case of causation are of their succession and contiguity. All of these questions are to be answered by an explanatory description of certain characteristic principles displaying the effect of memory upon imagination, "which associate together the ideas of these objects, and unite them in the imagination."[8] This explanation rests on the "general maxim in the science of human nature, *that when any impression becomes present to us, it not only transports the mind to such ideas as are related to it, but likewise communicates to them a share of its force and vivacity.*"[9] Essentially, the explanation consists in the application of the more specific version of this principle that the more often any impression is present to the mind, the greater the share of its force and vivacity it then communicates to the related idea. This then leads to Hume's final explanation of both our habit of making causal inferences and the inclusion of the idea of necessary connection in our complex idea of causation: "after a frequent repetition, I find, that upon the appearance of one of the objects, the mind is *determin'd* by custom to consider its usual attendant, and to consider it in a stronger light upon account of its relation to the first object."[10] Imagination's tendency to cast a strong light upon the idea of the effect, or to make it forceful and vivid, constitutes our belief that it must follow from its cause; and our "internal impression" of that "propensity" itself "which custom produces, to pass from an object to the idea of its usual" attendant,[11] is the impression that yields the idea of necessary connection, in accord with the other general maxim of human nature that the imagination produces an idea only when given some antecedent impression. Thus Hume reaches his explicit conclusion that "tho' causation be a *philosophical* relation . . . yet 'tis only so far as it is a *natural* relation, and produces an union among our ideas, that we are able to reason upon it."[12]

2. Let us now recall a paradigm example of a psychological *argument* (accompanied by a further psychological explanation). This is the (implausible) argument that Hume discusses under the rubric "Of scepticism with regard to reason." The argument seems to be this. Experience of "our fallible and uncertain faculties," or of "the inconstancy of our mental powers," informs us of a certain probability of error in any extended application of even the most "certain and infallible" rules of a "demonstrative science";[13] for example, even though the rules of geometry and arithmetic are themselves certain, the nature of human reasoning dictates that there is a determinate probability of error in the conclusion of any extended geometrical demonstration or arithmetical computation. So "our assurance in a

long enumeration [never] exceeds probability."[14] We might think to compensate for this possibility simply by checking our results a few times, thus giving "rise to a new species of probability to correct and regulate the first."[15] Here, however—and this is where his argument goes off the rails—Hume seems to think that the probability of error in each of our several attempts at the computation will be *added*, and thus become greater, rather than being *multiplied*, thus becoming less: after each check, he supposes, renewed reflection upon the fallibility of our faculties "must weaken still further our first evidence . . . and so on *ad infinitum*; till at last there remains nothing of the original probability, however great we may suppose it to have been, and however small the diminution by every new uncertainty."[16] Thus, the natural operation of the human capacity for computation would asymptotically reduce the probability of its own successful use toward zero, or a "total extinction of belief and evidence." Fortunately, we are saved from this epistemic annihilation by *another* "absolute and uncontroulable necessity" of our nature,[17] which is just that the mind cannot sustain reflection upon probabilities much past a "first and second decision," and that "where the mind reaches not its objects with easiness and facility, the same principles have not the same effect as in a more natural conception of the ideas."[18] Thus, the natural tendency of the mind to increase its estimation of the probability of error in any long calculation through reflection upon its own fallibility is counterbalanced by its equally natural disinclination to carry out any long calculations about the probability of error itself.

The obvious implausibility of the initial sceptical argument does not concern me; I am interested only in Hume's method for in this case generating as well as answering a sceptical argument by an explicit appeal to natural rather than rational principles of judgment—principles that cannot be validated by an appeal to reason but are as natural as our equally "uncontroulable necessity . . . to breathe and feel."[19] Such a strategy clearly demonstrates the role of alleged facts about the natural principles of human thinking as indispensable premises in arguments for as well as against sceptical conclusions. But before more fully drawing my morals from these two examples, let me add the one promised example from the *Philosophical Essays* of J. N. Tetens—whose psychologistic account of a wide range of central concepts and judgments should not be taken, as it traditionally is, as the *source* for the psychologistic theory of threefold synthesis in Kant's first edition of the transcendental deduction, but rather as a chief *target for criticism* by what is intended as nothing less than a nonpsychologistic theory of synthesis.

3. Early in his voluminous *Essays*, Tetens asks why in some cases we take the referent of a current representation to be a prior *representation*, which is the cause of the present one, whereas in other cases we judge that the present representation refers not to a prior representation but to the external object, which was the cause of the latter. I take it that this is a question that was of great interest to Kant as well. But Tetens's answer proceeds along very different lines from that which Kant was ultimately to offer. Following in the footsteps of Hume rather than blazing a trail for Kant, Tetens simply postulates that certain representations stimulate our tendency to recall past representations and others stimulate an equally natural tendency to think of the nonrepresentational objects of those representations. I will just illustrate this approach with Tetens's description of the latter tendency:

It is not difficult to find the ground of this phenomenon, or, as some call it, the natural tendency [*Hang*] to take representations for their objects.

When an absent object is represented again, we can perceive, [even though] the reawakened image is only somewhat lively, that a *tendency* to renew again the *complete* prior experience is connected with it. There arises an *impulse* [*Anwandlung*] to suffer again, to be so affected, to will, and to be active again as we previously were in the impression. . . . The powers of the soul thus contain a certain *proclivity* [*Richtung*], through which they are not determined nearly as much to the representation which otherwise belongs to their current modification as to the previous impression of the thing.

What goes on here is similar to what we experience when we have attentively directed our eyes to the *portrait* of a person who interests us, who is known to us from many sides; one soon forgets that it is a picture that stands before us: it is the person himself before our eyes.[20]

No concepts or rules are invoked to explain or justify the interpretation of our current representational state one way rather than another. Instead, just as Hume simply invokes certain natural tendencies of the mind to strengthen or weaken the vivacity of ideas under certain circumstances, so Tetens just postulates similar tendencies or proclivities of the mind to increase the vivacity of present representations by reawakening the larger context in which they were originally experienced or even getting us to overlook the experiences in favor of their external objects altogether. Such tendencies are simply facts about our nature.

With these examples before us, we may now state certain distinctive features of what Kant would have recognized as "physiological" or psychological explanations or arguments.

1. First, the premises of a psychological argument or explanation must postulate the actual occurrence, indeed at moments that are at least in principle determinable, of specific forms of experience or inputs to the mind as well as of specific acts of mental processing of or reaction to these inputs. Thus, the Humean mechanism for causal inference cannot produce a current belief that an event of type C will be followed by another of type E unless the individual reaching this belief has actually experienced previous instances of E's following C's and actually had his tendency to vividly represent E's upon impressions of C's caused by this prior experience.[21] And an accountant's confidence in some particular computation will not be shaken unless he actually engages in repeated reflection upon the fallibility of his mental powers, nor restored unless he actually cuts off such reflection after the first few judgments. Indeed, the character of the output of the psychological mechanism will be correlated to such features as the actual number of inputs or frequency of operation: thus, the strength of one's belief in a causal inference will on Hume's account be directly proportionate to the actual number of times one has previously experienced the appropriate impressions, and the degree of one's doubt about the probability of error in a given computation will be proportionate to the number of times one actually reflects upon the fallibility of our mental powers—that is why nature can save us from this form of scepticism precisely by limiting the number of such reflections. In other words, a genuinely psychological account requires the actual occurrence of specific mental acts, and on specific occasions. This is so even if, as Hume is the first to admit, we may well have failed to attend or even been able to attend to those specific occurrences—"the understanding or imagination can draw inferences from past experience, without reflecting upon it."[22]

2. Second, the assertions about the nature of the mental acts of input and processing that constitute the premises of psychological arguments are contingent rather than necessary truths. Precisely what is meant by so saying must, as usual, be spelled out; but we

should not be misled by Hume's remark that nature determines us to judge as well as to breathe and feel by an "absolute and uncontroulable necessity"; this does not mean that it is necessarily true that nature determines us to judge as Hume has described, but rather only that, if nature determines us to judge in the way that Hume says it does, then in any given instance it is necessary that we judge as we do—and even this conditional necessity must be qualified by Hume's general strictures on induction of the laws of nature. So it in fact means little more than that, given our experience to date, it seems highly probable that we will continue to judge in the way described. This said, we can perhaps make the general statement that psychological premises are ones to which there are conceivable alternatives. They cannot be truths entailed directly by a *concept* of human nature, nor even by any more general concept, such as that of a "cognitive system," but must, like the more particular propositions they support or explain, be "matters of fact." And "the contrary of every matter of fact is still possible; because it can never imply a contradiction."[23] So, for example, we can imagine with "facility and distinctness," as Hume would say, that we were not disposed to have ideas of increasing vivacity after having experiences of increasing frequency, or that we were not disposed to increase our assessments of the probability of error after repeated reflection upon our fallible mental powers. And there is nothing in logic or in any concept of our essence that excludes these fancies. That, indeed, is why we require a "science of man."[24]

3. This brings me back to my last criterion—or back to my opening point about Hobbes. This is just that psychological premises are ordinarily assumed to be discoverable only by some empirical method, even if that method be as easy as introspection of ourselves and observation of the manners of others. Hume makes this plain enough when he writes: "And as the science of man is the only solid foundation for the other sciences, so the only solid foundation we can give to this science itself must be laid on experience and observation," and then characterizes his own work as nothing other than "the application of experimental philosophy to moral subjects."[25] Tetens, too, makes this clear when he writes:

I hold it necessary first of all to declare myself concerning the method which I have employed. It is the [method of] *observing*, which was followed by Locke . . . and by our psychologists in empirical psychology [*erfahrende*

Paul Guyer

Seelenlehre]. To take the modifications of the soul as they may be known
through self-feeling; to observe these carefully, repeatedly, and with altera-
tions of their conditions noticed; to notice their manner of operation and
the laws of the operation [*Wirkungsgesetze*] of the powers which bring them
forth; then to compare [and] resolve the observations and from thence discover the simplest faculties and operations and their relation to each other;
these are the most essential procedures in the psychological analysis of the
soul, which rests on experiences. This method is the method of natural
philosophy.[26]

Of course, psychologists since Tetens have assumed that nonempirical methods of mathematics may be indispensable to the interpretation of their empirical observations (Kant too assumed that
mathematics is indispensable for any science, but also inapplicable to
inner sense, and therefore rejected the possibility of empirical as well
as rational psychology, MFNS 4:471); but the underlying assumption remains that since the basic "laws of the operation of the powers" of the mind are contingent, their discovery must be empirical.
And this, of course, is why psychological arguments "concludeth
nothing universally": their premises are unavoidably empirical, thus
limited by both the limits of observation and the limits of induction.

Kant's Transcendental Deduction

These three criteria hardly constitute a philosophy of psychology,
but will suffice for answering the question whether Kant's transcendental deduction is a psychological argument.

There is one line of argument in Kant's many attempts—unpublished as well as published—to produce a satisfactory deduction that
may well be psychological by at least the first two criteria I described.
This is the argument, which I have described elsewhere[27] and will
not linger over here, that the objective validity of the categories may
be derived from the act of a priori synthesis of any possible manifold,
which is necessary to explain our a priori certainty of the numerical
identity of the self (see A113, A116) in any such manifold. This is indeed an exercise in the "imaginary subject of transcendental psychology," as Professor Strawson so resoundingly called it.[28] But the problem with this argument is not that it is psychological, nor even that it
is transcendental, but that it is transcendent—it is based on a claim
to certitude in a priori knowledge, which Kant does not and cannot

sustain. In other words, it escapes my third criterion for a psychological argument, but only at the cost of its own implausibility.

What I will consider instead is a strategy for the deduction that does not depend upon any claim that transcendental apperception itself is synthetic a priori knowledge of the numerical identity of the self, but only on the more general premise that any form of knowledge (the alleged a priori certainty of the unity of the self here included) requires combination of a manifold. I have elsewhere described Kant as offering a variety of independent arguments based on this premise, and the historical evidence is indeed that he did; but for our purposes here we may more generously consider him as expounding this version of the deduction in three stages of increasing specificity. My argument then will be that even though this strategy for the deduction depends upon the premise that knowledge requires the combination of a manifold, it is not psychological in the sense I have outlined.

The premise of Kant's deduction certainly *sounds* psychological: "If every single representation was entirely alien to another, as it were isolated, and separated from the latter, such a thing as knowledge, which is a whole of compared and combined representations, could never arise" (A97). This sounds like something from Hume or Tetens; indeed, the similar statement of its premise in the second-edition deduction may sound even more overtly psychological:

The combination (*conjunctio*) of a manifold in general can never come to us through sense . . . for it is an act of spontaneity of the power of representation, and, since one must call this understanding in contrast to sensibility, so is all combination, whether we become conscious of it or not, whether it be a combination of the manifold of intuition, or of several concepts . . . an act of the understanding, which we will register with the general name *synthesis*, in order to make obvious that we can never represent anything as combined in the object without first having combined it ourself (B130).

This makes it sound as if Kant's argument must depend on nothing less than a supposition that knowledge is possible only after specific acts of mental processing have been performed. But although this is in a sense true, its truth is not reasonably regarded as a psychological fact; and it is certainly not to any real or alleged psychological laws that Kant appeals in order to show that the objective validity of the categories is a consequence of the need for such an act of synthesis.

57

Contrary to what may be their appearance, these statements describe only general and, as far as they go, conceptual truths about any representing or cognitive systems, human or otherwise, that work in time. To characterize such truths as psychological renders that notion virtually vacuous.

Kant attempts to exploit the underlying supposition that all knowledge requires the combination of a manifold into a unity by arguing that such combination necessarily employs certain rules, which can thus be known a priori, and that a priori knowledge of these rules implies a priori knowledge of the categories. The several stages of Kant's attempt to implement this strategy introduce varying amounts of information about both the data or manifold to be combined and the rules by which they must be combined. For present purposes it will suffice to sketch three levels of argument in Kant. The plausibility of the strategy will obviously increase with the increasing specificity of their characterization of the data to be synthesized for cognition and of the roles played by a priori rules in that synthesis; of course, some might argue that the power of the deduction must decrease as the amount of information it employs increases.

1. In its most general form, Kant's argument is simply that because the data to be synthesized for cognition of a manifold are given in separate episodes of sensible affection, neither the fact nor form of their combination can be given by any similar episode of sense, and must instead be supplied by an exercise of the combinatory capacity of the knower. He then assumes that because the *act* of combination is in this sense independent of the mere reception of the several data of sense, it must be characterized by some a priori concepts or rules. Suggestions of such an argument can be found in the introductory remarks to both the Transcendental Aesthetic ("while the matter of all appearance is given to us a posteriori only, its form must lie ready for the sensations in the mind," A20/B34) and the second-edition deduction (§15). In each of these cases, Kant's remarks could be taken as merely promissory notes for the subsequent argumentation rather than as self-sufficient arguments. But Kant's confidence that this simple argument should actually suffice to accomplish the transcendental deduction of the categories is clear in a letter written to his disciple J. S. Beck on October 16, 1792:

In my judgment everything comes to this: that, since in the empirical concept of the *composite* the composition is not given by means of the mere intuition and its apprehension but can only be represented through the *self-active connection* of the manifold in intuition and indeed in a consciousness in general (which is not empirical), this connection and the function thereof must stand under a priori rules in the mind, which constitute the pure thought of an object in general (C ɪɪ:376).

The problem with taking this as a complete argument, however, is obvious. It might seem clear that *if* any rule were needed for the mind to perform its act of combining its data, then since those rules could not be derived from sense they would have to be internal to the mind, and thus presumably known to it a priori (although this last, Cartesian presumption is a big one indeed). But it is not at all clear why *any* rules should be necessary for the act of combination to take place. Why cannot the mind simply collocate its several data as it chooses and call that the combination of the manifold? Why must representation of a whole of subsidiary representations be one in which the latter are "compared and combined" *according to rules*?

Kant frequently attempted to settle this point by a definition of *knowledge of an object*. In a seminal note from 1775, for instance, he says that "in order to set objects against my representations it is always requisite that the representation be determined according to a general law, for the object consists precisely in the universally valid point" (R4675, 17:648). But of course, a definition of knowledge of an object can yield at best analytic rather than synthetic a priori conclusions; in less polite terms, proving this point by definition begs the question. Without further details, it cannot be obvious that the mere fact that knowledge requires the combination of a manifold also implies that it requires rules, let alone a priori rules.

2. At his next level of argument, Kant attempts to extract the conclusion that combination must proceed in accord with determinate, a priori rules from the additional suppositions that any intellectual combination of a manifold must take place by means of an act of *judgment*, and that there is only a specific set of *forms of judgment* available for such acts. This strategy is clearly stated in a note written after the publication of the first edition of the *Critique*: if we ask

What can count as knowledge in general, then a concept is a representation which is related to an object in general, and designates it; and when we connect . . . one concept with another, in a judgment, we think something of the object that is designated through a given concept, that is, we cognize it. . . . Therefore experience is possible only through judgments (R5923, 18:386).

This strategy is also clearly laid out in the so-called metaphysical deduction, where Kant argues that the synthesis of representations requires both the synthesis of the manifold according to the forms of intuition and also the synthesis of these same intuitions in a judgment; he then argues that because there are fixed forms or "functions" of judgment, this means that all synthesis will proceed in accord with these functions:

> The same function which gives unity to different representations *in a judgment* also gives unity to the mere synthesis of different representations *in an intuition*. . . . The same understanding, therefore, and indeed by means of the very same acts through which . . . it produces the logical form of a judgment, also, by means of the synthetic unity of the manifold in intuition in general, brings a transcendental content to its representations (A79/B104–5).

The same line of reasoning is also prominent in the second-edition deduction, although its potential might seem to be weakened by the fact that Kant introduces it into his exposition only *after* rather than before what might appear to be a more controversial characterization of all *objectively valid* judgment as an assertion of the "*necessary unity*" of the terms connected in the judgment (§19 B141–42). One would have thought that Kant would have attempted to *deduce* the reality of such necessary unity—which of course will imply an a priori ground ("All necessity, without exception, is grounded in a transcendental condition," A106)—*from* the weaker claim, which he only subsequently introduces:

> The same act of the understanding, through which the manifold of given representations (be they intuitions or concepts) is brought under an apperception in general, is the logical function of judgments. Therefore all manifold, so far as it is given in one empirical intuition, is *determined* in respect of one of the logical functions for judging. . . . Now, however, the *categories* are nothing other than just these functions for judging (§20, B143).

Insofar as the several items in a manifold are combined into a single cognitive representation at all, then, they must be combined not only in accord with the pure forms of intuition but also in accord with the logical functions of judgment, and the latter are just identical to the categories. Therefore the categories can be known to hold a priori of any representations that can be synthesized at all.

The problems with this level of argument are themselves manifold. We can ask why in fact intuitions must be combined according to the forms of judgment as well as according to the forms of intuition. Kant's preferred, *mathematical* examples (see, for instance, A105 and B154) leave this very point obscure, since they do not seem to introduce any transcendental content into the construction of their objects except for mathematical concepts themselves—they certainly do not suggest how such concepts as *causation* or *interaction* might come into play. We can ask why the functions of judgment are those Kant lists, or, even more problematic, why *all* of the functions he lists must be used in synthesis—though an answer to this question must be forthcoming if Kant is to prove the objective validity of the categories of causation and interaction against Leibniz and of substance and causation against Hume. But perhaps the most pressing question is that of the identity of *logical* functions of judgment and categories on which this argument turns—for Kant elsewhere suggests that categories are required to fix what would be our otherwise *arbitrary* use of the *merely* logical forms of judgment.

This point is introduced only in passing in the *Critique*: only at the end of the "transition" to the actual deduction does Kant emphasize that the "merely logical employment of the understanding" leaves it entirely undetermined *how* a particular logical function of judgment is to be applied to given concepts or representations. Thus, for instance, *which* of the concepts *body* and *divisible* should be the subject and which the predicate is not determined by the logical requirement that we link them in *some* subject-predicate judgment. It is only when a category is employed, Kant suggests, that this becomes fixed: for example, "when the concept of body is brought under the category of substance, it is determined that its empirical intuition must always be regarded only as subject and never as mere predicate" (B129). But a number of texts make this point more emphatically, thereby suggesting that the argument for the objective validity of the categories only *begins* when the need for a ground for the nonarbitrary use of the logical functions of judgment is recognized. Thus, in his metaphysics lectures in 1784–85 Kant put the following at the center of his argument for synthetic a priori knowledge:

To all experiences there also belongs a relation of these representations of sense to the object, and in order to relate my representations to the object the forms of judgment must be made determinate. These concepts which contain the determination of an object in general in another form are called pure concepts of the understanding (*Metaphysik Volckmann*, 28:405).

And this point is equally central to the argument of the *Prolegomena*, where Kant explicitly argues that because even mere "judgments of perception" employ the logical forms of judgment, "it does not, as is commonly imagined, suffice for experience that perceptions are compared and connected in consciousness through judgment." Instead, experience is possible only when a "given intuition is subsumed under a concept which determines the form of judgment in general relatively to the intuition" (Prol §20, 4:300).

This may well explain why in the second-edition transcendental deduction Kant introduces the argument we were led to expect by the metaphysical deduction only after rather than before emphasizing the *necessary unity* asserted by objectively valid judgments: the logical forms of judgment are at most a necessary but not a sufficient condition of the objective validity of the categories; and some additional claim to necessity is needed to ground the a priori validity of these categories. The problem then becomes that of understanding Kant's justification for the introduction of the further claim of necessity. Kant's assertion in the second-edition deduction that objectively valid judgments themselves assert that the concepts they connect "belong to one another *in virtue of the necessary unity* of apperception" (§19, B142) comes perilously close to begging the question of a priori knowledge,[29] as does his similar statement in the *Prolegomena*: "when a judgment agrees with an object, all judgments concerning the same object must likewise agree among themselves, and thus the objective validity of the judgment of experience signifies nothing other than its necessary universal validity" (Prol §20, 4:298). In fact, it is my view that we cannot find a sufficient basis for the introduction of the categories other than an outright equation of objectivity with necessity until we turn to the last level of Kant's deduction, where he draws consequences from the specifically *temporal* nature of the manifold, which is to be synthesized in any claim to knowledge.

3. I will state the argument from the temporal nature of the manifold to the need for categories as briefly as possible. It begins with the claim that because the several members of any manifold of intuition are given only over some period of time longer than and preceding the moment at which a judgment about the manifold must be made, there must be some way in which the previously given mem-

bers of the manifold are reproduced at the moment of their synthesis. The temporally extended nature of the input of the manifold and the consequent need for the reproduction of its members are expressed by Kant's notions of the "synthesis of apprehension" and "synthesis of reproduction" respectively (A98–102). But since individual representations are "very variable and transitory" (Bxli), this reproduction cannot take the form of any literal combination of past with present representations—the past representations no longer exist when we come to the present. Instead, there must be some way in which the current representational state of the knower can be *interpreted* as including representation of its previous representational states. And this is possible only if the knower has some concepts or rules by which this current representational state can be interpreted, or a distinction drawn between what it represents *as* current and what it represents as having been previously represented. Only thus can we become conscious "that what we think is the same as what we thought a moment before," without which "all reproduction in the series of representations would be fruitless" (A103). This is what Kant calls the requirement for "synthesis of recognition in a concept." And the rules for this kind of interpretation turn out to be nothing other than the categories—or, more precisely, the synthetic a priori principles of empirical judgment that employ these categories. Thus, Kant's explanation why synthesis cannot simply consist in the ruleless combination of the manifold of data to be synthesized is that apart from rules for the interpretation of the manifold its members do not exist to be combined. The synthesis of reproduction cannot take place independently of the synthesis of recognition in a concept because it is only the application of appropriately interpretative concepts to the current representational state of any knower that reproduces the data to be synthesized.

Kant states the premise of this argument plainly enough at the beginning of the first-edition deduction: "Every intuition contains a manifold in itself which yet would not be represented as such if the mind did not distinguish the time in the sequence of impressions on one another: for as *contained in a single moment* each representation can never be anything other than absolute unity" (A99). This implies not only what Kant immediately adds, that representational input must occur at more than one moment for there to be any talk of a manifold, but also that the mere occurrence of the successive members in a manifold does not suffice for any representation *of* the manifold; for there is no one moment in which the mind actually has the whole manifold before it. Instead, it must "distinguish the time" that can be represented by its current representational state in accord with some scheme for such interpretation.

But only years as well as pages later does Kant make even minimally clear what the role of the categories in such interpretation is. This role is only spelled out when, several years after publishing the second edition of the *Critique*, Kant returns to its Refutation of Idealism and reveals its *nervus probandi*. Since I have discussed this at length elsewhere,[30] a few words will have to suffice here. Basically, Kant's idea is that concepts of independent and enduring substances with rule-governed states of succession in and among themselves as well as rule-governed effects on our perceptions of them, thus on the succession of our representations, are the only means by which we can judge that any of our current representational states does represent a sequence of past states, thus a manifold of intuition, as well:

Time itself is, to be sure, enduring, but it cannot be perceived by itself, consequently, there must be something which endures, against which one can perceive change in time. This enduring thing cannot be our self, for precisely as object of inner sense we are determined through time; that which endures can only be posited in that which is given through outer sense (R6311, 18:611);

and

Empirical consciousness (*apprehensio*) . . . can contain only succession. But this itself cannot be represented except by means of something which endures, with which that which is successive is simultaneous. This enduring thing, with which that which is successive is simultaneous . . . cannot in turn be a representation of the mere imagination (R6313, 18:614).

Only by determining that our current state represents successive states of a changing object can we determine that it must also represent a succession of representations of that object. But to determine this, we must introduce the concepts of, and principles by which to judge about, (i) an enduring object distinct from our representation of it, (ii) states of that object that must succeed one another in a determinate manner, and (iii) rules that correlate the successive states of such an object with a succession of representational states in ourself. This means that reproduction of the manifold of intuition is only possible by means of the concept of enduring independent substances whose states stand in rule-governed relations of succession and have determinate effects upon the succession of our states as well—which is pretty much what has to be proved for a deduction of the objective validity of the a priori categories.

Is Kant's Deduction Psychological?

All of this may still sound as if it reaches deep into the same territory of cognitive psychology presumed upon by Tetens and Hume. But I shall now argue that this is not so. To be sure, Kant's argument ultimately depends on an assumption of what may have to be regarded as a matter of fact: that the input or data for cognition are temporally successive, and thus that earlier items in a manifold can be reproduced only by being recognized to be represented by its current member. But to call this fundamental fact psychological, however contingent it may in the end be (if indeed we have any clear grasp of what is contingent and what not at this level), is to trivialize the concept of psychology. After all, this claim is also true of a computer, whose current distribution of electrical charges can be interpreted as a representation of previously acquired data only by a suitable program (and of course programmer). Kant's premise is not a psychological claim but a basic constraint on any system for synthesizing data that are only given over time.

i. Let me expand upon this assertion by reviewing the three criteria I extracted from my discussion of Hume and Tetens. The most delicate issue is raised by the first of these, which stated that a psychological argument or explanation premises the actual and at least theoretically datable occurrence of particular types of mental acts, and can even make reference to such a fact as the frequency of the occurrence of such acts. Kant's argument does seem to satisfy this criterion at least insofar as it refers to the actual input of the original representations in a succession and an actual act of recognition of what is reproduced at a subsequent time. However, that different representations are originally successive rather than coexistent seems more a fact about time than about our psyches; it is on the same plane as the fact that successive entries of data into a computer do not themselves subsequently exist simultaneously, but are at best represented by charges simultaneously existing at a later moment at different spots on its memory chips. Or, to put it in a different way, it is trivially true that data entered into a human (or mechanical) knower at different moments are indeed entered at different moments, and can only be recovered with the aid of a proper procedure. This is not comparable to the by no means trivial claim that repeated entry of similar impressions tends to increase the vivacity with which a correlated idea is subsequently entertained.

The more difficult issue is whether the end stage of Kant's model, the rule-guided act of synthesizing and thus both recognizing and reproducing the successively given manifold, should be characterized as ineluctably psychological. Kant certainly seems to write as if he were describing a datable mental occurrence, which must take place if a further occurrence, the mental or verbal issuance of a knowledge-claim, is to be explained. But here there is also some room for doubt as to whether Kant is describing a psychological occurrence in which the manifold is interpreted or an epistemological requirement that it be interpretable in the light of certain rules. At least one remark may make it seem as if Kant simply wishes to fudge the distinction between the psychological and the epistemological, between claims about mental history and about the conceptual structure of self-interpretation, by invoking the Leibnizian dodge of perceptions which are not apperceived: a concept, he writes,

is *one* consciousness which unites the manifold, successively intuited and then also reproduced, into one representation. This consciousness can often be only weak, so that we connect it only [with] the effect, not [with] the act itself, that is, immediately with the generation of the representation; but, regardless of these differences, [this] consciousness must always be found (A104).

But other remarks make it look as if Kant is not interested in postulating the actual occurrence, whether faintly or vividly apperceived, of any act of interpretation, but is rather insisting only upon the availability of concepts by which the interpretation of the present representational state of the knower could be justified. On this account, his claim would not be that the categories are always used in actual events of synthesis, but only that the categories must be available to sustain the judgments by which the reproduction and recognition of the manifold can be expressed:

We cognize the object if we have produced synthetic unity in the manifold of intuition. This however is impossible if the intuition could not have been produced through such a function of synthesis according to a rule which makes the reproduction of the manifold a priori necessary and a concept in which it is united possible. So we think a triangle as an object insofar as we are conscious of three straight lines according to which such an intuition can always be presented (A105).

Here Kant's point seems to be that it must be possible for us to produce the rule by which the reproduction of the manifold is guided and interpreted if we are to justify our claim to knowledge of an object, not that any actual assertion of a knowledge-claim must be preceded or accompanied by some datable act of mental processing that literally tokens the rule. Indeed, it would even be compatible with such an account that the psychological explanation of the knowledge-claims that we actually think and utter involve Humean processes of association and vivification, and that it is only the epistemic justification of them that requires reference to the pure concepts of the understanding.

Even if this conclusion seems too strong, room remains for some differentiation between the method of Kant's deduction and the psychological approach typified by Hume. In Hume's arguments and explanations the alleged maxims of the science of man are essential premises, whereas in Kant's deduction the postulation of even the actual occurrence of an act embodying the synthesis of recognition is only the conclusion of an argument, the premises of which—the successive input of the manifold of intuition and the need for an interpretative reproduction of it—are not themselves psychological. Thus Kant's deduction may even have a psychological conclusion without being a psychological argument. Somewhat more strongly, we might put the point thus: while the essential steps in Kant's arguments—that the manifold must be successively experienced and subsequently interpreted—may be matters of fact, these are facts of life rather than facts of psychology. After all, computers, too, must subsequently process the data that have been antecedently and successively entered into them—and they need some rules to do this. We certainly should not give a nominal answer to the question whether computers can think by calling this a psychological fact.

2. I can now deal more briefly with the remaining criteria. The second criterion for a psychological claim was contingency: if the premise of an argument is genuinely psychological, then we ought to be able to imagine an alternative to it, as we certainly can imagine that human beings might repeatedly experience conjunctions of impressions without thereby winning livelier ideas. It is far from obvious that the premises—or conclusion—of Kant's deduction have

conceivable alternatives in this sense. That a knower that receives its data over time must reproduce them in order to derive knowledge from them, but can only do so by interpreting its current state according to a rule, does not seem contingent, and seems to apply to computers as well as to ourselves precisely because it is not a contingent fact about our own psychologies but some sort of necessary truth about information-processing in time. And even Kant's more specific claims that our interpretation of temporal succession in our manifolds requires postulation of a realm of rule-governed, causally active external objects does not fit the model of a Humean custom or an inclination as conceived by Tetens. It is not just a fact about our own mental habits that this is what we appeal to in order to justify our judgments about the succession of our own experiences; rather, any set of objects that we *could* appeal to would have to be characterized by these very general categories.

3. My recurring claim that Kant's argument turns on what are constraints for a computer's reproduction of its data as well as for our own interpretation of our experience should also make it clear that Kant's transcendental deduction violates the third criterion for a psychological argument: its premises are clearly not empirical—at least not in the sense of being drawn from any observation or induction about ourselves that we have subsequently learned applies to computers as well. (I did not learn them in a computer science course.) Instead, the argument has to do with the necessary conditions for any cognitive system working in time. Such constraints may be discovered by reflection upon the structure of knowledge and the nature of time—this conjoint origin is what makes them synthetic rather than analytic propositions—and even if the relevant claims, especially about time, are in some sense ultimately contingent or factual, this does not make them psychological.

I conclude, then, that the basic premises of Kant's transcendental deduction, even if derived from his most "subjective" presentation of it, indeed from what is often called the "subjective deduction," namely the theory of the threefold synthesis, are not psychological in any nontrivial sense. They may well place constraints on anything that would count as human cognitive psychology—but that would be another story.

Sensibility, Understanding, and the Doctrine of Synthesis: Comments on Henrich and Guyer

P. F. STRAWSON

Professor Henrich has given us a most illuminating and instructive account of the methodology of the transcendental deduction and of Kant's transcendental strategy in general. He begins with the juridical analogy, which, as he shows, there is conclusive reason to think Kant had in mind. A deduction in the relevant sense aims to justify an acquired title, or claim of right, by tracing it back to *origins*, to origins which are such as to confer legitimacy on it. In application to the *Critique* this is a matter of elucidating crucial *basic facts* by virtue of which our *knowledge-claims* are justified and upon which our possession of knowledge depends. These basic facts relate to *specific cognitive capacities* of which we have, in reflection, an *implicit* awareness or knowledge. The deduction is then said to proceed, not by linear demonstration, but by a variety of argumentative strategies that will systematize and render explicit the functioning of our cognitive capacities and, in doing so, will, it is hoped, exhibit the necessary "validity of the categories for all objects of experience."

Given this program, with its emphasis on crucial basic facts regarding our specific cognitive capacities or faculties, it is obviously important to be clear what exactly those basic facts *are*. Crucial here is the distinction between sensibility and understanding: on the one hand, the (intuitive) faculty of receptivity through which the materials of knowledge are given to us; and, on the other, the (discursive) faculty of thought through which they are conceptualized and through which judgment is possible—both faculties being indispensable to beings like us who lack the power of intellectual intuition. To these must surely be added, as Professor Henrich stresses, the self-consciousness (the "I think") that can accompany all our cognitive operations, but is not merely an accompaniment or correlate of other thoughts; but rather something pervasively indispensable in the elaboration of the argument that is to lead, it is hoped, to the conclusion that the categories are necessarily valid of objects.

However, in these brief comments, I do not propose to attempt an analysis of the stages of the argument. I wish, rather, to raise what might be called a metacritical point: a point concerning those "crucial basic facts" about the dual faculties of sensibility and understanding; specifically about the a priori forms of sensibility and about the forms or functions, and hence the pure concepts, of understanding.

In a well-known sentence at B145–46, Kant writes: "This peculiarity of our understanding, that it can produce a priori unity of apperception solely by means of the categories, and only by such and so many, is *as little capable of further explanation as why we have just these and no other functions of judgment or why space and time are the only forms of our possible intuition.*"

The clear implication of this passage seems to be that we must take it as a basic *fact* indeed about human cognitive faculties—as something fundamentally *contingent*, given and inexplicable—that we have just the forms and functions of judgment, and just the (spatial and temporal) forms of sensibility, that we do have. If this is so as regards the forms of judgment, then it will indeed follow that no *further* explanation can be given of why we have just the pure concepts of an object in general, the categories, that we do have; for the latter are precisely held to be derived from the former. Moreover, the inexplicable givenness or bare contingency, of our possessing just these and no other functions of judgment and forms of intuition will constitute no objection, from the *critical* point of view, to bestowing the title "a priori" both on the pure concepts and on the spatio-temporal forms of sensibility; for, as conditions of the possibility of empirical knowledge of objects—as virtually defining what can count as objects *for us* and our purposes—they will certainly not be themselves empirical, that is, derived from within experience. Again, it may not *matter* from the critical point of view, that the possibility of synthetic a priori knowledge is seen to rest on a contingent foundation, a human "peculiarity" (*Eigentümlichkeit*), to use Kant's word; though the fact that what is a priori is represented as having a *contingent* foundation will be found at least worthy of remark (and perhaps, to some, disturbing).

But if we shift our stance, if we stand just a little outside the critical point of view, we may legitimately wonder whether it really *is* quite inexplicable that we have just the functions of judgment (the logical forms) and just the spatio-temporal forms of intuition that we do have. First, as to the logical forms. The fundamental logical operations or forms of judgment recognized in Kant's table are such as are, and must be, recognized in any general logic worthy of the name. By "the fundamental logical operations" I mean: predication (subject and predicate), generalization (particular and universal forms), sentence-composition (including negation, disjunction, conditionality, etc.). Now it is not a mysterious but an analytic truth that judgment involves concepts, that concepts are such as to be applicable or inapplicable to one or more instances, that judgments or propositions are capable of truth or falsity. From such considerations as these it is not too difficult to show that the possibility of the fundamental logical operations is inherent in the very nature of the judgment or proposition. Wittgenstein expressed the point with characteristic epigrammatic obscurity when he wrote in the *Tractatus*: "One could say that the sole logical constant was what *all* propositions, *by their very nature*, had in common with one another. But that is the general propositional form."[1] Of course there are differences between the notational devices and forms recognized in different systems of general logic, notably between the forms listed by Kant and those that we find in modern (standard) classical logic. But in spite of their differences in perspicuity and power, the same fundamental logical operations are recognized in both systems. It does indeed seem pretty clear that Kant himself regarded the truths of logic and the principles of formal inference as analytic. Why, one may ask, did he not also see the forms of logic, the fundamental logical operations, as themselves analytically implicit in the very notion of judgment? Had he done so, he could scarcely have said that it was *beyond explanation* why we had "just these and no other functions of judgment." The only answer I can think of to my question—the question why he didn't see it this way—refers to the idea of an intellect that is not discursive at all, but purely intuitive: to the idea of "intellectual intuition." But that is really no answer. For a nondiscursive, an intuitive intellect, which had no need of sensible intuition, which as it were created its own objects of knowledge, would presumably have no need of *judgment* either. (I say this tentatively, however, having no more conception than Kant had of what intellectual intuition would be like.)

What now of the doctrine that it is a bare inexplicable fact of human sensibility that we have just the spatial and temporal forms of intuition that we do have? Is it really inexplicable? Does it simply inexplicably *happen* to be the case that the spatial and the temporal are the modes in which *we* are sensibly affected by objects? Well, one very simple explanation, or ground of explanation, would be this: that the objects, including ourselves, *are* spatio-temporal objects, are *in* space and time—where by "objects" is meant not *just* "objects of possible knowledge" (though that is also meant) but objects, and ourselves, as they really are or are in themselves. The reason why this would be an adequate explanation is fairly straightforward, granted only that we are indeed creatures whose intellects are discursive and whose intuition is sensible. For such creatures must, in judgment, employ and apply general concepts to the objects of sensible intuition; the very notion of the generality of a concept implies the possibility of numerically distinguishable individual objects falling under one and the same concept; and, once granted that objects are themselves spatio-temporal, then space and time provide the uniquely necessary media for the realization of this possibility in sensible intuition of objects. I say "uniquely necessary," because, although distinguishable spatio-temporal objects falling under the same general concept could certainly be distinguishable in many other ways, the one way in which they *could not fail* to be distinguishable—the one way in which they are *necessarily* distinguishable—is in respect of their spatial and/or temporal location. (I repeat here an argument I have used elsewhere,[2] but it seems sufficiently important to be worth repeating.)

I have argued that *both* our possession of just the logical functions of judgment (and hence, arguably, just the pure concepts) that we do possess *and* our possession of just the spatio-temporal forms of intuition that we do possess—I have argued that, on certain assumptions, both of these admit of perfectly adequate explanation. Two of these assumptions—viz. that our intellect is discursive and our intuition sensible—are admitted, indeed proclaimed, by Kant himself. The third assumption—namely that objects and ourselves are, as they are in themselves, spatio-temporal things—is an assumption that he would, it seems, reject, although the significance of this rejection is not, perhaps, entirely clear.

But there is a more important point to be made, which is this. Nothing in what I have said is, in itself, sufficient to challenge for one moment the status of space and time as a priori forms of intuition. For spatio-temporal intuition of objects, through whatever sensory modalities it may be empirically mediated, appears even more strongly than before as a uniquely fundamental *condition* of any empirical knowledge of objects. Similarly, given the status I have claimed for the logical functions of judgment, then, if the derivation of the categories from the forms of judgment and their ensuing deduction are both sound, it will follow that they, too, have a parallel status to that of the forms of sensible intuition as a priori conditions of empirical knowledge. So nothing in what I have so far said threatens this aspect of Kant's transcendentalism. Equally, and still more obviously, nothing threatens his empirical realism.

What, then, of his version of idealism, the apparently sharp distinction between things in themselves and appearances, the latter alone being objects of empirical knowledge? The question here is one of interpretation. *If,* in accordance with the purely negative concept of the noumenon, the thought of things in themselves is to be understood simply and solely as the thought of the very things of which human knowledge is possible, but the thought of them *in total abstraction* from what have been shown (or at least argued) to be the conditions of the very *possibility* of any such knowledge, then it must surely be concluded that the thought is empty; for the doctrine that we can have no knowledge of things *as they are in themselves* reduces to the tautology that no knowledge of things is possible *except under the conditions under which it is possible*; or: we can know of things only what we can know of them. In that case, though the empirical realism is secure, the "idealism" in Kant's "transcendental idealism" would appear as little more than a token name, or as, at most, the acknowledgment that though indeed we can have knowledge of things, there may be more to the nature of those things than what we can know about them—an acknowledgment that most of us would be perfectly happy to make.

However, it must, I think, be admitted that it is far from clear that this is the intended, or at least the consistently intended, interpretation of the distinction between appearance and thing in itself. And if it is not, then we are faced with a host of familiar difficulties (regarding the relations between a supersensible and a sensible world) which it would be irrelevant now to recall.

In his paper Professor Guyer confronts the question whether Kant's transcendental deduction of the categories is to be understood as "psychological" in character. There is a sense of that word in which to understand the deduction as "psychological" would certainly be damaging to its claim to establish the a priori objective validity of the pure concepts of an object in general. Drawing on examples from Hume and J. N. Tetens, Professor Guyer mentions three connected characteristics or arguments or explanations that are psychological in this sense.

First, such explanations or arguments refer or appeal to the actual occurrence at determinable moments of specific mental experiences and mental acts. Second, it is only contingently true that acts of these types occur. And, third, it is only empirically that their occurrences can be established or certified.

Two things are immediately clear. First, any account or argument that did indeed have these characteristics would be quite alien to the aims of the deduction and quite unable to fulfil its purposes. But, second, it is only too easy to read some passages of the deduction (especially in the first-edition version) as if what were being spoken of were actual occurrences of mental acts and processes of reproducing and synthesizing or combining sequential elements of the sensory manifold. Such a reading runs into the obvious difficulty that, on the one hand, it is hard to see how there could be any but *empirical* knowledge of any such occurrences; whereas, on the other, the argument of the deduction seems to require their occurrence to be an antecedent condition of the possibility of any empirical knowledge at all.

Professor Guyer aims to show that the deduction is not psychological in the damaging sense; consequently that the reading above referred to is incorrect and the difficulties inherent in it do not arise. I think he is substantially successful in this aim and I will endeavor, first, to state very summarily what seem to me to be the main points of his argument. First, it has to be admitted that the sensory input that supplies us with all the materials of knowledge comes to us over time, as a series of "variable and transitory data," a temporal manifold. A mere series of transitory, and *unconnected*, representations or receptions of successive elements of such a manifold would not amount to cognition or knowledge. To achieve the latter, some form of representation is required that *holds together* the successive elements of the manifold. Or, in Professor Guyer's own words, "there must be some way in which the current representational state of the knower can be interpreted to include representation of its previous representational states." And this in its turn is possible only if the knower deploys, in his current representational state, concepts that themselves exemplify or incorporate the crucial categories or concepts of an object in general, specifically those of substance and cause; that is, the concepts to be deployed are concepts "of enduring independent substances whose states stand in rule-governed relations of succession and have determinate effects upon the succession of our states as well." (This is most clearly spelled out, Professor Guyer suggests, in Kant's subsequent reflections on the Refutation of Idealism.)

However, the line of thought I have so drastically—no doubt too drastically—abbreviated here does, I think, require some interpretation if the shades of Hume and Tetens are to be finally dismissed. It is true, of course, that the sensory input we receive is extended over time and hence that it can in principle be thought of as a series of successive impressions, each with its own intrinsic instantaneous character. But, if the *intrinsic* character of each single successive impression were thought of (on Hume-like lines) as *not* already involving the objective concepts to be argued for, then it would seem that something like a retrospective *act* of reproducing past impressions and *combining* them with a present one by the *imposition* of a unifying objective concept would be called for. But *that* story would be altogether too reminiscent of the dreaded psychological model, with its attendant difficulties, for it to be acceptable to Professor Guyer (or, for that matter, to me). Rather we must insist—and to do so is, incidentally, to be quite faithful to the actual character of our ordinary perceptual experience—we must insist, I say, that at *any instant* in the ongoing stream of "episodes of sensible affection" (as Professor Guyer calls them) our perceptual experience involves the deployment of concepts of objects of the desired sort; that our representational states *at each moment* are thoroughly permeated by such concepts. The truth that perceptual experience *at any given moment* is to be thus characterized is precisely what is necessary and sufficient to link the actual current perception or representational state to other, not actually current, past, or possible future representational states; to effect, if you like, their necessary combination. Concepts of enduring objects with causal powers have precisely this nature: any actual current perception, or representation, of something as falling under such a concept is essentially linked to other nonactual, noncurrent perceptions of the same kind. As I have put it elsewhere, nonpresent perceptions "are in a sense represented in, alive in, the present perception." This is why Kant gives such an important role to the faculty of imagination, qualified as "transcendental"; for imagination, as more commonly understood, is just the faculty of representing the nonactual.[3] And I think, and hope, that much of the same thought is present in Professor Guyer's mind when he writes: "The synthesis of reproduction cannot take place independently of the synthesis of recognition in a concept because it is only the application of appropriately interpretative concepts to the current representational state of any knower that reproduces the data to be synthesised."

However, given the present state of research in cognitive psychology, there is something to be added to this. As far as our *conscious* experience is concerned, it is right to insist, as I have done, and as I think Professor Guyer implicitly does, that our successive states of conscious perceptual experience are, throughout, such that they cannot (in general) be accurately characterized without employing concepts of enduring objects with causal powers; and it is true, too, as the deduction is designed to show (or to prepare the ground for showing), that so much is a necessary condition of knowledge arising from perceptual experience. But we have also learned, from the results of studies in physiological psychology, that our *conscious* perceptual experience is causally dependent on neuro-physiological processes of immense complexity, processes of which we are *not* conscious at all while we are enjoying the conscious experience that depends upon them. The studies in question are empirical, as are their results. They relate to particular occurrences and processes in the brain and nervous system, themselves occasioned by impingements on the external organs. Perhaps—though I speak in ignorance—the phrase "information-processing" is correctly applied to these internal operations. Now, as I earlier remarked, much of the language of Kant's deduction—notably in the theory of the three-fold synthesis—does invite and encourage interpretation in terms of particular occurrences of events and processes—of reproduction and combination—that culminate in the application of concepts falling under the categories. May it not be that the Kantian theory of synthesis, interpreted in this style, has at least analogues—and perfectly respectable analogues—in the empirical theories of the physiological psychologists? If so, and even if (as seems likely) very little can be made out in the way of detailed parallels, the Kantian theory of synthesis, understood in *this* way, could be seen as a brilliantly imaginative anticipation of the results of scientific investigation—indeed of what might, with peculiar, unexpected, and certainly *unintended* appropriateness, be called "the physiology of inner sense." I think that Professor Guyer perhaps hints at something of the kind himself when he remarks that the Kantian theory "may well place constraints on anything that would count as human cognitive psychology."

If both parts of these comments of mine on Professor Guyer's paper are on roughly the right lines, then a certain inevitable tension in our understanding of Kant's deduction can be satisfactorily resolved. On the one hand we can safely deny that Kant's theory is psychological in that damaging sense that Professor Guyer illustrates by reference to Hume and Tetens. At the same time we can construe those passages in Kant's work that undeniably *suggest* such a reading as pointing, rather, toward developments in what is undoubtedly empirical (and physiological) psychology—developments of which it was impossible to form an accurate or detailed conception at the time at which he wrote. Both views of the matter are perfectly compatible with each other—they can be held simultaneously—and both may be seen as underlining his genius. Neither constrains us to see Kant as conducting an exercise in what I once somewhat rudely called "the imaginary subject of transcendental psychology" and which, as Professor Guyer rightly remarks, might more correctly be described as "transcendent" rather than "transcendental ."

PART II

The *Critique of Practical Reason*

Themes in Kant's Moral Philosophy

JOHN RAWLS

I shall discuss several connected themes in Kant's moral philosophy, in particular what I shall refer to as moral constructivism and the fact of reason, and how that fact connects with the authentication of the moral law and the moral law as a law of freedom. These are each large topics and I can only survey them; but perhaps something can be gained from a brief synoptic view. I would like to have concluded with some comments about what Kant means by the practical point of view but that proved impossible for lack of space.

To set the background for these topics, I begin with a schematic outline of how Kant understands the moral law, the categorical imperative and the procedure by which that imperative is applied. Some account of that procedure is an essential preliminary to understanding his constructivism. Plainly a full account is out of the question but I believe many intriguing details of interpretation are not crucial so long as the account meets certain conditions (cf. §1.5). My hope is that the reading suggested is accurate enough to bring out the more central elements of Kant's constructivism and to connect this doctrine with the other topics.

My discussion has five parts: the first covers the procedure for applying the categorical imperative, or the CI-procedure, as I shall call it; the second surveys six conceptions of the good, and how these conceptions are constructed in an ordered sequence; whereas the

John Rawls

third, based on the preceding two parts, examines the aspects of Kant's doctrine that make it constructivist and specify a conception of objectivity. The fourth and fifth parts take up, respectively, the kind of justification, or authentication, that can be given for the moral law, and how the moral law as an idea of reason is seen as a law of freedom and how this connects with Kant's idea of philosophy as defense.

§1. The Four-Step CI-Procedure

1. I begin with a highly schematic rendering of Kant's conception of the categorical imperative.[1] I assume that this imperative is applied to the normal conditions of human life by what I shall call the "categorical imperative procedure," or the "CI-procedure" for short. This procedure helps to determine the content of the moral law as it applies to us as reasonable and rational persons endowed with conscience and moral sensibility, and affected by, but not determined by, our natural desires and inclinations. These desires and inclinations reflect our needs as finite beings having a particular place in the order of nature.

Recall that the moral law, the categorical imperative, and the CI-procedure are three different things. The first is an idea of reason and specifies a principle that applies to all reasonable and rational beings whether or not they are like us finite beings with needs. The second is an imperative and as such it is directed only to those reasonable and rational beings who, because they are finite beings with needs, experience the moral law as a constraint. Since we are such beings, we experience the law in this way, and so the categorical imperative applies to us. The CI-procedure adapts the categorical imperative to our circumstances by taking into account the normal conditions of human life and our situation as finite beings with needs in the order of nature.

Keep in mind throughout that Kant is concerned solely with the reasoning of fully reasonable and rational and sincere agents. The CI-procedure is a schema to characterize the framework of deliberation that such agents use implicitly in their moral thought. He takes for granted that the application of this procedure presupposes a certain moral sensibility that is part of our common humanity.[2] It is a misconception to think of it either as an algorithm that yields more or less mechanically a correct judgment, or on the other hand, as a

82

set of debating rules that will trap liars and cheats, cynics and other scoundrels, into exposing their hand.

2. The CI-procedure has four steps as follows.[3] At the first step we have the agent's maxim, which is, by assumption, rational from the agent's point of view: that is, the maxim is rational given the agent's situation and the alternatives available together with the agent's desires, abilities, and beliefs (which are assumed to be rational in the circumstances). The maxim is also assumed to be sincere: that is, it reflects the agent's actual reasons (as the agent would truthfully describe them) for the intended action. Thus the CI-procedure applies to maxims that rational agents have arrived at in view of what they regard as the relevant features of their circumstances. And, we should add, this procedure applies equally well to maxims that rational and sincere agents might arrive at given the normal circumstances of human life. To sum up: the agent's maxim at the first step is both rational and sincere. It is a particular hypothetical imperative (to be distinguished later from *the* hypothetical imperative) and it has the form:

(1) I am to do X in circumstances C in order to bring about Y. (Here X is an action and Y a state of affairs.)

The second step generalizes the maxim at the first to get:

(2) Everyone is to do X in circumstances C in order to bring about Y.

At the third step we are to transform the general precept at (2) into a law of nature to obtain:

(3) Everyone always does X in circumstances C in order to bring about Y (as if by a law of nature).

The fourth step is the most complicated and raises questions that I cannot consider here. The idea is this:

(4) We are to adjoin the law of nature at step (3) to the existing laws of nature (as these are understood by us) and then calculate as best we can what the order of nature would be once the effects of the newly adjoined law of nature have had a chance to work themselves out.

It is assumed that a new order of nature results from the addition of the law at step (3) to the other laws of nature, and that this new order of nature has a settled equilibrium state the relevant features of which we are able to figure out. Let us call this new order of nature a "perturbed social world," and let's think of this social world as associated with the maxim at step (1).

Kant's categorical imperative can now be stated as follows: We are permitted to act from our rational and sincere maxim at step (1) only if two conditions are satisfied: First, we must be able to intend, as a sincere reasonable and rational agent, to act from this maxim when we regard ourselves as a member of the perturbed social world associated with it (and thus as acting within that world and subject to its conditions); and second, we must be able to will this perturbed social world itself and affirm it should we belong to it.

Thus, if we cannot at the same time both will this perturbed social world and intend to act from this maxim as a member of it, we cannot now act from the maxim even though it is, by assumption, rational and sincere in our present circumstances. The principle represented by the CI-procedure applies to us no matter what the consequences may be for our rational interests as we now understand them. It is at this point that the force of the priority of pure practical reason over empirical practical reason comes into play. But let's leave this aside for the moment.

3. To illustrate the use of the four-step procedure, consider the fourth example in the *Grundlegung* (Gr 4:423). The maxim to be tested is one that expresses indifference to the well-being of others who need our help and assistance. We are to decide whether we can will the perturbed social world associated with this maxim formulated as follows.

I am not to do anything to help others, or to support them in distress, unless at the time it is rational to do so, given my own interests.

The perturbed social world associated with this maxim is a social world in which no one ever does anything to help others for the sake of their well-being. And this is true of everyone, past, present, and future. This is the relevant equilibrium state; and we are to imagine that this state obtains, like any other order of nature, in perpetuity, backwards and forwards in time. Kant takes for granted that everyone in the perturbed social world knows the laws of human conduct that arise from generalized maxims and that everyone is able to work out the relevant equilibrium state. Moreover, that everyone is able to do this is itself public knowledge. Thus, the operation at step (3) converts a general precept at step (2) into a publicly recognized law of (human) nature. That Kant takes these matters for granted is clearest from his second example, that of the deceitful promise.

Now Kant says that we cannot will the perturbed social world associated with the maxim of indifference because many situations may arise in that world in which we need the love and sympathy of others. In those situations, by a law originating from our own will, we would have robbed ourselves of what we require. It would be irrational for us to will a social world in which every one, as if by a law of nature, is deaf to appeals based on this need. Kant does not say much about how the idea of a rational will works in this example. In addition, the test as he applies it to the maxim of indifference is too strong: that is, the same test rejects those maxims that lead to any form of the precept (or duty) of mutual aid. The reason is this: any such precept enjoins us to help others when they are in need. But here also, in the perturbed social world associated with a precept to help others in need, situations may arise in which we very much want not to help them. The circumstances may be such that helping them seriously interferes with our plans. Thus, in these cases too, by a law originating from our own will, we would have prevented ourselves from achieving what we very much want. The difficulty is clear enough: in any perturbed social world all moral precepts will oppose our natural desires and settled intentions on at least some occasions. Hence the test of the CI-procedure, as Kant apparently understands it, is too strong: it appears to reject all maxims that lead to moral precepts (or duties).

4. One way out, I think, but I don't say the only one, is to try to develop an appropriate conception of what we may call "true human needs," a phrase Kant uses several times in the *Metaphysics of Morals* (MM 6:393, 432; see also 452–58).[4] Once this is done, the contradiction in the will test as illustrated by the fourth example might be formulated as follows:

Can I will the perturbed social world associated with the precept of indifference rather than the perturbed social world associated with a precept of mutual aid, that is, a maxim enjoining me to help others in need? In answering this question I am to take account only of my true human needs (which by assumption, as part of the CI-procedure, I take myself to have and to be the same for everyone).

Thus, in applying the procedure as now revised we understand that any general precept will constrain our actions prompted by our

John Rawls

desires and inclinations on some and perhaps many occasions. What we must do is to compare alternative social worlds and evaluate the overall consequences of willing one of these worlds rather than another. In order to do this, we are to take into account the balance of likely effects over time for our true human needs. Of course for this idea to work, we require an account of these needs. And here certain moral conceptions, rooted in our shared moral sensibility, may be involved.

I believe that Kant also assumes that the evaluation of perturbed social worlds at step (4) is subject to at least two limits on information. The first limit is that we are to ignore the more particular features of persons, including ourselves, as well as the specific content of their and our final ends and desires (Gr 4:433). The second limit is that when we ask ourselves whether we can will the perturbed social world associated with our maxim, we are to reason as if we do not know which place we may have in that world (see the discussion of the Typic at CP 5:69–70). The CI-procedure is misapplied when we project into the perturbed social world either the specific content of our final ends, or the particular features of our present or likely future circumstances. We must reason at step (4) not only on the basis of true human needs but also from a suitably general point of view that satisfies these two limits on particular (as opposed to general) information. We must see ourselves as proposing the public moral law for an ongoing social world enduring over time.

5. This brief schematic account of the CI-procedure is intended only to set the background for explaining the sequence of conceptions of the good in §2 and Kant's moral constructivism in §3. To serve this purpose, the procedure must meet two conditions: (1) it must not represent the requirements of the moral law as merely formal; otherwise, the moral law lacks sufficient content for a constructivist view; and (2) it must have features that enable us to see what Kant means when he says that the moral law discloses our freedom to us (considered in §5); for this, too, is an essential part of Kant's constructivism, since freedom of moral thought and action is required if the constructivist procedure is to be authenticated as objective, as the work of reason (considered in §4).

It turns out that for the second condition to be met, the CI-procedure must display in how it works, on its face as it were, the way in which pure practical reason is prior to empirical practical reason. This enables us to understand the distinctive structure of Kant's moral conception and how it is possible for our freedom to be made manifest to us by the moral law. What this priority means will become clearer as we proceed. For the present let's say that pure practical reason restricts empirical practical reason and subordinates it absolutely. This is an aspect of the unity of reason. The way in which pure practical reason restricts and subordinates empirical practical reason is expressed in imperative form by the CI-procedure: this procedure represents the requirements of pure practical reason in the manner appropriate for the conditions of human life. Empirical practical reason is the principle of rational deliberation that determines when particular hypothetical imperatives are rational. The CI-procedure restricts empirical practical reason by requiring the agent's rational and sincere deliberations to be conducted in accordance with the stipulations we have just surveyed. Unless a maxim passes the test of that procedure, acting from the maxim is forbidden. This outcome is final from the standpoint of practical reason as a whole, both pure and empirical. The survey of six conceptions of the good in Kant's doctrine in the next part (§3) will supplement these remarks about how the two forms of practical reason are combined in the unity of practical reason.

6. Before turning to this survey, a few comments on the sketch of the CI-procedure. In characterizing human persons I have used the phrase "reasonable and rational." The intention here is to mark the fact that Kant's uses *vernünftig* to express a full-bodied conception that covers the terms "reasonable" and "rational" as we often use them. In English we know what is meant when someone says: "Their proposal is rational, given their circumstances, but it is unreasonable all the same." The meaning is roughly that the people referred to are pushing a hard and unfair bargain, which they know to be in their own interests but which they wouldn't expect us to accept unless they knew their position is strong. "Reasonable" can also mean "judicious," "ready to listen to reason," where this has the sense of being willing to listen to and consider the reasons offered by others. *Vernünftig* can have the same meanings in German: it can have the broad sense of "reasonable" as well as the narrower sense of "rational" to mean roughly furthering our interests in the most effective way. Kant's usage varies but when applied to persons it usually covers being both reasonable and rational. His use of "reason" often has the even fuller sense of the philosophical tradition. Think of what *Vernunft* means in the title the *Critique of Pure Reason*! We are worlds

away from "rational" in the narrow sense. It's a deep question (which I leave aside) whether Kant's conception of reason includes far more than reason.

It is useful, then, to use "reasonable" and "rational" as handy terms to mark the distinction that Kant makes between the two forms of practical reason, pure and empirical. The first is expressed as an imperative in *the* categorical imperative, the second in *the* hypothetical imperative. These forms of practical reason must also be distinguished from particular categorical and hypothetical imperatives (the particular maxims at step (1)) that satisfy the corresponding requirements of practical reason in particular circumstances. The terms "reasonable" and "rational" remind us of the fullness of Kant's conception of practical reason and of the two forms of reason it comprehends.

7. I conclude with some remarks about the relation between Kant's three different formulations of the categorical imperative. Some may think that to rely, as I shall, on the first formulation alone gives an incomplete idea of the content of the categorical imperative. It may be incomplete, but nevertheless I believe it is adequate for our purposes. Kant says (Gr 4 : 436–37) that the three formulations are "so many formulations of precisely the same law." He also says that there is a difference between the formulations, which is only subjectively rather than objectively practical. The purpose of having several formulations is to bring the idea of reason (the moral law) nearer to intuition in accordance with a certain analogy and so nearer to feeling. At the end of the passage (pars. 72–75 of ch. II), Kant says that if we wish to gain access (or entry) for the moral law[5] it is useful to bring one and the same action under all three formulations, and in this way, so far as we can, to bring "it [the action] nearer to intuition." We are also instructed that it is better when making a moral judgment to "proceed always in accordance with the strict method and take as our basis the universal formula of the categorical imperative." This imperative we have interpreted in accordance with the law of nature formula (Gr 4 : 421); we noted also the *Critique of Practical Reason* with its account of the Typic at CP 5 : 67–71.

There are certain obscurities in Kant's view here. I shall not discuss them but simply state what I regard as his two main points. First, we are to use the four-step CI-procedure whenever we are testing whether our maxim is permitted by the categorical imperative. The other formulations cannot add to the content of the moral law as it applies to us. What is important here is that, however we interpret them, the second and third formulations must not yield any requirement that is not already accounted for by the CI-procedure. In particular, this holds for the second formulation concerning treating persons always as ends and never as means only (see Gr 4 : 429). With its use of the term "humanity" (*Menschheit*), this formulation seems strikingly different from the first and third. This appearance is misleading, since it is clear from the Introduction to the *Metaphysics of Morals* that "humanity" means the powers that characterize us as reasonable and rational beings who belong to the natural order. Our humanity is our pure practical reason together with our moral sensibility (our capacity for moral feeling). These two powers constitute moral personality, and include the power to set ends (MM 6 : 392); they make a good will and moral character possible. We have a duty to cultivate our natural capacities in order to make ourselves worthy of our humanity (MM 6 : 387). Thus, the duty to treat humanity, whether in our own person or in the person of others, always as an end, and never simply as a means, is the duty to respect the moral powers both in ourselves and in other persons, and to cultivate our natural capacities so that we can be worthy of those powers. Modulo shifts of points of view as described in the next paragraph, what particular duties are covered by this duty are ascertained by the first formulation of the categorical imperative. The first principle of the doctrine of virtue (MM 6 : 395) is a special case of this formulation. I think we cannot discern what Kant means by the second formulation apart from his account in the *Metaphysics of Morals*.

8. A second point about the relation of the three formulations: I believe that the purpose of the second and third formulations is to look at the application of the CI-procedure from two further points of view. The idea is this: each formulation looks at this procedure from a different point of view. In the first formulation, which is the strict method, we look at our maxim from our point of view. This is clear from how the procedure is described. We are to regard ourselves as subject to the moral law and we want to know what it requires of us. In the second formulation, however, we are to consider our maxim from the point of view of our humanity as the fundamental element in our person demanding our respect, or from the point of view of other persons who will be affected by our action. Humanity both in us and in other persons is regarded as *passive*: as that which will be affected by what we do. As Kant says (CP 5 : 87), in an

apparent reference to the second formulation of the *Grundlegung*, the autonomy of a reasonable and rational being is to be "subjected to no purpose which is not possible by a law which could arise from the will of the passive subject itself." But when this passive subject considers which laws can arise from its will, it must apply the CI-procedure. The point is simply that all persons affected must apply that procedure in the same way both to accept and to reject the same maxims. This ensures a universal agreement which prepares the way for the third formulation.

In this formulation we come back again to the agent's point of view, but this time we no longer regard ourselves as someone who is subject to the moral law but as someone who makes that law. The CI-procedure is seen as the procedure adherence to which with a full grasp of its meaning enables us to regard ourselves as legislators—as those who make universal public law for a possible moral community. This community Kant calls a realm of ends—a commonwealth and not a kingdom—the conception of which is also an idea of reason.

Finally, using all three formulations of the moral law is subjectively practical in two ways: first, having these formulations deepens our understanding of the moral law by showing how it regards actions from different points of view, and second, our deeper understanding of that law strengthens our desire to act from it. This is what Kant means, I think, by gaining entry or access for the moral law.[6]

§2. The Sequence of Six Conceptions of the Good

1. In order to understand Kant's constructivism and how he thinks that the moral law discloses our freedom to us, we need to look at the priority of pure practical reason over empirical practical reason, and to distinguish six conceptions of the good in Kant's doctrine. These conceptions are built up in a sequence one by one from the preceding ones. This sequence can be presented by referring to the four steps of the CI-procedure, since each conception can be connected with a particular step in this procedure. This provides a useful way of arranging these conceptions and clarifies the relations between them. It also enables us to explain what is meant by calling the realm of ends the necessary object of a will determined by the moral law, as well as what is meant by saying of this realm that it is an object given a priori to such a pure will (CP 5:4).

The first of the six conceptions of the good is given by unrestricted empirical practical reason. It is the conception of happiness as organized by the (as opposed to a particular) hypothetical imperative. This conception may be connected with step (1) of the CI-procedure, since the maxim at this step is assumed to be rational and sincere given that conception. Thus the maxim satisfies the principles of rational deliberation that characterize the hypothetical imperative, or what we may call "the rational." There are no restrictions on the information available to sincere and rational agents either in framing their conceptions of happiness or in forming their particular maxims: all the relevant particulars about their desires, abilities, and situation, as well as the available alternatives, are assumed to be known.

The second conception of the good is of the fulfillment of true human needs. I have suggested that at the fourth step of the CI-procedure we require some such idea. Otherwise the agent going through the procedure cannot compare the perturbed social worlds associated with different maxims. At first we might think this comparison can be made on the basis of the agent's conception of happiness. But even if the agent knows what this conception is, there is still a serious difficulty, since Kant supposes different agents to have different conceptions of their happiness. On his view, happiness is an ideal, not of reason but of the imagination, and so our conception of our happiness depends on the contingencies of our life, and on particular modes of thought and feeling we have developed as we come of age. Thus, if conceptions of happiness are used in judging social worlds at step (4), then whether a maxim passes the CI-procedure would depend on who applies it. This dependence would defeat Kant's view. For if our following the CI-procedure doesn't lead to approximate agreement when we apply it intelligently and conscientiously against the background of the same information, then that law lacks objective content. Here objective content means a content that is publicly recognized as correct, as based on sufficient reasons and as (roughly) the same for all reasonable and sincere human agents.

Observe that this second conception of the good based on true human needs is a special conception designed expressly to be used at step (4) of the CI-procedure. It is formulated to meet a need of reason: namely, that the moral law have sufficient objective content. Moreover, when this procedure is thought of as applied consistently by everyone over time in accordance with the requirement of complete determination (Gr 4:436), it specifies the content of a conception of right and justice that would be realized in a realm of ends. This conception, as opposed to the first, is restricted: that is, it is framed in view of the restrictions on information to which agents are subject at step (4).

The third conception of the good is the good as the fulfillment in everyday life of what Kant calls "permissible ends" (MM 6:388), that is, ends that respect the limits of the moral law. This means in practice that we are to revise, abandon, or repress desires and inclinations that prompt us to rational and sincere maxims at step (1) that are rejected by the CI-procedure. Here it is not a question of balancing the strength and importance to us of our natural desires against the strength and importance to us of the pure practical interest we take in acting from the moral law. Such balancing is excluded entirely. Rather, whenever our maxim is rejected, we must reconsider our intended course of action, for in this case the claim to satisfy the desires in question is rejected. At this point the contrast with utilitarianism is clear, since for Kant this third conception of the good presupposes the moral law and the principles of pure practical reason. Whereas utilitarianism starts with a conception of the good given prior to, and independent of, the right (the moral law), and it then works out from that independent conception its conceptions of the right and of moral worth, in that order. In Kant's view, however, unrestricted rationality, or the rational, is framed by, and subordinated absolutely to, a procedure that incorporates the constraints of the reasonable. It is by this procedure that admissible conceptions of the good and their permissible ends are specified.

2. The first of the three remaining conceptions of the good is the familiar conception of the good will. This is Kant's conception of moral worth: a completely good will is the supreme (although not the complete) good of persons and of their character as reasonable and rational beings. This good is constituted by a firm and settled highest-order desire that leads us to take an interest in acting from the moral law for its own sake, or, what comes in practice to the same thing, to further the realm of ends as the moral law requires. When we have a completely good will, this highest-order desire, however strongly it may be opposed by our natural desires and inclinations, is always strong enough by itself to insure that we act from (and not merely in accordance with) the moral law.

The next conception of the good is the good as the object of the moral law, which is, as indicated above, the realm of ends. This object is simply the social world that would come about (at least under reasonably favorable conditions) if everyone were to follow the totality of precepts that result from the correct application of the CI-procedure. Kant sometimes refers to the realm of ends as the necessary object of a will, which is determined by the moral law, or alternatively, as an object that is given a priori to a will determined by that law (CP 5:4). By this I think he means that the realm of ends is an object—a social world—the moral constitution and regulation of which is specified by the totality of precepts that meet the test of the CI-procedure (when these precepts are adjusted and coordinated by the requirement of complete determination). Put another way, the realm of ends is not a social world that can be described prior to and independent of the concepts and principles of practical reason and the procedure by which they are applied. That realm is not an already given describable object the nature of which determines the content of the moral law. This would be the case, for example, if this law were understood as stating what must be done in order to bring about a good society the nature and institutions of which are already specified apart from the moral law. That such a teleological conception is foreign to Kant's doctrine is plain from ch. II of the Analytic of the *Critique of Practical Reason*. The burden of that chapter is to explain what has been called Kant's "Copernican Revolution" in moral philosophy (CP 5:62–65).[7] Rather than starting from a conception of the good given independently of the right, we start from a conception of the right—of the moral law—given by pure (as opposed to empirical) practical reason. We then specify in the light of this conception what ends are permissible and what social arrangements are right and just. We might say: a moral conception is not to revolve around the good as an independent object, but around a conception of the right as constructed by our pure practical reason into which any permissible good must fit. Kant believes that once we start from the good as an independent given object, the moral conception must be heteronomous, and this is as true of Leibniz's perfectionism as it is of the psychological naturalism that underlies Hume's utilitarianism. In these cases what determines our will is an object given to it and not principles originating in our pure reason as reasonable and rational beings.

Finally, there is Kant's conception of the complete good. This is the good that is attained when a realm of ends exists and each member of it not only has a completely good will but is also fully happy so far as the normal conditions of human life allow. Here, of course, happiness is specified by the satisfaction of ends that respect the requirements of the moral law, and so are permissible ends. Often Kant refers to this complete good as the highest good. This is his preferred term after the *Grundlegung*, especially when he is presenting his doctrine of reasonable faith in the second *Critique*. I shall use the secular term "realized realm of ends," and I assume that this complete good can be approximated to in the natural world, at least under reasonably favorable conditions. In this sense it is a natural good, one that can be approached (although never fully realized) within the order of nature.

Kant holds that in the complete good, the good will is the supreme good, that is, we must have a good will if the other goods we enjoy are to be truly good and our enjoyment of them fully appropriate. This applies in particular to the good of happiness, since he thinks that only our having a good will can make us worthy of happiness. Kant also believes that two goods so different in their nature, and in their foundations in our person, as a good will and happiness are incommensurable; and, therefore, that they can be combined into one unified and complete good only by the relation of the strict priority of one over the other.

3. The preceding sketch of conceptions of the good in Kant's view indicates how they are built up, or constructed, in an ordered sequence one after the other, each conception (except the first) depending on the preceding ones. If we count the second (that of true human needs) as part of the CI-procedure itself, we can say that beginning with the third (that of permissible ends), these conceptions presuppose an independent conception of right (the reasonable). This conception of right is represented by the CI-procedure as the application of pure practical reason to the conditions of human life. Only the first conception of the good is entirely independent of the moral law, since it is the rational without restriction. Thus the sequence of conceptions beginning with the second exemplifies the priority of pure practical reason over empirical practical reason and displays the distinctive deontological and constructivist structure of Kant's view. We start with two forms of practical reason, the reasonable and the rational. The unity of practical reason is grounded in how the reasonable frames the rational and restricts it absolutely.

Then we proceed step by step to generate different conceptions of the good and obtain at the last two steps the conceptions of the good will and of a complete good as a fully realized realm of ends. The contrast between the deontological and constructivist structure of Kant's doctrine and the linear structure of a teleological view starting from an independent conception of the good is so obvious as not to need comment.

§3. Kant's Moral Constructivism

1. We are now in a position to see what is meant in saying that Kant's moral doctrine is constructivist, and why the term "constructivist" is appropriate.

One way to bring out the features of Kant's moral constructivism is to contrast it with rational intuitionism. The latter doctrine has, of course, been expressed in many ways; but in some form it dominated moral philosophy from Plato and Aristotle onwards until it was challenged by Hobbes and Hume, and, I believe, in a very different way, by Kant. To simplify things, I take rational intuitionism to be the view exemplified in the English tradition by Samuel Clarke and Richard Price, Henry Sidgwick and G. E. Moore, and formulated in its minimum essentials by W. D. Ross. With qualifications, it was accepted by Leibniz and Christian Wolff in the guise of perfectionism, and Kant knows of it in this form.

For our purposes here, rational intuitionism may be summed up in three theses, the first two of which it has in common with a number of other views, including Kant's. These three theses are: *First*, the basic moral concepts of the right and the good, and the moral worth of persons, are not analyzable in terms of nonmoral concepts (although possibly they are analyzable in terms of one another). *Second*, first principles of morals (whether one or many), when correctly stated, are true statements about what kinds of considerations are good reasons for applying one of the three basic moral concepts: that is, for asserting that something is (intrinsically) good, or that a certain institution is just or a certain action right, or that a certain trait of character or motive has moral worth. *Third* (and this is the distinctive thesis for our purposes), first principles, as statements about good reasons, are regarded as true or false in virtue of a moral order of values that is prior to and independent of our conceptions of person and society, and of the public social role of moral doctrines.

This prior moral order is already given, as it were, by the nature of things and is known by rational intuition (or in some views by moral sense, but I leave this possibility aside). Thus, our agreement in judgment when properly founded is said to be based on the shared recognition of truths about a prior order of values accessible to reason. Observe that no reference is made to self-evidence; for although intuitionists have often held first principles to be self-evident, this feature is not essential.

It should be observed that rational intuitionism is compatible with a variety of contents for the first principles of a moral conception. Even classical utilitarianism, which Sidgwick in his *Methods of Ethics* was strongly inclined to favor, was sometimes viewed by him as following from three more fundamental principles, each grasped by rational intuition in its own right. Of the recent versions of rational intuitionism, the appeal to rational intuition is perhaps most striking in Moore's so-called ideal utilitarianism in *Principia Ethica*. A consequence of Moore's principle of organic unity is that his view is extremely pluralistic: there are few if any useful first principles, and distinct kinds of cases are to be decided by intuition as they arise. Moore held a kind of Platonic atomism:[8] moral concepts (along with other concepts) are subsisting and independent entities grasped by the mind. That pleasure and beauty are good, and that different combinations of them alone, or together with other good things, are also good, and to what degree, are truths known by intuition: by seeing with the mind's eye how these distinct objects (universals) are (timelessly) related.

Now my aim in recalling these familiar matters is to indicate how rational intuitionism, as illustrated by Sidgwick, Moore, and Ross, is distinct from a constructivist moral conception. That Kant would have rejected Hume's psychological naturalism as heteronomous is clear. But I believe that the contrast with rational intuitionism, regardless of the specific content of the view (whether utilitarian, perfectionist, or pluralist) is even more instructive. It has seemed less obvious that for Kant rational intuitionism is also heteronomous. Perhaps the reason is that in rational intuitionism basic moral concepts are conceptually independent of natural concepts, and first principles as grasped by rational intuition are viewed as synthetic a priori, and so independent of any particular order of nature. They give the content of an ethics of creation, so to speak: the principles God would use to ascertain which is the best of all possible worlds. Thus, it may seem that for Kant such principles are not heteronomous.

Yet in Kant's moral constructivism it suffices for heteronomy that first principles obtain in virtue of relations among objects the nature of which is not affected or determined by our conception of ourselves as reasonable and rational persons (as possessing the powers of practical reason), and of the public role of moral principles in a society of such persons. Of particular importance is the conception of persons as reasonable and rational, and, therefore, as free and equal, and the basic units of agency and responsibility. Kant's idea of autonomy requires that there exists no moral order prior to and independent of those conceptions that is to determine the form of the procedure that specifies the content of first principles of right and justice among free and equal persons. Heteronomy obtains not only when these first principles are fixed by the special psychological constitution of human nature, as in Hume, but also when they are fixed by an order of universals, or of moral values grasped by rational intuition, as in Plato's realm of forms or in Leibniz's hierarchy of perfections.

Thus an essential feature of Kant's moral constructivism is that the first principles of right and justice are seen as specified by a procedure of construction (the CI-procedure) the form and structure of which mirrors our free moral personality as both reasonable and rational. This conception of the person he regards as implicit in our everyday moral consciousness. A Kantian doctrine may hold (as Kant did) that the procedure by which first principles are specified, or constructed, is synthetic a priori. This thesis, however, must be properly understood. It simply means that the form and structure of this procedure express the requirements of practical reason. These requirements are embedded in our conception of persons as reasonable and rational, and as the basic units of agency and responsibility. This conception is found in how we represent to ourselves our free and equal moral personality in everyday life, or in what Kant in the second *Critique* calls "the fact of reason."

It is characteristic of Kant's doctrine that a relatively complex conception of the person plays a central role in specifying the content of his moral view. By contrast, rational intuitionism requires but a sparse conception of the person, based on the idea of the person as knower. This is because the content of first principles is already given, and the only requirement is that we be able to know what these principles are and to be moved by this knowledge. A basic psychological assumption is that the recognition of first principles as true of a prior and antecedent order of moral values gives rise, in a being capable of rationally intuiting those principles, to a desire to act from them for their own sake. Moral motivation is defined by reference to desires that have a special kind of causal origin, namely, the intuitive grasp of first principles. This sparse conception of the person together with this psychological assumption characterizes the moral psychology of Sidgwick, Moore, and Ross. Of course, intuitionism is not forced to so sparse a conception. The point is rather that, since the content of first principles is already given, it is simply unnecessary to have a more elaborate moral psychology or a fuller conception of the person of a kind required to specify the form, structure, and content of a constructivist moral view.

2. So much for explaining Kant's moral constructivism by the contrast with rational intuitionism. Let's turn to a more specific account of the constructivist features of his view. But I should mention first that the idea of constructivism arises within moral and political philosophy. The term "constructivist" is not used because of analogies with constructivism in the philosophy of mathematics, even though Kant's account of the synthetic a priori nature of arithmetic and geometry is one of the historical sources of constructivist accounts of mathematical truth. There are also important constructivist elements in Kant's account of the basis of Newtonian mechanics.⁹ The roots of constructivism lie deep in Kant's transcendental idealism; but these parallels I cannot discuss here.

My aim is to see the way in which Kant's moral doctrine has features that quite naturally lead us to think of it as constructivist, and then how this connects with the themes of the unity of reason and the moral law as an idea of freedom. To this end, let's consider three questions.

First, in moral constructivism, *what* is it that is constructed? The answer is: the *content* of the doctrine.¹⁰ In Kant's view this means that the totality of particular categorical imperatives (general precepts at step (2)) that pass the test of the CI-procedure are seen as constructed by a procedure of construction worked through by *rational* agents subject to various *reasonable* constraints. These agents are rational in that, subject to the reasonable constraints of the procedure, they are guided by empirical practical reason, or the principles of *rational* deliberation that fall under *the* hypothetical imperative.

A *second* question is this: Is the CI-procedure itself constructed? No, it is not. Rather, it is simply *laid out*. Kant believes that our everyday human understanding is implicitly aware of the requirements of practical reason, both pure and empirical; as we shall see, this is part of his doctrine of the fact of reason. So we look at how Kant seems to reason when he presents his various examples and we try to *lay out* in procedural form *all* the conditions he seems to rely on. Our aim in doing this is to incorporate into that procedure *all* the relevant criteria of practical reasonableness and rationality, so that the judgments that result from a *correct* use of the procedure are *themselves* correct (given the requisite true beliefs about the social world). These judgments are correct because they meet all the requirements of practical reason.

Third, what, more exactly, does it mean to say, as I said a while back, that the form and structure of the CI-procedure *mirrors* our free moral personality as both reasonable and rational? The idea here is that not everything can be constructed and every construction has a basis, certain materials, as it were, from which it begins. While the CI-procedure is not, as noted above, constructed but laid out, it does have a *basis*; and this basis is the conception of free and equal persons as reasonable and rational, a conception that is *mirrored* in the procedure. We discern how persons are mirrored in the procedure by noting what powers and abilities, kinds of beliefs and wants, and the like, they must have as agents who are viewed as implicitly guided by the procedure and as being moved to conform to the particular categorical imperatives it authenticates. We look at the procedure as laid out, and we consider the use Kant makes of it, and from that we elaborate what his conception of persons must be. This conception, along with the conception of a society of such persons, each of whom can be a legislative member of a realm of ends, constitutes the basis of Kant's constructivism. Thus, we don't say that the conceptions of person and society are constructed. It is unclear what that could mean. Nor do we say they are laid out. Rather, these conceptions are *elicited* from our moral experience and from what is involved in our being able to work through the CI-procedure and to act from the moral law as it applies to us.

To illustrate: that we are both reasonable and rational is mirrored in the fact that the CI-procedure involves both forms of reasoning. We are said to be rational at step (1), and indeed at all steps, since the deliberations of agents within the constraints of the procedure always fall under the rational. We are also said to be reasonable, since if we weren't moved by the reasonable, we would not take what Kant calls a pure practical interest in checking our maxims against the procedure's requirements; nor when a maxim is rejected would we have such an interest in revising our intentions and checking whether our revised maxim is acceptable. The deliberations of agents *within* the steps of the procedure and subject to its reasonable constraints mirror our rationality; our motivation as persons in caring about those constraints and taking an interest in acting in ways that meet the procedure's requirements mirrors our being reasonable.

The conception of free and equal persons as reasonable and rational is the *basis* of the construction: unless this conception and the powers of moral personality it includes—our humanity—are animated, as it were, in human beings, the moral law would have no basis in the world. Recall here Kant's thought that to commit suicide is to root out the existence of morality from the world (MM 6:422–23).

3. It is important to see that the contrast between rational intuitionism and Kant's moral constructivism is not a contrast between objectivism and subjectivism. For both views have a conception of objectivity; but each understands objectivity in a different way.

In rational intuitionism a correct moral judgment, or principle, is one that is true of a prior and independent order of moral values. This order is also prior to the criteria of reasonableness and rationality as well as prior to the appropriate conception of persons as autonomous and responsible, and free and equal members of a moral community. Indeed, it is that order that settles what those reasonable and rational criteria are, and how autonomy and responsibility are to be conceived.

In Kant's doctrine, on the other hand, a correct moral judgment is one that conforms to all the relevant criteria of reasonableness and rationality the total force of which is expressed by the way they are combined into the CI-procedure. He thinks of this procedure as suitably joining together all the requirements of our (human) practical reason, both pure and empirical, into one unified scheme of practical reasoning. As we saw, this is an aspect of the unity of reason. Thus, the general principles and precepts generated by the correct use of that procedure of deliberation satisfy the conditions for valid judgments imposed by the form and structure of our common (human) practical reason. This form and structure is a priori, rooted in our pure practical reason, and thus for us practically necessary. A judgment supported by those principles and precepts will, then, be acknowledged as correct by any fully reasonable and rational (and informed) person.

A conception of objectivity must include an account of our agreement in judgments, how it comes about. Kant accounts for this agreement by our sharing in a common practical reason. For this idea to succeed, we must suppose, as Kant does, that whoever applies the CI-procedure, roughly the same judgments are reached, provided the procedure is applied intelligently and conscientiously, and against the background of roughly the same beliefs and information. Reasonable and rational persons must recognize more or less the same reasons and give them more or less the same weight. Indeed, for the idea of judgment even to apply, as opposed to the idea of our simply giving voice to our psychological state, we must be able to reach agreement in judgment, not of course always, but much of the time. And when we can't do so, we must be able to explain our failure by the difficulties of the question, that is, by the difficulties of surveying and assessing the available evidence, or else the delicate balance of the competing reasons on opposite sides of the issue, either or both of which leads us to expect that reasonable persons may differ. Or, alternatively, the disagreement arises from a lack of reasonableness or rationality or conscientiousness on the part of one or more persons involved, where of course the test of this lack cannot simply be the fact of disagreement itself, or the fact that other persons disagree with us. We must have independent grounds for thinking these causes of disagreement are at work.

Finally, to prevent misunderstanding, I should add that Kant's constructivism does not say that moral facts, much less all facts, are constructed. Rather, a constructivist procedure provides principles and precepts that specify *which* facts about persons, institutions, and actions, and the world generally, are relevant in moral deliberation. Those norms specify which facts are to *count* as reasons. We should not say that the moral facts are constructed, since the idea of constructing the facts seems odd and may be incoherent; by contrast, the idea of a constructivist procedure generating principles and precepts singling out the facts to count as reasons seems quite clear. We have only to recall how the CI-procedure accepts some maxims and rejects others. The facts are there already, so to speak, available in our everyday experience or identified by theoretical reason, but apart from a constructivist moral conception they are simply facts. What is needed is a way to single out which facts are relevant from a moral point of view and to determine their weight as reasons. Viewed this way, a constructivist conception is not at odds with our ordinary idea of truth and matters of fact.

§4. What Kind of Authentication Has the Moral Law?

1. In the first appendix to chapter 1 of the Analytic of the *Critique of Practical Reason*, Kant says that the moral law can be given no deduction, that is, no justification of its objective and universal validity, but rests on the fact of reason. This fact (as I understand it) is the fact that in our common moral consciousness we recognize and acknowledge the moral law as supremely authoritative and immediately directive for us. Kant says further that the moral law needs no justifying grounds; to the contrary, that law proves not only the possibility but also the actuality of freedom in those who recognize and acknowledge that law as supremely authoritative. The moral law thus gives objective, although only practical, reality to the idea of freedom, and thereby answers to a need of pure speculative reason, which had to assume the possibility of freedom to be consistent with itself. That the moral law does this is sufficient authentication, or credential, as Kant says, for that law. And this credential takes the place of all those vain attempts to justify it by theoretical reason, whether speculative or empirical (CP 5:46–50).

This is a fundamental change from the *Groundwork*, where in the last part Kant tries to derive the moral law from the idea of freedom. Now what is the significance of this change?[11] It signals, I believe, Kant's recognition that each of the four forms of reason in his critical philosophy has a different place and role in what he calls the unity of reason. He thinks of reason as a self-subsistent unity of principles in which every member exists for every other, and all for the sake of each (see Bxxiii, and CP 5:119–21). In the most general sense, the authentication of a form of reason consists in explaining its place and role within what I shall call the constitution of reason as a whole. For Kant there can be no question of justifying reason as such; for reason must answer all questions about itself from its own resources (A476–84/B504–12), and it must contain the standard for any critical examination of every use of reason (CP 5:16): the constitution of reason must be self-authenticating.

Themes in Kant's Moral Philosophy

Now once we regard the authentication of a form of reason as an explanation of its role within the constitution of reason, then, since the forms of reason have different roles, we should expect their authentications to be different. Each fits into the constitution of reason in a different way, and the more specific considerations that explain their role in that constitution will likewise be different. The moral law will not have the same kind of authentication that the categories do, namely, the special kind of argument Kant gives for them in the transcendental deduction of the first *Critique*, an argument designed to show the concepts and principles in question are presupposed in some kind of experience, or consciousness, in contrast, for example, to their being regulative of the use of a faculty.

Pure speculative reason also has what Kant calls a deduction (A670/B698), that is, a justification (or authentication) of the objective validity of its ideas and principles as transcendental principles (A651/B679). But what is important here is that the moral law as an idea of pure practical reason has an even different authentication than pure speculative reason. To elaborate: for Kant, pure reason, as opposed both to the understanding and to empirical practical reason, is the faculty of orientation.[12] Whereas reason's work in both spheres is similar, it performs its work differently in the theoretical than in the practical sphere. In each sphere, reason provides orientation by being normative: it sets ends and organizes them into a whole so as to guide the use of a faculty, the understanding in the theoretical sphere, the power of choice in the practical. In the theoretical sphere, pure reason is regulative rather than constitutive; the role of its ideas and principles is to specify an idea of the highest possible systematic unity, and to guide us in introducing this necessary unity into our knowledge of objects and our view of the world as a whole. In this way the work of reason yields a sufficient criterion of empirical truth (A651/B679).[13] Without pure reason, general conceptions of the world of all kinds—religion and myth, and science and cosmology—would not be possible. The ideas and principles of reason that articulate them, and that in the case of science provide a criterion of empirical truth, would not exist, for their source is reason. The role of speculative reason in regulating the understanding and organizing into a unity our empirical knowledge authenticates its ideas and principles.

By contrast, in the practical sphere, pure reason is neither constitutive nor regulative but directive: that is, it immediately directs

John Rawls

the power of choice, which does not provide independent material of its own to be organized, as the understanding does. In this sphere, it is empirical practical reason that is regulative; for empirical practical reason organizes into a rational idea of happiness, by the principle of the hypothetical imperative, the various desires and inclinations belonging to the lower faculty of desire (CP 5:120). In contrast, the power of choice, as the higher faculty of desire, is directed *immediately* by pure reason's idea of the moral law, a law by which reason constructs for that power its practically necessary object, the realm of ends.

In a way suitable to the theoretical and the practical spheres, pure reason tries to fashion what Kant calls the unity of reason. There are three such unities: the first, in the theoretical sphere, is the greatest possible systematic unity of the knowledge of objects required for a sufficient criterion of empirical truth; the second, in the practical sphere, is the greatest possible systematic unity of ends in a realm of ends. The third unity is that of both theoretical and practical reason in one constitution of reason with theoretical reason subordinate to practical reason, so that practical reason has primacy (CP 5:119–21).

2. I turn from these general remarks to consider why Kant might have given up the attempt to give an argument from theoretical reason for the moral law by examining several forms such an argument might take.

During the 1770's, Kant made a number of efforts in this direction. Dieter Henrich divides them into two groups.[14] In the first, Kant tries to show how the theoretical use of reason, when applied to the totality of our desires and ends of action, necessarily gives rise in a rational agent not only to the characteristic approval of moral judgment but also to incentives to act from that judgment. In the second group, Kant tries to derive the essential elements of moral judgment from what he takes to be a necessary presupposition of moral philosophy, but a presupposition that can be seen to be necessary by the use of theoretical reason alone, namely, the concept of freedom.

For each group, Henrich describes a few examples. I leave aside these details. The relevant point is that Kant tries to ground the moral law solely in theoretical reason and the concept of rationality. He tries to derive the reasonable from the rational. He starts from a conception of a self-conscious rational (versus reasonable) agent with all the powers of theoretical reason and moved only by natural needs and desires. These arguments bear witness to Kant's effort over a number of years to find a derivation of the moral law from theoretical reason.

Another kind of argument for the moral law, one resembling the kind of argument Kant gives for the categories, might be this: we try to show the moral law to be presupposed in our *moral consciousness* in much the same way that the categories are presupposed in our *sensible experience* of objects in space and time.[15] Thus, we might argue that no other moral conception can specify the concepts of duty and obligation, or the concepts needed to have the peculiarly moral feelings of guilt and shame, remorse and indignation, and the like. Now that a moral conception include the necessary background for these concepts is certainly a reasonable requirement. But the argument tries for too much: it is implausible to deny that other conceptions also suffice for this background. The conceptions of two societies may differ greatly even though people in both societies are capable of moral consciousness. Many doctrines satisfy this condition besides that specified by the moral law.

A fault in this kind of argument is that it assumes the distinction between concept and pure intuition, whereas in moral consciousness there is no such distinction. Theoretical reason concerns the knowledge of objects, and sensory experience provides its material basis. But practical knowledge concerns the reasonable and rational grounds for the production of objects. The complete good is the realization of a constructed object: the realm of ends as the necessary object of a will immediately determined by the moral law. Moral consciousness is not sensible experience of an object at all and this kind of argument has no foothold.

Consider a further argument. One might say: since the deduction of the categories shows that their objective validity and universal applicability is presupposed in our unified public experience of objects, a parallel argument for the moral law might show it to constitute the only possible basis for a unified public order of conduct for a plurality of persons who have conflicting aims and interests. The claim is that without the moral law, we are left with the struggle of all against all as exemplified by the pledge of Francis I (CP 5:28). This would allow us to say that the moral law is constitutive of any unified public order of a social world.[16]

This approach, I think, is likewise bound to fail. The requirement that a moral conception specify a unified and shared public order of conduct is again entirely reasonable. The obvious difficulty is that utilitarianism, perfectionism, and intuitionism, as well as other doctrines, can also specify such an order. The moral law is, as we have seen, a priori with respect to empirical practical reason. It is also a priori as an idea of reason, but it is not a priori in the further sense that any unified public order of conduct must rest on it.

Kant does not, I believe, argue that the moral law is a priori in this further sense. What, in effect, he does hold is that the moral law is the only way for us to construct a unified public order of conduct without falling into heteronomy. Kant uses the idea of autonomy implicit in a constructivist conception of moral reason to eliminate alternative moral doctrines. Although Kant never discusses utilitarianism,[17] perfectionism, and intuitionism as we view them today, it is clear that he would also regard these contemporary doctrines as forms of heteronomy. His appeal would be to the moral law as a principle of free constructive reason.

3. Finally, let's return briefly to the second *Critique*, where Kant explains why the moral law has no deduction (CP 5:46–50). Here he stresses the differences between theoretical and practical reason. Theoretical reason is concerned with the knowledge of objects given to us in our sensible experience; whereas practical reason is concerned with our capacity as reasonable and rational beings to bring about, or to produce, objects in accordance with a conception of those objects. An object is understood as the end of action, and for Kant all actions have an object in this sense. Acting from pure practical reason involves first, bringing about an object the conception of which is framed in the light of the ideas and principles of pure practical reason, and second, our being moved (in the appropriate way) by a pure practical interest in realizing that conception. Since it is in virtue of our reason that we can be fully free, only those actions meeting these two conditions are *fully* free.

Now from what we have said the authentication of the moral law can seem highly problematic. This sets the stage for Kant's introducing the doctrine of the fact of reason in the second *Critique*. For the moral law cannot be derived from the concepts of theoretical reason together with the concept of a rational agent; nor is it presupposed in our moral experience, or necessary to specify a unified order of public conduct. It cannot be derived from the idea of freedom since no intellectual intuition of freedom is available. Moreover, the moral law is not to be regulative of a faculty with its own material. This kind of authentication holds for speculative reason and, within the practical sphere, for empirical practical reason, which regulates the lower faculty of desire. Yet there is still a way, Kant now holds, in which the moral law is authenticated:

The moral law is given, as an apodictically certain fact, as it were, of pure reason, a fact of which we are a priori conscious, even if it be granted that no example could be found in which it has been followed exactly, [while] the objective reality of the moral law can be proved through . . . no exertion of the theoretical reason, whether speculative or empirically supported. . . . Nevertheless, it is firmly established of itself.

He adds:

Instead of this vainly sought deduction of the moral principle, however, something entirely different and unexpected appears: the moral principle itself serves as a principle of the deduction of an unscrutable faculty which no experience can prove but which speculative reason had to assume as at least possible (in order not to contradict itself . . .). This is the faculty of freedom, which the moral law, itself needing no justifying grounds, shows to be not only possible but actual in beings that acknowledge the law as binding upon them (CP 5:47).

To conclude: each form of reason in Kant's critical doctrine has its own distinctive authentication. The categories and principles of the understanding are presupposed in our experience of objects in space and time, and pure speculative reason is authenticated by its role in organizing into a systematic unity the empirical knowledge of the understanding, thereby providing a sufficient criterion of empirical truth. Empirical practical reason has a similar role with respect to our lower faculty of desire organizing its inclinations and wants into a rational conception of happiness. It is *pure* practical reason the authentication of which seems the most elusive: we long to derive its law, as Kant did for many years, from some firm foundation, either in theoretical reason or in experience, or in the necessary conditions of a unified public order of conduct; or failing all of these, from the idea of freedom itself, as Kant still hopes to do in the *Grundlegung*.

But none of these authentications are available within Kant's critical philosophy. In the second *Critique*, Kant recognizes this and accepts the view that pure practical reason, with the moral law as its first principle, is authenticated by the fact of reason and in turn by that fact's authenticating, in those who acknowledge the moral law as binding, the objective reality of freedom, although always (and this needs emphasis) only from a practical point of view. In the same way the moral law authenticates the ideas of God and immortality. Thus, along with freedom, the moral law is the keystone of the whole system of pure reason (CP 5:3). Pure practical reason is authenticated finally by assuming primacy over speculative reason and by cohering into, and what is more, by *completing* the constitution of reason as one unified body of principles: this makes reason self-authenticating as a whole (CP 5:119–21).

Thus by the time of the second *Critique* Kant has developed, I think, not only a constructivist conception of practical reason but a coherentist account of its authentication. This is the significance of his doctrine of the fact of reason and of his abandoning his hitherto vain search for a so-called deduction of the moral law. This doctrine may look like a step backward into intuitionism, or else into dogmatism. Some have tried to interpret it away so as to make it continuous with Kant's earlier views; others have lamented it. Here I think that Kant may be ahead of his critics. A constructivist and coherentist doctrine of practical reason is not without strengths as a possible view; and as such it is part of the legacy Kant left to the tradition of moral philosophy.

§5. The Moral Law as a Law of Freedom

1. The distinctive feature of Kant's view of freedom is the central place of the moral law as an idea of pure reason; and pure reason, both theoretical and practical, is free. For Kant there is no essential difference between the freedom of the will and freedom of thought. If our mathematical and theoretical reasoning is free, as shown in free judgments, then so is our pure practical reasoning as shown in free deliberative judgments. Here in both cases free judgments are to be distinguished from verbal utterances that simply give voice to, that are the (causal) upshot of, our psychological states and of our wants and attitudes. Judgments claim validity and truth, claims that can be supported by reasons. The freedom of pure reason includes the freedom of practical as well as of theoretical reason, since both are freedoms of one and the same reason (Gr 4:391; CP 5:91, 121). Kant's approach requires that the moral law exhibit features that disclose our freedom, and these features should be discernible in the CI-procedure, on its face, so to speak. The moral law serves as the *ratio*

cognoscendi of freedom (CP 5:4n). Our task is simply to recall the features of this procedure (surveyed in §1) which Kant thinks enables us to recognize it as a law of freedom.[18]

Consider first the features through which the CI-procedure exhibits the moral law as unconditional. These are evident in the ways that the reasonable restricts the rational and subordinates it absolutely. The CI-procedure (the reasonable) restricts empirical practical reason (the rational) by requiring that unless the agent's rational and sincere maxim is accepted by the procedure, acting from that maxim is forbidden absolutely. This outcome is final from the standpoint of practical reason as a whole, both pure and empirical. Thus, the moral law, as represented by the CI-procedure, specifies a scope within which permissible ends must fall, as well as limits on the means that can be adopted in the pursuit of these ends. The scope and limits that result delineate the duties of justice. The moral law also imposes certain ends as ends that we have a duty to pursue and to give some weight to. These duties are duties of virtue. That the moral law as represented is unconditional simply means that the constraints of the CI-procedure are valid for all reasonable and rational persons, no matter what their natural desires and inclinations.

We might say: pure practical reason is a priori with respect to empirical practical reason. Here the term "a priori" applies, of course, to pure practical knowledge and not to the knowledge of objects given in experience. It expresses the fact that we know in advance, no matter what our natural desires may be, that the moral law imposes certain ends as well as restrictions on means, and that these requirements are always valid for us. This fits the traditional epistemological meaning of a priori once it is applied to practical knowledge, and it accords with Kant's definition of the a priori at CP 5:12. Kant uses the unconditional and a priori aspects of the moral law to explain the sense in which our acting from that law shows our independence of nature and our freedom from determination by the desires and needs aroused in us by natural and psychological causes (so-called negative freedom).

2. Next, let's ask how the CI-procedure exhibits the moral law as sufficient of itself to determine the will. Here we should be careful not to interpret this feature too strongly. I do not think Kant wants to say, and certainly he does not need to say, that the moral law determines all the relevant aspects of what we are to do. Rather, the moral law specifies a scope *within* which permissible ends must fall,

and also *limits* the means that may be used in their pursuit, and this goes part way to make the moral law sufficient of itself to determine the will. (Of course, particular desires determine which permissible ends it is rational for us to pursue, and they also determine, within the limits allowed, how it is rational for us to pursue them. This leeway I view as compatible with Kant's intentions.)

But beyond specifying a scope for permissible ends and limiting means in their pursuit, the moral law must further provide sufficient grounds to determine the will by identifying certain ends that are also duties and by requiring us to give at least some weight to those ends. Since the moral law determines both aspects of action, both ends and means, pure practical reason, through the moral law as an idea of reason, is *sufficient* to determine the will.[19] The point here is that for Kant action has an end; if the moral law failed to identify certain ends as also duties, it would not suffice to determine an essential feature of actions.

What is crucial for Kant's view is that the moral law must not be merely formal but have enough content to be, in a natural meaning of the word, sufficient of itself to determine ends: pure reason is not merely finding the most effective way to realize given ends but it criticizes and selects among proposed ends. Its doing this is what Kant has in mind when he says that the moral law specifies a positive concept of freedom. We are free not only in the sense that we are able to act independently of our natural desires and needs, but also free in the sense that we have a principle regulative of *both* ends and means from which to act, a principle of autonomy appropriate to us as reasonable and rational beings.

3. So much for the way in which the CI-procedure exhibits the moral law as unconditional and sufficient of itself to determine the will. In addition to this procedure exhibiting how the moral law imposes ends that are also duties, it exhibits that law as doing reason's work in setting ends and in securing their ordered unity, so that it is not merely a principle of rationality. We can also see how the moral law constructs the realm of ends and thereby specifies the conception of its object. In short, the CI-procedure in its constructions models all the essential features of a principle doing the work of pure reason in the practical sphere.

This procedure also clarifies the more general aspects of pure practical reason to which Kant refers in a passage from the first *Critique*. Kant says:

Reason does not . . . follow the order of things as they present themselves in appearance, but frames for itself with perfect spontaneity an order of its own according to ideas [of pure reason], to which it adapts the empirical conditions, and according to which it declares actions to be [practically] necessary (A548/B576).

We can grasp what Kant has in mind: namely, that pure practical reason constructs out of itself the conception of the realm of ends as an order of its own according to ideas of reason; and given the historical and material circumstances under which society exists, that conception guides us in fashioning institutions and practices in conformity with it.

The particular characteristics of a realm of ends are, then, to be adapted to empirical, that is, to historical and social conditions. What in particular is the content of citizens' permissible ends, and what specific institutions are best suited to establish a moral community regulated by the moral law, must wait upon circumstances. But what we do know in advance are certain general features of such a moral community: the nature of ends that are also duties, and the arrangement of these ends under the duty to cultivate our moral and natural perfection, and the duty to further the happiness (the permissible ends) of others. We also know that under favorable conditions, a realm of ends is some form of constitutional democracy.

4. Now consider the two examples Kant presents in sec. 6 of ch. I of the Analytic (CP 5:30). Kant's first example is that of a man who claims to have a natural desire so overwhelmingly strong that if the object desired were vividly placed before him, this desire would be irresistible. Kant thinks that the man must be exaggerating or else mistaken. If he knew that he would be executed immediately upon satisfying his desire, and the instruments of execution (for example, the gallows) were as vividly placed before him as the attractive object, surely he would realize that there are other desires, if necessary his love of life—the sum total of all natural desires as expressive of life—which would intervene to resist this alleged irresistible desire. In the last resort the love of life, when equally vividly aroused, is able to control all other natural desires. Kant thinks that as purely rational and natural beings we cannot act against the love of life.

The second example is that of a man who is ordered by his sovereign to make a false deposition against an honorable subject whom the sovereign wishes to be rid of on some plausible pretext. This

John Rawls

order, we are to assume, is backed up by a threat of sudden death as vividly present as in the previous case. This time, however, it is the desire to act from the moral law that opposes the love of life. Here Kant thinks that while perhaps none of us would want to say what we would do in such a situation, we do know, as this man would know of himself, that it would be *possible* for us to disobey the sovereign's order. Of this man Kant says: "He judges . . . that he can do something because he knows that he ought, and he recognizes that he is free—a fact which, without the moral law, would have remained unknown to him" (CP 5:30).

Kant's aim in these examples is to convince us that although as purely natural beings, endowed with the powers of the rational but not the reasonable, we cannot oppose the love of life, nevertheless we can do so as natural beings endowed with *humanity*, that is, the powers of the reasonable in union with moral sensibility.[20] Moreover, our consciousness of the moral law discloses to us that we can stand fast against the totality of our natural desires; and this in turn discloses our capacity to act independently of the natural order. Our consciousness of the moral law could not do this unless that law was not only unconditional and sufficient of itself to determine our will, but also had all the features of a principle of pure practical reason. These features must be exhibited in our moral thought and feeling in some such manner as the CI-procedure represents them. Knowledge that we *can* act from a law of *that* kind—a law that is a principle of autonomy—is what discloses our freedom to us.

5. To conclude, one other passage should be mentioned. It is found at CP 5:94: here Kant says that there are writers who think they can explain freedom by empirical principles. They regard it as a psychological property that can be accounted for by an exact investigation of the mind and the incentives of the will as discerned in sense experience. Those writers do not regard freedom as a transcendental predicate of the causality of persons who also have a place in the natural order but who, Kant implies, are not entirely of it. He writes:

They deprive us of the great revelation which we experience through our practical reason by means of the moral law—the revelation of an intelligible world through realization of the otherwise transcendent concept of freedom; they deprive us of the moral law itself, which assumes absolutely no empirical ground of determination. Therefore, it will be necessary to add

112

something here as a protection against this delusion and to expose empiricism in its naked superficiality.

This severe passage expresses the depth of Kant's conviction that those without a conception of the moral law and lacking in moral sensibility could not know they were free. They would appear to themselves as purely natural creatures endowed with rationality, without the essentials of humanity. If by some philosophical or other doctrine we were to be convinced that the moral law is a delusion, and our moral sensibility simply an artifact of nature to perpetuate the species, or a social contrivance to make institutions stable and secure, we would be in danger of losing our humanity, even though we cannot, Kant thinks, lose it altogether. The empiricist "delusion," as Kant calls it, must not be allowed to take from us the glorious disclosure of our autonomy made known to us through the moral law as an idea of pure reason. Philosophy as defense (apology in the traditional sense)—the role Kant gives it—is to prevent this loss.

Justification and Freedom in the *Critique of Practical Reason*

HENRY E. ALLISON

I

In an earlier paper, I defended Kant's seemingly paradoxical claim that "freedom and unconditional practical law reciprocally imply each other" (CP 5:59). This claim, which I call the Reciprocity Thesis, seems paradoxical because it entails that freedom is a sufficient, not merely a necessary condition of the possibility of standing under moral laws. In the present paper, I shall assume this result and attempt, on the basis of it, to sketch the outlines of the Kantian justification of the moral law.

Since the Reciprocity Thesis looms large in the present discussion, it should be helpful to begin with a brief summary of my defense of it. This defense was based on three main assumptions: (1) a fairly standard view of rational justification to the effect that if a rule of action (a "maxim" in Kant's sense) is deemed "right" for an agent in given circumstances, it must also be deemed right for all agents in relevantly similar circumstances; (2) that a transcendentally free agent is not free merely from determination by any *particular* sensuous inclination, drive, or desire (this being the mark of practical freedom), but also free from determination by desire or inclination *überhaupt*; (3) that since, *ex hypothesi*, the selection of a maxim by a transcendentally free agent must always be regarded as an act of freedom, even the highest maxims or most fundamental practical principles of such an agent are subject to the justification requirement. On this basis, it was then argued that the assumption of transcendental freedom blocks certain familiar types of justification, namely, those that appeal to "human nature" or some given determinant of behavior, for example, an instinct for self-preservation. This, in turn, led to the positive result that the maxims of a transcendentally free agent can be justified only if they can be shown to be compatible with an unconditionally valid practical law. Since it turns out that the moral law (as defined by Kant) is the only conceivable candidate for such a law, it follows that all transcendentally free agents are subject to the moral law. This does not, of course, mean that they necessarily obey that law, but merely that it functions as the ultimate norm governing their choice of maxims.

Although only a first step in Kant's justification of morality (albeit one that is common to both the *Groundwork* and the *Critique of Practical Reason*), this result suffices to answer the familiar objection that Kant is engaged in a futile endeavor to derive substantive moral conclusions from morally neutral premises about the nature of rationality or rational agency. More specifically, it shows that Kant's actual starting point is the thick concept of a transcendentally free rational agent rather than the thin concept of a rational being, or even a rational agent *simpliciter*. Clearly, however, most critics would regard this as a Pyrrhic victory; since by connecting Kantian morality so intimately to the presumably disreputable notion of transcendental freedom, it undermines any attempt to defend essential elements of the former without accepting the latter.

In addition to affirming the inseparability of the moral law and transcendental freedom, the Reciprocity Thesis also makes it clear that a Kantian justification of morality must move in one of two possible directions: (1) it can attempt to provide an independent proof of transcendental freedom and infer from this the validity of the moral law; or (2) it can attempt to establish the moral law and infer from this the reality of freedom.

As Dieter Henrich has demonstrated, Kant was attracted to the former approach for a considerable period of time, and only abandoned it with the recognition of the impossibility of providing a theoretical proof of freedom.[1] Indeed, even after this recognition, he still attempted a version of it in *Groundwork* III, by arguing from the necessity of presupposing the idea of freedom. Although the issue is controversial, I think it reasonable to assume that Kant's recognition of the failure of the argument in *Groundwork* III led to the adoption of the second approach in the *Critique of Practical Reason*.[2]

This alternative approach consists in an appeal to the notorious "fact of reason." Instead of trying to deduce the moral law from freedom (or from the necessity of presupposing freedom), Kant now claims that the law, as the "sole fact of pure reason," needs no deduction because it is self-validating and that it can serve as the basis for a deduction of freedom (CP 5:31, 47–48). Not surprisingly, this dual claim has struck many students of Kant as an act of desperation, a lapse into a dogmatism that is hopelessly at odds with the whole spirit of the "critical" philosophy.[3] In what follows, I shall argue to the contrary that the appeal to the "fact of reason" is not only the move dictated by the logic of Kant's position, but also that it is far more plausible than is generally assumed.

II

The initial problem confronting any would-be defender of the fact of reason is to determine the nature of this "fact." This is far from a trivial task because, as Lewis White Beck notes, Kant provides six distinct formulations of it within the *Critique of Practical Reason* alone. Following Beck, these are: (1) "consciousness of the moral law," (2) "consciousness of freedom of the will," (3) "the law," (4) "autonomy in the principle of morality," (5) "an inevitable determination of the will by the mere conception of the law," and (6) "the actual case of an action presupposing unconditional causality."[4] Elsewhere, Kant identifies it with freedom, the practical law of freedom, and the categorical imperative.[5] To complicate the situation further, Kant sometimes refers to it simply as the "fact of reason" (or pure reason) and other times as the "fact as it were" (*gleichsam als ein Faktum*).[6]

As Beck indicates, the various characterizations of the "fact" or "fact as it were" fall into roughly two classes. One (the objective class) identifies it with either the moral law or freedom (or their equivalents), the other (the subjective class) identifies it with the *consciousness* of the law (or its equivalents).[7] Leaving aside for the present the complexities introduced by the reference to freedom, the problem raised by this classification is obvious. If the "fact" is construed subjectively as a mode of consciousness, its existence is readily granted, but no inference to the validity of the law is warranted thereby. Conversely, if the "fact" is construed objectively and equated with the law itself, then the existence of this fact becomes the very point at issue and can hardly be appealed to in order to ground the reality of moral obligation.

Beck's strategy for resolving this problem involves the introduction of a further distinction between a "fact for" and a "fact of" pure reason.[8] By the former is to be understood a pregiven, transcendentally real value that is somehow apprehended by pure reason, that is, by a direct nonsensuous insight or "intellectual intuition." Although Kant sometimes appears to construe the "fact" in this way and is frequently interpreted as having done so, such a reading stands in blatant contradiction with Kant's denial of a capacity for intellectual intuition.[9] Moreover, as Beck points out, if Kant is interpreted in this way, then his doctrine is subject to all the well-known difficulties of intuitionism.[10]

Beck also claims, however, that these problems do not arise if we take Kant to be referring to the fact *of* pure reason, which he equates with the fact that pure reason is practical.[11] According to Kant, the claim that pure reason is practical means that of itself, that is, independently of any antecedent interest or desire, it is capable of determining the will (CP 5:15–16). This, in turn, means that pure reason provides both a rule or principle of action and a motive to act or refrain from acting in ways specified by this principle. Expressed in the terms of the *Lectures on Ethics*, it means that pure reason must furnish both a *principium iudicationis bonitatis* and a *principium executionis bonitatis*.[12] Although this does not correspond precisely to any of the characterizations of the fact of reason cited above, it seems to be a reasonable interpretation of Kant's doctrine.[13]

It would also appear, however, that this solution to the exegetical problem makes the appeal to the fact of reason completely question-begging. After all, the practicality of pure reason is hardly obvious, as is evidenced by the fact that it has been explicitly denied by "empiricists of practical reason" from Aristotle to Bernard Williams. Indeed, if Kant had thought that it was obvious, he would not have thought it necessary to devote a whole critique to the topic. Accordingly, even though Kant himself contends that it is a fact or "fact as it were" that pure reason is practical, it still seems necessary to provide an argument in support of this contention.

Henry E. Allison

III

Since it is virtually the only serious attempt in the recent literature
to provide such an argument, Beck's formulation is a natural place to
begin. The gist of it is contained in the following claim:

> Only a law which is given by reason itself to reason itself could be known a
> priori by pure reason and be a fact for pure reason. The moral law expresses
> nothing else than the autonomy of reason . . . it is a fact for pure reason only
> inasmuch as it is the expression of the fact of pure reason, i.e., of the fact that
> pure reason can be practical. That is why the moral law is the sole fact
> of pure reason and for pure reason.[14]

In his attempt to spell out this allegedly "tricky" argument, Beck
appeals to moral experience. He begins by suggesting that a moral
principle is not binding on a person who is ignorant of it; but that "if
he believes that an imperative is valid for him, then it is in so far forth
valid for him, and he shows that reason is practical even in the awareness of this aspect of a valid claim."[15] At first glance at least, this
seems both strange and un-Kantian. The simple fact that someone
believes that something is a duty hardly makes it so. As almost any of
the familiar cases of moral disagreement makes clear, many people
are mistaken in their beliefs about duties.

Beck does not really deny this, however, for he proceeds to add
that this principle holds "whether the imperative expresses a claim
that is in fact valid or not."[16] The point, then, is not that merely
thinking that something is one's duty makes it so; it is rather that
"only a being with an a priori concept of normativity could ever
make a mistake about this."[17] Beck's reasoning is highly compressed,
but it appears to involve two contentions: (1) In order to argue
against a putative duty claim, or even mistakenly to make such a
claim, it is necessary to appeal to a rational norm. More generally,
such a norm is a presupposition of all rational choice. (2) In appealing to such a norm, one is presupposing the moral law because, as
Beck puts it, "the moral law—the fact for pure reason—expresses
nothing but the law-giving of reason itself."[18]

This looks quite promising. We appear to be on the way to a
transformation of the moral law from a pregiven, transcendentally
real principle, totally independent of the human will, in the manner
of seventeenth- and eighteenth-century ethical rationalism, to one
that is presupposed by and immanent in the will. This, in turn,

would enable us to see the appeal to the fact of reason as the culmination of the "critical" program or the transcendental turn in the practical sphere, rather than, as it first appeared, as a lapse into a sort of precritical dogmatism of practical reason.

Unfortunately, things are not that simple. The most that the argument establishes is that a rational agent must presuppose *some* universally valid norm or principle as a condition of rational choice. It does not show that such an agent must (on pain of denial of rationality) presuppose the moral law as defined by Kant. Moreover, in one place at least, Beck acknowledges this problem and defends only the weaker claim.[19]

Elsewhere, however, he uses virtually the same argument in support of the stronger claim. He does so by appealing to the "metaphysical deduction" in order to show that the Kantian version of the moral law qualifies as the required principle.[20] But this puts more weight on the "deduction" than it can possibly support. It begins with the concept of a universally and unconditionally valid practical law and argues that the moral law is the only conceivable candidate for such a law. This is a reasonable claim, given Kant's definitions; but it is also quite distinct from Beck's suggestion that the moral law is the only conceivable candidate for a rational norm.[21]

Nevertheless, Beck's analysis is on the right track. The crucial point around which his discussion revolves, without ever making it fully explicit, is the self-imposed or, equivalently, self-legislated nature of moral obligation. As autonomous, the will gives the law to itself (or *Wille* gives it to *Willkür*), and only so is it morally obligated. Correlatively, it is in and through this self-imposition or self-legislation that pure reason becomes practical. Moreover, this feature of the fact of reason is the key to the self-justifying nature of moral obligation.

In order to begin to grasp these points, it should be noted that, from the standpoint of a heteronomous ethic, moral skepticism remains a real possibility, just as theoretical skepticism does for transcendental realism. This is most obvious in divine command theories, where one's belief that one has a duty to act in a certain way is a function of one's beliefs about God and what God has commanded. But such skepticism is not limited to a theologically based ethic. In all heteronomous theories, that is, all theories that do not regard moral obligation as self-imposed, one is morally obligated if and only if x, where "x" stands for some claim about God, human nature, one's own desires or feelings, etc. Thus, with respect to all such theories, it is always possible to question the justification of ethical principles and even the reality of moral obligation. Correlatively, from the motivational side, in all such theories there is an implicit need to assume some extrinsic incentive in order to motivate obedience to the law (to provide a reason to be moral). That is why Kant contends that all such theories effectively reduce categorical to hypothetical imperatives (see Gr 4 : 432–33, CP 5 : 39–41).

The situation is quite different, however, under the assumption of the autonomy of the will. First, insofar as I spontaneously impose the law upon myself, I cannot reasonably doubt that I am subject to it. In that sense, then, Beck is perfectly correct to suggest that insofar as one believes that one stands under moral laws one really does so stand, even if one is mistaken about particular obligations. Second, in acknowledging the law as the ultimate norm governing my conduct, which is what I do when I impose it upon myself, I *ipso facto* recognize that I have a motive to follow its dictates. Thus, I can no longer reasonably ask, as I can from the standpoint of any heteronomous theory, "Why should I be moral?" Finally, insofar as I recognize it as a law for me (on the grounds that it is a law for all rational beings), I cannot doubt that I have the capacity to obey it, that is, the capacity not only to do what duty requires, but to do it because duty requires it.

The overall point can be clarified by a consideration of Jaakko Hintikka's analysis of the logic of performatives in his well-known interpretation of Descartes's *cogito* argument.[22] According to Hintikka, the *sum* is not to be construed as an inference from the *cogito*, as if the denial of one's existence generated a logical contradiction. Instead, the argument turns on a presumed existential inconsistency in such a denial, which is itself a consequence of the logic of first-person sentences. Thus, while I could perfectly well deny that De Gaulle exists, De Gaulle himself could not coherently do so. The indubitability of his own existence was evident to him in the very act of thinking it. As Hintikka puts it: "The indubitability of my own existence results from my thinking of it almost as the sound of music results from playing it or (to use Descartes's own metaphor) light in the sense of illumination (*lux*) results from the presence of a source of light (*lumen*)."[23]

The analogy between this and the self-imposed nature of moral obligation is apparent. To submit oneself to the moral law is to "perform" in a certain manner. Moreover, since in the very act of submitting to it I take it as valid for me, I cannot coherently doubt that I am subject to it; nor can I doubt what follows immediately from being subject to it: namely, that I have both an incentive to do what the law requires and the capacity to do it. From my (first-person) perspective, then, my subjection to the law and, therefore, its objective (practical) reality, has the status of an undeniable fact, a "fact of reason" as it were. Certainly, I can doubt that a given action is obligatory, permissible, or prohibited; although Kant himself sometimes suggests otherwise. Given the self-imposition of the law, however, I cannot doubt my status as a rational agent with duties, which limit "in the eyes of reason" my pursuit of interests stemming from inclination, and with an incentive and the capacity to do what these duties require of me.

IV

As it stands, this reconstruction of the fact of reason doctrine seems to suffer from the obvious and presumably fatal defect that it limits the scope of the demands of duty to those who are already willing to recognize those demands. If moral obligation is self-imposed, then it appears to be possible to avoid and even to deny all such obligations by the simple expedient of refusing to impose them on oneself. Morality, on this view, becomes a kind of game, the rules of which are certainly binding on those who play (this is the force of the performative response to the skeptic), but which we are all free to play or not to play as we choose. Accordingly, whereas it may be senseless for those who are already engaged in the moral enterprise to ask why they should be moral, it would seem to remain a very pertinent question for those who are not already so committed.

This brings into focus a point noted by W. T. Jones, namely, that a Kantian justification of morality must deal with two distinct issues: one is the "objectivity question," that is, whether one who believes himself to be morally obligated really is obligated; the other is the "universality question," that is, whether all rational agents are subject to the demands of the moral law, regardless of their beliefs.[24] The analysis of the fact of reason in terms of self-imposition has answered the former, but in a way that exacerbates the difficulties of the latter.

Before we are in a position to sketch the Kantian response to the universality challenge, we must determine more precisely the form that this challenge takes. Since the fact of reason has already been established, at least in the attenuated form noted above, the opponent at this stage of the dialectic must acknowledge that moral requirements are in some sense legitimate; that there is an incentive to follow them; and that one has the capacity to do so, if one so chooses. At the same time, however, he will also insist that it is "legitimate," that is, reasonable, to allow other considerations to override the demands of duty. But since a duty is, by definition, an unconditional requirement, this means that such a person acts on the principle of not acknowledging any duties.[25] For convenience sake, I shall henceforth characterize the position of our dialectical opponent as amoralism.

Now, since the justification requirement is still in place and since it can be assumed that the amoralist is a rational agent, the essential question is whether the principle implicit in this position can be rationally justified. As before, I shall assume that the justification of a practical principle requires showing that it is "right" (in a morally neutral sense) or at least "reasonable" for any rational agent to adopt it in the relevant circumstances.

Presumably, the amoralist would accept this minimal result. In fact, he could even claim that everyone "ought" to adopt his principle, meaning thereby simply that it would be in the interest of each agent not to recognize any overriding moral requirements. But he would deny that this entails that he is constrained to subject his principle to the test of its compatibility with a universal law binding on all rational agents independently of their interests. The latter amounts to the claim that he must assume an impartial, "moral point of view" with respect to his own interests, which is, of course, precisely what he denies. This does not mean that the amoralist is necessarily a crude sort of rational egoist (certainly he is not a psychological egoist, since he acknowledges the possibility of acting from duty), but merely that he rejects any reason for acting that is independent of his own interests. In short, he is an "internalist" in Bernard Williams's sense.[26]

It is just at this point that the Reciprocity Thesis comes into play. Having acknowledged the fact of reason, albeit in the attenuated sense, the amoralist must also acknowledge the capacity to act from duty, namely, transcendental freedom. It follows from this, however, that the demand for justification cannot be satisfied by the brute appeal to the amoralist's interests, no matter how refined or worthy they may be. Since the taking of an interest in something is equivalent to the adoption of a maxim to pursue a certain end, it must be regarded as an act of freedom, imputable to the subject *qua* rational agent (see Gr 4:459n, CP 5:79). Consequently, rather than serving as the ultimate sources of justification for actions, interests themselves require justification.

Finally, if interests, so construed, require justification, then, presumably, so must the amoralist's principle of not allowing any considerations to override his interests (of not recognizing any duties). The question, then, is where this justification is to come from. Since the principle amounts to a fundamental maxim or highest order subjective principle, it obviously cannot stem from any higher order subjective principle or maxim. By elimination, then, it can be derived only from an objectively valid principle that is applicable to all rational agents independently of their desires or interests. But the "metaphysical deduction" of the *Critique of Practical Reason* has shown that the only viable candidate for such a principle is the moral law. The amoralist therefore cannot provide rational grounds for refusing to recognize the authority of this law. That is to say, he cannot reasonably refuse to play the "moral game."

V

Unfortunately, this is far from the end of the story. The problem is that it has been assumed throughout that the fact of reason entails transcendental freedom; but this assumption is hardly self-evident. Certainly, the amoralist would deny it and affirm instead that all that he need concede is the familiar compatibilist conception of freedom, namely, a capacity to act from duty, if one so chooses. Moreover, in rejecting transcendental freedom, the amoralist will also reject the appeal to the Reciprocity Thesis and with it the requirement to justify his fundamental principle by reference to an "objective," interest-independent norm.

What resources does the Kantian have to counter this obvious line of response? To begin with, we have Kant's own claim in his presumed "deduction" of freedom from the moral law that "the moral law, itself needing no justifying grounds, shows [the faculty of freedom] to be not only possible but actual in beings which acknowledge the law as binding upon them" (CP 5:47). The root idea here seems to be that the very act of the self-imposition of the moral law shows pure reason to be practical; and this, in turn, establishes the reality of a causal power (that of pure practical reason) that is unconditioned by anything in the phenomenal world.

Nevertheless, this is not likely to satisfy the critic, who will still insist that Kant has overstated his case, and that the most that can be derived from the fact of reason is the compatibilist conception of freedom. The problem is exacerbated by Kant's best-known characterizations of transcendental freedom. For example, in the Dialectic of the *Critique of Pure Reason*, Kant construes it as absolute spontaneity, by which is meant a causal power that is independent of determination by antecedent conditions.[27] Similarly, in the *Critique of Practical Reason*, he defines it as "independence from everything empirical and hence from nature generally," which turns out to include everything that can be an object of either outer or inner sense (CP 5:97).[28] There would seem to be little reason to accept the claim that the fact of reason, construed as the capacity for the self-imposition of the moral law, requires anything like this conception of freedom.

An adequate response to this line of objection would require a detailed treatment of Kant's conception of agency, a task that is obviously beyond the scope of this paper. Nevertheless, it does seem possible to sketch the outlines of this response. Such a sketch will probably not convince the confirmed compatibilist, but it should at least help to clarify the connection between the fact of reason and transcendental freedom.

Let us begin with a consideration of Kant's characterization of transcendental freedom in the Canon of the *Critique of Pure Reason*. In contrast to the formulations cited above, Kant is there concerned to juxtapose transcendental to practical freedom. Whereas practical freedom is described as "one of the causes in nature, namely . . . a causality of reason in the determination of the will," transcendental freedom is said to demand "the independence of this reason—in respect of its causality, in beginning a series of appearances—from all determining causes of the sensible world" (A803/B831).

The contrast with practical freedom underscores the fact that, from the point of view of Kant's moral philosophy, the operative question regarding transcendental freedom is not whether we are rational agents at all, as opposed, let us say, to extremely complex mechanisms; it is rather whether we are agents of a particular sort.[29] More specifically, the question is whether the "causality of reason" is always in the service of inclination (which is compatible with practical freedom), or whether reason is capable of determining the will independently of the desires and inclinations of the agent. In the latter case, the "causality of reason" is "independent" or "unconditioned" in the relevant sense; otherwise it is "conditioned." Consequently, what must be shown is that the mere capacity to impose the law upon oneself presupposes such an unconditioned causality of reason.

What is initially strange about the suggestion that the self-imposition of the moral law reveals or presupposes transcendental freedom is that it is not itself an action, that is, it is not something that one can intend to do. Nevertheless, it would be a mistake to dismiss it for this reason. First, although not an action (*Handlung*), self-imposition is nonetheless an act (*Aktus*) that is to be attributed to the spontaneity of the subject rather than to the receptivity of sense.[30] Specifically, it can be understood as equivalent to what Kant sometimes describes as taking an interest in morality. The point here is that to take an interest in morality is not merely to find it interesting, as if this were somehow a matter of how one is constituted; it is rather to take or to recognize the demands of morality as unconditionally binding.[31] Moreover, as I have argued elsewhere, since intellectual acts such as "taking as" or recognition (in a concept) are expressions of the spontaneity of the subject, they are not themselves to be regarded as causally conditioned.[32]

Second, as already noted, imposing the law upon oneself involves acknowledging it as an incentive (*Triebfeder*). Kant is thus an "internalist" in that he holds that the very recognition of the moral law as the supreme norm implies the existence of a motive for following its dictates.[33] But to acknowledge that the law is itself an incentive is to recognize that one can be motivated by respect for it. This remains the case even if one never acts on the basis of such motivation.

Third, the capacity to be motivated by respect for the law entails the capacity to act out of respect for it. Normally, of course, the claim that one is susceptible to a certain kind of motivation must be sharply distinguished from the claim that one has the capacity for the corresponding kind of action. Thus, I might be strongly motivated to save a drowning child, but, being unable to swim, I would not be capable of doing so. In the present case, however, what is at stake is not the physical (or mental) capacity to perform a certain kind of action; it is rather the capacity to be motivated appropriately. Since we have this capacity, we can do what is required (CP 5:30).

Finally, to be able to act out of respect for the law is to be free in the transcendental sense. In short, Kant's basic claim is that the fact of reason establishes our transcendental freedom in that it reveals a capacity for a certain kind of agency that itself requires such freedom. Moreover, apart from our recognition of moral demands we would have no grounds for attributing to ourselves such agency. That is why Kant insists that the moral law is the *ratio cognoscendi* of freedom and claims that "had not the moral law already been distinctly thought in our reason, we would never have been justified in assuming anything like freedom" (CP 5:5n).

The key element in the preceding, which I take to be the gist of the Kantian "deduction" of freedom, is the contention that the mere fact that we can be motivated by, and act out of respect for, the moral law suffices to establish our transcendental freedom. This replaces the initial assertion that the capacity to impose the law upon ourselves establishes such freedom, since it spells out what is really involved in self-imposition. Unfortunately, it is not likely that the confirmed compatibilist would find this any more convincing than the original claim. We still need an argument to take us from respect to transcendental freedom and Kant does not appear to provide one for us.

Nevertheless, the materials for an indirect argument against the compatibilist are implicit in Kant's account of moral agency. Its main thrust is that the compatibilist cannot make good on the initially plausible assumption that actions supposedly motivated by respect for the law are (*qua* taken under that description) causally conditioned. The proviso regarding the description under which such actions are taken is necessary here for a number of reasons, not the least of which being that, given his transcendental idealism, Kant himself must insist that these very same actions, taken under a different description (as occurrences in the phenomenal world), are causally conditioned.

To begin with, it should be noted that neuro-physiological or, more generally, physicalistic explanations are not at issue. This is important because Kant's account of transcendental freedom is frequently criticized on the grounds that it considers only psychological causes such as inclinations and desires, thereby leaving open the possibility that allegedly "free" actions could be explained physicalisticly. Although it is impossible to pursue the matter here, I believe that Kant would reject this criticism on the familiar grounds that physi-

Justification and Freedom

calistic explanations cannot account for an action *qua* action.[34] But even if that sweeping claim be questioned, it still seems clear that such explanations cannot account for an action *qua* taken under the appropriate description, namely, as motivated by respect for the law.

Moreover, certain familiar kinds of psychological explanations that "rationalize" (in the Davidsonian sense) an action by providing a reason (in the sense of a motive) can likewise be readily dismissed as inappropriate. The point here is that causal explanation in terms of such reasons effectively explains away the very motivation (respect for the law) for which it is supposed to account. Consequently, the action allegedly explained is no longer taken under its original description. Consider, for example, an explanation of the form: Jones believed that acting in morally appropriate ways and even developing a morally good disposition are likely to make him happier in the long run than behaving in self-serving ways. Because of this belief and the desire to achieve happiness, Jones took the demands of duty with the utmost seriousness, that is, he came to "respect" the law and to act accordingly. The belief and the desire thus supposedly "rationalize" the action.

It is obvious, however, that explanations of this form cannot be regarded as accounts of actions motivated by respect for the law. Insofar as one's interest in morality is a consequence of such belief and desire, one's interest is not in the law itself; it is rather in the desired end (happiness) that is supposed to explain the putative "interest" in the law. In Kant's familiar terms, on this assumption we would be acting heteronomously, not autonomously; our actions would have legality but not morality; we would be following a hypothetical rather than the categorical imperative (see, for example, Gr 4:400–44, CP 5:33–40, 71).

But not all causal explanations of human actions are either physicalistic or rationalizations that change the character of the *explanandum*.[35] Thus, the compatibilist can still insist on the possibility of providing perfectly acceptable and broadly psychological explanations of actions that are putatively motivated by respect for the law. Typically, such explanations might include a combination of environmental factors, such as education, and innate dispositions or character traits. Given these conditions, so the argument goes, it is perfectly possible to provide a naturalistic causal account of morally praiseworthy action that does not reduce it to a disguised form of self-love.

The issue here is extremely tricky because, as already noted, Kant does not deny that causal explanations are possible for all free actions. Admittedly, Kant's best-known examples involve immoral actions, for which the agent can be held morally responsible in spite of the possibility of providing a causal account that shows the action to have been inevitable.[36] Nevertheless, there is nothing in Kant's theory to preclude the possibility of providing empirical explanations of morally praiseworthy actions as well (see R5612, 18:252–54). In fact, leaving aside the complications introduced by his denial of scientific status to empirical psychology, Kant would seem to be committed to the possibility of such explanations by the central tenets of the Transcendental Analytic, particularly the Second Analogy.[37] At the very least, he is committed to the proposition that such actions, considered as events in the phenomenal world, have empirical causes. At the same time, however, his conceptions of moral agency and worth require him to deny that any explanation in terms of such causes is capable of accounting for an action as motivated by respect for the law.

The argument in support of this denial turns crucially on the unique, nonempirical nature of respect, considered as an incentive or "determining ground" of the will.[38] First, it is noted that the data for any such empirical explanation would necessarily include inclinations or desires. Second, it is granted that such factors, together with the relevant belief, background conditions, etc., are perfectly capable of accounting for what, in the contemporary jargon, can be called a "proattitude" toward morality. To that extent Kant is in agreement with the compatibilist. Because of his understanding of the nature of respect, however, Kant would part company with the compatibilist in denying that an explanation of an action in terms of an empirically conditioned "proattitude" could count as an explanation of it as motivated by respect.

To put basically the same point somewhat differently, the distinction between an action motivated by a kindly disposition, perhaps in conjunction with a complex set of prudential considerations, and one motivated by respect for the law or the pure thought of duty is empirically vacuous. In both cases we have an action that is accounted for in terms of a "proattitude" toward morality, and it is certainly possible, even for Kant, to give a causal explanation of such an attitude and of the actions stemming therefrom. But since there is no observable difference between the two types of "proattitude," it can never be claimed that the action being explained is one that is motivated by respect for the law. In short, although the action might very well be one that is motivated in the morally appropriate way, no empirical explanation could ever account for it as so motivated.

At first glance at least, this account of Kant's position appears to play into the compatibilist's hands, since it gives grounds to dismiss the contrast between the two types of "proattitudes" toward morality as a distinction without a difference. This is especially true if one keeps in mind Kant's well-known and sharply stated agnosticism regarding the ultimate grounds of actions that accord with duty. In no case, he insists, can we ever be certain that we were moved to act by the pure thought of duty (respect for the law) rather than by some secret inclination (see Gr 4 : 407 and MM 6 : 392–93). Given this admission, the compatibilist critic might well ask: if we can never be certain that this unique motive, respect for the law, is operative in a particular instance, what need is there to account for it at all? More germanely, if we can never be certain that such a motive is operative, how can one appeal to it as an aspect of an alleged fact of reason?

The Kantian response to this verificationist attack is twofold. First, it does not follow from the fact that the distinction between actions based on inclination and those based on the thought of duty or respect for the law is of no explanatory significance and, therefore, theoretically null, that it is of no significance at all. On the contrary, its significance is purely practical, since it is crucial for the evaluation (not the explanation) of actions. Moreover, this practical significance suffices to block the otherwise tempting application of Ockham's razor. Second, what the fact of reason establishes is not the existence of actions motivated by respect for the law, but merely the capacity to act on the basis of such motivation. This is sufficient to establish the reality of transcendental freedom, at least from the practical point of view, which is alone of concern here.

This, in outline at least, is the argument linking the fact of reason with the possession of transcendental freedom. Although Kant does not present it as such, we have seen that this linkage constitutes the final and decisive stage in the justification of the moral law. As reconstructed here, this argument has a number of presuppositions. These include a conception of rational agency that is reflected in the contention that reason is practical or, in the language of the *Groundwork*, that we act according to the conception of laws or on principles, as well as interpretations of the fact of reason and of transcendental freedom. In addition, it was claimed that the self-imposition of the law involves the recognition of the law as binding, that this entails that there is a reason or incentive to act for the sake of the law (Kant's internalism) and that this, in turn, entails the possibility of acting in the required manner (the peculiarly Kantian version of the "ought implies can" principle). Admittedly, all of these points are extremely controversial and it has been impossible to deal adequately with them here. Nevertheless, I think that these assumptions and claims are plausible, both in their own right and as interpretations of Kant. Moreover, granting them, the "deduction" of transcendental freedom does seem to work, which, in turn, makes possible the validation of the moral law.

Justification and Objectivity: Comments on Rawls and Allison

BARBARA HERMAN

In the recent resurgence of work on Kant's ethics, one notices the quiet avoidance of the issue of justification. This is to some extent the harmless by-product of new enthusiasm generated by success with the substantive ethical theory. But the other thing at work, I believe, is the suspicion that the project of justification in Kantian ethics is intractable. What these two papers do, decisively, is to dispel this sort of anxiety. With their focus on the often ignored fact of reason argument in the *Critique of Practical Reason,* they provide a much clearer picture of what is at stake for Kant in the sections that deal with foundational questions, and, in addition, offer guides to resources in Kant's work that one might need in trying to understand Kant's project. Professors Allison and Rawls return from these scarcely charted regions with convincing reports that it is possible to work and prosper on even this redoubtable frontier. What I thought I might do, on this occasion, is to try to make more perspicuous the different ambitions of their respective expeditions, and, of course, to express some respectful puzzlement about what they say they have found.

The problem Henry Allison sees in reconstructing Kant's justification of the moral law in the *Critique of Practical Reason* is in understanding how the fact of reason could serve as part of an argument for the objective validity of the moral law, since it is hard to read it as not assuming it. The idea is that the fact of reason can serve as the basis for a deduction of *transcendental freedom* since it reveals the *possibility* of our acting out of respect for the moral law. And if it is possible that we can so act, then we must be transcendentally free. For, if it is possible to act out of respect for the moral law, it is possible to act on a principle that has no foundation in inclinations, empirical interests, or desires. Then, given the Reciprocity Thesis (which I will accept for the purposes of this discussion), the objective validity of the moral law follows from the deduction of transcendental freedom.

What the fact of reason does, as I understand Allison's reconstruction, is allow us to argue from the conditions of will of an agent accepting the moral law, *to* transcendental freedom (and so justification of the moral law via the Reciprocity Thesis) *without assuming* that there is such a law valid for the agent, or for rational beings in general. This is a very bold interpretive claim, but one that initially fits with the idea that there is a deduction of the moral law, for we expect Kantian deductions to begin with some "given" element of experience and argue to its necessary conditions.

To support this, Allison thinks we must (and can) argue the following: First, the fact of reason reveals, to anyone conscious of the moral law, that he can act out of respect for the moral law. And if we can act out of respect for the moral law, we are free. Second, since there can be no compatibilist account of this capacity, this freedom, we may conclude from what the fact of reason reveals that we are transcendentally free. Third, since there are no rational grounds for refusing the authority of the moral law, as acknowledged, transcendental freedom is not just a property of wills who (subjectively) take themselves to be under the moral law, but of rational wills as such. I will focus primarily on the first element of the argument.

Let us then consider what the fact of reason is. Allison (following Lewis White Beck) construes the fact of reason as (or as reporting?) a *performance,* not just a mode of consciousness or belief. It is not just that as a moral agent I believe or feel that the moral law is a valid practical law, but I *submit* myself to the moral law, and in submitting myself, I cannot coherently doubt that it is valid for me, and that I am able to act out of respect for it. (There is some small uncertainty here as to whether the fact of reason is the submitting, or the consciousness that I have submitted myself.) The key interpretive question is whether we are to conclude that in submitting myself to the moral law, it is the case—not just "it is the case to me"—that I am under the authority of the moral law; and that it is the case—not just "it is the case to me"—that I am able to act as and in the way the moral law requires.

In construing the submission as a performative, Allison wants to make use of an analogy with Jaakko Hintikka's doubt-dispelling interpretation of the *cogito*. But what doubt is to be dispelled? There are two possibilities: I can doubt that the moral law is objectively valid (that it is a universal norm of pure practical reason), and I can doubt that I am able to act from a motive of respect for such a law when the motive cannot be based in any empirical desire or interest. It might seem that the fact of reason could only be addressed to the latter: if I submit myself to any authority A, I cannot reasonably doubt that I can do what A requires.

In the ordinary case, in submitting myself to an authority, I will, intend, or commit myself to do what it says. Such submission cannot make the authority valid (think of My Lai-type cases, submissive housewives, etc.), although it looks as though the submission might explain how I take it as valid. But let us ask further: In what sense does that act of submission make me able to do what the authority says I am to do? There are a number of things to think about here. (1) Is the submission more than an expression of intention and willingness to obey or to accept some negative sanction if I disobey? (2) Have I submitted if the authority to which I submit is not valid? Is "submitting" like consent? Do certain conditions need to be met for "submitting" to be valid? And if so, what are they? ("I do" only marries me if it is the phrase of assent in an otherwise valid marriage ceremony.) (3) Can the submission be unconditional? Spontaneous? Must it be given for reasons? Could there be reasons for submitting to the moral law that do not make the submission conditional? (4) Can I submit and be required to do something that is not possible for me? If not, does this mean that submission is conditional in this sense—that I have not submitted unless I can do what is required, or that I have submitted only insofar as I can do what is required? Or is it that the performance of submitting doesn't guarantee the possibility of performance?

The worry that these questions produce is this. If submitting myself to the moral law is to show that I can act from respect for the moral law, either the submitting makes it the case that I can so act, or the submission wouldn't be valid unless I could so act. The first is implausible, for it would imply that by submitting I make myself transcendentally free. The second seems to beg the question, for it supposes that there are criteria of a valid submission that are neither the validity of the authority submitted to, nor the capacity to act as the authority requires. Perhaps there is some further piece of work that the performative is supposed to do.

Let us look at a more ordinary case. I tell my son that he is wrong to question the authority of his soccer coach. Given the structure of things, he is free to doubt the wisdom of his coach's decisions, but he cannot doubt the coach's authority over the team, and so over him, as a member of the team. That doubt was foregone on joining. Thus if he is on the team, he has submitted. And if he has submitted, he cannot doubt that he has a certain intention and commitment. But that is not enough.

There are two more things to consider here. First, the needed connection between submission and ability is not present. Not everything that is commanded can the player do. But perhaps what the analogy (and the coach) requires is willingness—and surely if the player has submitted and committed himself to the authority of the coach, he is, and has sufficient reason to be, willing to try to act as the coach requires. Second, both the coach's position and the players' qualifications must be valid for this submission to work. Thus the analogy does not dispel the thought that transcendental freedom is like a membership qualification: you cannot submit to the authority of the moral law unless you are transcendentally free. That is, *if* my will is autonomous, and I submit, I can act (will) as the moral law requires.

I chose the sports analogy in part because of Allison's concern to show that there cannot be valid reasons for not submitting to the authority of the moral law. One may evade the authority of coaches by refraining from participating in organized sports. One may not evade the moral law. The scope of submission must extend beyond those who take themselves to have submitted. What Kant would have to show is *either* that all persons *have submitted* to the moral law (and the fact of reason is then consciousness of this submission, not a way of submitting), *or* that no one can, on rational grounds, refrain from submitting to the moral law (where the argument removing such grounds does not involve the claim that the moral law *is* universally valid). I doubt there is any argument that could show this.

Allison's strategy at this point is to imagine what it would be both to accept the force of the fact of reason *and* to question its authority. The figure he conjures here is an amoralist who acknowledges duty in an attenuated sense. That is, the amoralist acknowledges that there is such a thing as duty, but would insist that moral reasons are not overriding of considerations of self-interest. The sense in which he acknowledges duty is that he agrees with the fact of reason argument: moral requirements are legitimate, and one is able to follow them, if one submits to the moral law (Allison says, "if one so chooses"). The further submission of the amoralist is to come from the recognition that (a) if he chose to submit to the moral law, he could submit to the moral law; (b) if he is able to submit to the moral law, he is capable of acting from reasons that are not interest-based—that is, he is transcendentally free; and (c) if he is transcendentally free, and the Reciprocity Thesis is accepted, then the moral law is the only possible principle that can provide ultimate justification for actions. But there is no reason why the amoralist must accept this, if as we have seen, the transition from (a) to (b) is unsupported. Indeed, I would have thought this is just the position an amoralist ought to hold: that is, he does not take moral reasons as overriding because he rejects the authority of the moral law. He can meet the minimal "justification requirement" because he has been given no reason to acknowledge the existence of principles that are not interest-based. In short—he has not been forced away from the doctrine of practical heteronomy.

If the fact of reason could show that I *can* act out of respect for the moral law if I choose to, transcendental freedom would follow. What I cannot see is how any performance of submitting could show that acting from respect for the moral law was possible, when it is just the possibility of so acting that is in question. What the fact of reason so understood could show is that in submitting to the moral law we cannot doubt that acting from respect for the moral law is possible. The fact of reason might thus explain why many *believe* we are able to act from respect for the moral law. Such conviction, however, does not bootstrap us up to transcendental freedom.

If Allison has correctly interpreted Kant's ambition with the fact of reason, then the difficulties we have found with the attempt to

Barbara Herman

provide Kant with some kind of argument to transcendental freedom through the fact of reason suggest that Kant's strategy in the *Critique of Practical Reason* provides no real advance over the disappointing third chapter of the *Groundwork*.

John Rawls sees the order and the point of the argument based on the fact of reason differently. The moral law is an idea of reason—the fact of reason its expression in our experience. The argument of the *Critique of Practical Reason* that culminates in the fact of reason is that the principle of morality must be a principle of autonomy. As reasonable and rational beings, we encounter the moral law as a law of autonomy in our everyday experience—it presents itself to us in a spontaneous and forceful way—*as* a principle of autonomy. This is the fact of reason. The analysis of the conception of morality presented by the fact of reason is represented by the CI-procedure (a formal construction based on the manner of moral thought and judgment that is appropriate to us *as* reasonable and rational beings), and the CI-procedure exhibits in its stages that it is a principle of autonomy.

So understood, the fact of reason cannot guarantee that the moral law as a principle of autonomy has objective reality. The moral phenomena we encounter are susceptible to a variety of explanations. What we can say is that none of these other explanations would support the idea of morality as a principle of autonomy. Through the fact of reason we have a view of ourselves as under the authority of an autonomous principle. Because our dignity and our humanity are at stake in our acknowledging the moral law, it is reasonable for us to accept the validity of the moral law (as a principle of autonomy)— not just for ourselves, but for all reasonable and rational beings.

The acceptance of the objective reality of the moral law—a practical law of reason according to which we are able both to limit our principles of desire and to bring about objects that are in some sense given by reason—sets the terms for the deduction of transcendental freedom. The way Rawls sees Kant closing this argument, what in the end shows that this is the right way to account for our moral experience, is the role transcendental freedom (or the autonomy of the will under a law of pure practical reason) plays in resolving the Third Antinomy and the fit of the moral law in the "unity of reason." In the end, then, according to Rawls, the moral law "is justified by answering to a need of speculative reason and by its cohering into the constitution of reason."

This has Kant saying both less and more than one might wish, especially if one is looking for an answer to skepticism about morality or its complementary concept, transcendental freedom. Although the moral law has a foundation (or "authentication" as Rawls calls it) when seen this way, it is only within a much larger and itself difficult conception of reason.

Where does this leave us? There is no deduction of the moral law nor any bootstrapping our way into transcendental freedom. We are instead clearer about the place of the moral law in Kant's critical philosophy, and thereby in a position to see why, for Kant, the conditions for scientific knowledge could not be used as grounds for moral skepticism. Moreover, morality so conceived is not vulnerable to the challenge of the amoralist. Amoralism is a practical matter, the choice of self-interest as the ultimate determining ground of one's will. From the fact that amoralism is (practically) possible, it does not follow that it is correct, or justified. This is shown in the rejection of empiricism about practical reason.

I want to turn now to Rawls's substantive interpretation of Kantian ethics: what he calls "Kant's constructivism." In particular, I want to look at the practical side of objectivity, or, in Rawls's phrase, the problem of "objective content."

According to Rawls, the idea of constructivism makes explicit and explains why we cannot know in advance what the output of the CI-procedure will be. This does not mean that the output of the CI-procedure could be just anything, or that we have no idea what sorts of moral results will issue. We are not to mistake the idea of construction for some form of creation. The CI-procedure represents (for purposes of judgment) an idea of reason, an idea that Kant contends is before the mind in ordinary moral consciousness or conscience. We therefore have good reason to expect that what we take the content of morality to be *is* the content of morality, as it will emerge from employment of the CI-procedure. What remains to be seen is the precise nature of these requirements and prohibitions, *and* their justifying reason.

The idea of construction suggests the bringing into being of a moral world that is intelligible to us and expressive of our nature as reasonable and rational beings. Thus, the CI-procedure must offer more than an algorithm for permissibility that spits out well-formed moral results. The *procedure* must have moral content: actions should be rejected as morally impermissible for reasons that explain what is wrong with them. This is part of the importance of the conceptions of "goodness" that Rawls sees built into the stages of the CI-procedure. What the CI-procedure should allow us to say is that an action or maxim is impermissible (wrong) because it fails to realize a certain kind of goodness. (This is not to turn Kant's theory into a teleological theory of the good—for it is still the moral law that sets the good as the object of a rational will, and the formal CI-procedure that determines what is good willing.)

Further reason why the CI-procedure must not work as a black box but provide substantive guidance for moral thought as well as judgment derives from the fact that the CI-procedure assesses maxims. Maxims are constructed from the material of agents' beliefs and circumstances, including agents' moral beliefs, some of which may be wrong. The CI-procedure must be able to challenge these moral beliefs, for they are the basis of an agent's moral understanding and perception. It cannot do this if it is silent about the nature of the error in an impermissible maxim.

As Rawls elaborates Kantian constructivism, features are built into the CI-procedure to secure "objective content." He speaks of the public role of moral principles in a society of reasonable and rational persons, and of the need for agreement in judgment. It may therefore seem that the task of the CI-procedure is to yield a list of duties, to play the role of such public principles or rules. I am not sure this must be so.

Agreement in judgment is secured if two agents, in the same circumstances, possessing the same information, will arrive at the same moral judgment using the CI-procedure. The conditions for agreement in judgment (in this formal sense) will yield substantive and thoroughgoing agreement in judgment (agreement in a material sense) if agents also agree on the nature of what is to be judged (and the information that is relevant, etc.). In such circumstances, disagreement can be explained by appeal to error, lack of rationality, or some such deviation.

But there may not be reason to expect (or require) widespread *material* agreement in judgment in Kantian theory. This again has to do with the fact that judgment is maxim-based. An agent's maxim presents her action (the kind of thing she would do) as she conceives it to be good—say as promoting some end she has an interest in, or takes to be good in itself. The maxim, in a sense, presents the agent's justification for doing what she does. What the CI-procedure assesses, then, are action and justifying reason *pairs*. This leaves room for widely divergent maxims of quite similar actions, as agents conceive them to be good in different ways (for different reasons). And if the maxims diverge, so may the results of employing the CI-procedure.

In order to get a list of duties from the employment of the CI-procedure, then, one might have to *begin* with agreement in judgment. That is, where a culture was deeply uniform, where people share a set of concepts (and agree on their employment), the output of the CI-procedure would be like a list of duties—but it would be like that because the input was (morally) uniform. But in a culture in which prevailing moral concepts were not uniform, or unstable, where there was moral change and criticism—different values, if you like—it would not be likely that the CI-procedure would yield duty-like results (public principles).

Is this a problem? Would it deprive Kantian theory of "objective content"? I find two strands of thought in what Rawls says. One strand focuses on the need for public rules and agreement in judgment in the strong sense, to be secured by certain restrictions on information that agents can bring to the CI-procedure. I am uneasy about this; one of the tasks I think the CI-procedure can perform is to reveal to agents when the special features of their situation that they take to justify their action do not have the justificatory power they take them to have. Restricting information secures uniformity of output by eliminating some forms of diversity from the input. Since I do not think these restrictions are necessary to get the CI-procedure to work (that is, we need not worry that the CI-procedure, without restrictions, would permit people in special circumstances to exempt themselves from otherwise general moral requirements), there is only a problem if material uniformity of outcome is required.

There is another strand in Rawls's remarks that suggests it is not. "Reasonable and rational persons," he says, "must recognize more or less the same reasons and give them more or less the same weight." This much is secured by the sincere and intelligent employment of the CI-procedure. For if we disagree, we are able to explain our dis-

Barbara Herman

agreement to one another, in terms of what we have seen in the circumstances of action, and the ways we conceived of our action as good. This is to suggest that even stubborn disagreement may not mark any weakness in the procedures of moral judgment.

Imagine a race of pure (not Holy) wills—each of whom has no reason to doubt the moral conscientiousness of the others. Suppose further that they are personally sensitive and morally creative. Why wouldn't they find their disagreements occasion for further reflection, for appreciation of moral diversity, as an occasion to appreciate the possibilities of moral insight?

We need not understand "the world that reason would bring forth" as an ideal world of agents acting according to uniform substantive principles, a world that we at best imperfectly realize through acting morally. The idea of reason is to manifest itself in the way we will, and so in the way we value what we value for our own reasons. The world that practical reason could bring forth is a world in which agents deliberate and reflect according to the CI-procedure. We should not imagine that we know what this world would look like.

That is not quite right. For we know that the CI-procedure will reject certain sorts of maxims and introduce certain minimal requirements—prohibiting deception for the sake of self-interest, say, or the total neglect of the needs of others. In that sense there are certain base-line requirements—no world that reason would bring forth could resemble the Hobbesian war of all against all.

There are two further features one might think call for restrictions to generate material agreement in judgment. First is the idea that we are to use the CI-procedure to generate principles (or duties) of justice. Second, and connected to this, is the thought that we must always view ourselves as (legislating) members of a possible social order. Rawls suggests that we are to think of the output of the CI-procedure as the totality of general precepts that satisfy the test of whether they can be jointly willed as universal laws for a realm of ends.

In the *Rechtslehre,* Kant identifies the problem of justice as the problem of justifying coercion of "external" actions. Duties of justice require performances, not maxims. There are problems, special to the circumstances of justice, that may not extend to moral judgment in general. It may be these, and not the need for objective content, that introduce restrictions into the CI-procedure.

The requirements of mutual intelligibility through commitment to judgment via the CI-procedure seem to me to be enough to secure

Justification and Objectivity

the idea of the moral agent as legislating for a kingdom of ends. A given agent's permissible maxim is one that could so serve, but so might others, adopted in relevantly similar circumstances. The totality of precepts that can be willed a universal law may not then resemble the principles of a public order. What I would suggest is that "formal agreement in judgment" may be enough to claim objective content for the theory. It's a bit like thinking that if we had the spirit we could do without the letter of the law.

What remains is the idea of the totality of general precepts that can be "jointly willed." I am not sure where this last requirement comes from, or what sort of further constraint it actually introduces. Perhaps there are limitations drawn from the need to constitute a moral community that are stronger than mutual intelligibility. Perhaps it is our distance from "purity of will." These possibilities need exploration but I cannot do that here. Part of the great power of Rawls's interpretation of Kant is that he opens Kantian moral theory to such questions and investigations.

PART III

The *Critique of Judgment*

The Social Spirit of Mankind

STUART HAMPSHIRE

Many British accounts of Kant's philosophy, unduly concentrated on the *Groundwork of the Metaphysics of Morals* and on the first *Critique*, leave his influence on Friedrich Schiller and the *Letters on Aesthetic Education* hard to explain. How can Schiller have been inspired by the harsh and bleak oppositions of nature on the one side and freedom on the other, of feeling and sensibility versus pure reason, of the universal moral law versus the contingent values and interests in human life? It is inconceivable that this British, Scottish, rationalistic, Kant, theorist of the divided self and of the solitary dominance of reason, could have inspired the precursor of romanticism from Weimar. In fact Kant launched a theory of the imagination and of genius that deserves to be taken at least as seriously as his doctrine of the free, because rational, will and of the categorical imperative: taken seriously both as a guide in politics and as a guide to the ideal life of an individual person. We have in the third *Critique* at least a sketch of another kind of freedom of mind, quite different from the rational ideal of the *Groundwork* and complementary to it: a different conception also of an attainable unity of mankind, which is not the unity attainable through either theoretical or practical reason. In the *Critique of Judgment* we learn that there is a bridge that conducts us from unreclaimed nature to rational freedom, a bridge prepared and ready for all mankind, even though earlier critical writings may suggest that there could be no such bridge.

First it is necessary to understand the construction of the *Critique of Judgment* itself, and to raise the old question: how do the two parts of it, the discussion of teleology and the aesthetics, fit together? Not, why did Kant put them together in a single volume, as a matter of fact, ascertainable from the biographical record: but rather, did he have good reasons, within his philosophy, for putting them together within a single volume? I think that he did.

Consider first Leibniz's principle of sufficient reason, in one of its stronger forms, sometimes called the principle of the best. This principle can be seen, casting its shadow, throughout the third *Critique*. Leibniz had argued in "On the Ultimate Origin of Things," and in several other places, that no explanation of natural processes can be a complete explanation, no theory a finally acceptable and complete theory, unless it conforms to the principle of the best: that is, unless it introduces such normative notions as perfect fit and ideal coherence, and unless it introduces the notion of perfection. The notion of final perfection—the maximum amount of being—is for Leibniz the shortest bridge that leads us from fact to value, and from acceptance of the various causal connections and natural laws in nature that we discover to a full understanding of why these causal connections and lawlike necessities must be as they are, when we survey them as a whole. We do not understand the connections that we observe if they remain a mere list or catalog of laws, and if we have not grasped the interconnections between them, and their perfect coherence within a larger and complete design. To grasp the interconnections is not just to add further and more comprehensive lawlike connections to the list, as an empiricist would think. It is to see or to grasp (a metaphor from the senses has to be used) the total pattern and the design, the natural adaptation of parts, and the principles of coherence between the already known causal connections: we move to another level of explanation. In order to understand completely, one needs to see an overarching system of mutually adapted parts and therefore to be in a position to reason counterfactually about what would have been imperfect in the world if any one of these causal connections or natural laws had been missing: imperfect, because existence would have been greatly impoverished elsewhere, with many other possibilities consequently unrealized: a traceable imperfection.

The Social Spirit of Mankind

Leibniz derived this doctrine of explanation, which holds that so-called mechanical explanations are incomplete until teleological explanation is added, from two sources: sources that he held to be inseparable though distinct. They were the theory of truth and the theory of a transcendent creator, which Christian theology requires. To say of a contingent proposition that it is true is just to say that there is a reason why of the several possibilities that the concept of the subject evidently leaves open, this one actual possibility was reasonably chosen: chosen by God.

In Kant's Copernican revolution, the whole of this Leibnizian apparatus is turned on its head, but the apparatus itself is still intact. More specifically, the tight connection between truth and explanation, or truth and intelligibility, is preserved, and this will always be the crucial point that separates Kant from empiricists of all kinds. Kant is to argue in the third *Critique* that explanations of nature in terms of causal connections and nomic necessities alone are always incomplete as explanations, however complete they may seem to be in their own quasi-mechanical terms. Even if we had arrived at a unified field theory in beautiful mathematical shape, so that we might claim to have come to the end of physics, at least as that science is now circumscribed, we would still need to know why this particular possibility was chosen from among all the logically coherent possibilities that there are. Leibniz says that we step outside the series of causal explanations to the extramundane creator, to the intentions and designs of "the divine mathematician," or (in a metaphor more significant for Kant) the perfect cunning of the supreme formal games-player, which is the allotted role of Leibniz's God. After the Copernican revolution, this jump into another domain of explanation cannot be so literally and metaphysically interpreted; but still the key notions of the principle of sufficient reason are to be preserved as regulative principles and in understanding living creatures: we need the notions of perfect coherence and mutual adaptation, and above all the notion of the systematic interdependence of the mechanisms involved, and involved in different degrees in all natural processes. But where are these explanatory notions to be anchored if not in the actual existence, demonstrable beyond doubt, of a benevolent and transcendent God? Kant has abandoned Leibniz's theory of truth as an internal, and in the last analysis a formal, property of propositions, without returning to earlier Cartesian doctrines of correspondence. He can preserve the notion of choice, as a necessary condition of human understanding alongside the category of cause, without attaching the notion of choice to a known transcendent chooser: just as he need not attach the notion of cause in a cosmological argument to a known first cause in order to claim an a priori assurance of the notion's universality.

Taking the three *Critiques* as a whole, Kant argues that we have an a priori assurance, without an independent metaphysical guarantee, that human understanding requires the universality both of the notion of cause, marking mechanical explanation, and the notion of choice, more specifically choice of the best, marking teleological explanation. If you claim a priori assurance of an extramundane first cause, as Leibniz did, you can also claim that the best explanation of natural processes that you find, conforming to the principle of sufficient reason, must fit into that unattainable complete knowledge that would express God's original and chosen design. For Kant a discovered explanatory truth about nature is not a fragment of complete knowledge, but it is a proposition found to be adequate to our experience of the world, as we constitute the world of phenomena in accordance with the category of causality and in accordance also with the presumption of a final coherence and adaptation of parts in Nature. Inevitably, we associate the category of causality with the choice of means toward ends of our actions, since we are necessarily active as well as theoretical creatures. We therefore associate mechanical explanation with the discovery of techniques and of technology: with our learnable rules and prescriptions for action. Correspondingly, we think of causal explanations as revealing "the technic of nature." We explain our actions by reference to means toward ends that were themselves chosen from possible alternatives. The ends constrain the choice of means, which is therefore not a free choice, because the specification of the ends and known causal connections dictate what are the right means. But the ends themselves have to be chosen, and chosen from a set of possibilities. The reasons that explain any choice of this kind do not necessitate the outcome, leaving only one possibility as still a possibility after the reason is supplied. The reason, once supplied, still leaves other possibilities open as still possibilities, but as less eligible possibilities, less inclined to be taken, on the assumption that the choice is for the best, or putative best.

Both Leibniz and Kant claim to know two things about the created world, though they arrive at the two truths by different routes:

first, we must look to it to exhibit universal laws tying causes to effects, effective means toward ends, in necessary connections; second, we must look to it to exhibit the most reasonably eligible systems of laws, taking the system as a whole. The emphasis falls on "taken as a whole." We shall never reach any vision of the systematic whole, though we shall continuously pursue the idea of it as a receding idea of reason. But still we are guided in theory-building by the regulative principle that the most elegant and tightly coherent arrangement of causal necessities will be the actually preferred arrangement. If there is a beautiful simplicity and formal rigor in a physical theory, and if we can compare it to other, less pleasing, more cumbersome theories that are still adequate to the phenomena, we shall immediately be drawn to the first theory. This is our intellectual assurance that nature is adapted to our powers of cognition.

In aesthetic enjoyment we derive the same satisfaction more vividly and directly, and through the senses, when we look out upon a Tuscan valley that we can take in within a single vision, and when we see how the immense complexity of the scene can still yield a beautifully coherent pattern and a patent design. This is more than an analogy. In responding with pleasure to the beauty of the scene, we are seeing it as adapted in form and in scale to human powers of cognition, when we allow our imagination to be free from the constraints of inquiry into causes.

From where can we derive the assurance that both these orders of explanation, the mechanical and the teleological, are indispensable to our understanding of nature, the second complementing and completing the first? Some quotations from both parts of the third *Critique* will yield the beginnings of an answer. From the second part: (1) "We find an original capacity of selection and construction on the part of natural beings (sc. trees) such as infinitely outdistances all the efforts of art" (CJ §64, 5:371). (2) "The first requisite of a being, considered as a physical end, is that its parts, both as to their existence and their form, are only possible by their relation to the whole" (CJ §65, 5:373). Therefore, (3) "We are entitled, rather we are incited, by the example that nature affords us in its organic products, to expect nothing from nature and its laws but what is purposive when things are viewed as a whole. It is evident that this is a principle to be applied not by the determinant, but only by the reflective judgment, that it is regulative and not constitutive, and that it is a clue to guide us in the study of natural things" (CJ §67, 5:379). "The word design,

149

as used here, . . . is not meant to introduce any special ground of causality, but only to assist the employment of reason by supplementing investigation of mechanical laws by the addition of another method of investigation, so as to make up for the inadequacy of the former even as a method of empirical research that has for its object all particular laws of nature" (CJ §68, 5 : 383).

What we are looking for is "a unity of nature in its empirical laws." "Strictly speaking, we do not observe the ends in nature as designed. We only read this conception into the facts as a guide to judgment in its reflection upon the products of nature" (CJ §75, 5 : 399). "We can never get a sufficient knowledge of organized beings and their inner possibility, much less get an explanation of them, by looking merely to mechanical principles of nature" (CJ §75, 5 : 400). Most revealing of all: "The production in a rational being of an aptitude for any ends whatever of his own choosing, consequently of the aptitude of a being in its freedom, is culture. Hence it is only culture that can be the ultimate end which we have cause to attribute to nature in respect of the human race. His individual happiness on earth, and, we may say, the mere fact that he is the chief instrument for instituting order and harmony in irrational external nature, are ruled out" (CJ §83, 5 : 431). Culture, *Kultur,* is neither freedom nor happiness, but something intermediate: it has neither the supersensible, unconditioned value of freedom as an end, nor is it as empty and trivial as happiness conceived as an end. "The value of life for us, measured simply by what we enjoy (by the natural end of the sum of all our inclinations, that is, by happiness) is easy to decide. It is less than nothing. For who would enter life afresh under the same conditions?" (CJ §83, 5 : 434n). Culture is the natural development of mankind into a new unity, not the overcoming of the given nature of mankind as in moral aspiration. Culture is the bridge that leads from nature to freedom and rationality. "Fine art and the sciences, if they do not make man morally better, yet, by conveying a pleasure that admits of universal communication, and by introducing polish and refinement into society, make him civilized" (CJ §83, 5 : 433).

Viewing itself as one natural kind among others, and as an entity for biological study, mankind might set before itself as its inevitable end the satisfaction of its naturally produced desires, and therefore happiness. But this is to ignore man's "capacity for setting before himself ends of his deliberate choice," ends that must be sought in the natural order. Culture is "the production in a rational being of an aptitude for any ends whatever of his own choosing"; and this requires for its development skill (*Geschicklichkeit*), also a negative discipline that frees a person from his immediate and natural impulses. The point of culture, so interpreted, is to constitute from the biological unit, the animal species, a new unity, which is humanity, the humanity that is held together through communication in art and in literature and in aesthetic enjoyment generally.

The error of classical philosophies, particularly Aristotle's, is that they had claimed to read off a determinate end for humanity from the mechanisms of the natural kind. But only the indeterminate end, of freedom to choose an end, can single out and constitute humanity as itself an end in relation to nature as a whole. So culture, as Kant interprets it here, as binding humanity together, is neither a naturally occurring phenomenon, like happiness, nor a supernatural ideal, like the rational will, but is something intermediate between them.

We can now turn back to the first part of the *Critique of Judgment* and see the concepts involved in the Kantian version of the principle of sufficient reason unlocking the aesthetic domain: the concepts of mechanism and teleology, of determinate and indeterminate ends, of the diversity and unity of nature, of nature as "adapted to our powers of cognition" and nature as exceeding them in sublimity.

First, creation and design, mechanism and teleology. Creative genius is to be contrasted with mere talent, the free and imaginative arts are to be contrasted with the crafts, the fulfillment of a determinate function is to be contrasted with the satisfaction of an indeterminate end. "The product of fine art, intentional though it be, must not have the appearance of being intentional: fine art must be clothed with the aspect of nature, although we recognize it to be art" (CJ §45, 5 : 307). The adaptation of means to ends must not be perceptible. The works of genius, products of creative imagination, do not exhibit "the marks of contrivance." You cannot say how the effect is produced, or even think of the object as a set of means toward a determinate end, as in a work of mere talent or in an achievement of craftsmanship. If you can separate the means from the end, you destroy the beauty of the work, as you can kill a joke by analyzing it. Yet it is also true that there is still no fine art with which something mechanical and academic does not enter in (cf. CJ §47, 5 : 310). There is a learnable craft of means toward ends, even in the free and liberal arts. Genius is the added, unanalyzable element that "gives the rule as nature." The adaptation of means toward a determinate end is the fulfilment of a function. It is a technology: finality under a concept. The fulfilment of function and beauty are related, but they must not be identified, as in some early theories of modern architecture. We can design means to produce a psychological effect, an effect of charm and agreeableness, but the work will fall short of true art, unless we see in the work "self-propagating formative power which cannot be explained by mechanism" (CJ §65, 5:374). This refers to a living organism, but also to a beautiful thing that must seem to be alive; "The beautiful is directly attended with a feeling of the furtherance of life" (CJ §23, 5:244). A thing may be visibly efficient, streamlined, visibly adapted to its specific purpose, a beautiful solution of a statable problem. If it is a beautiful work of the imagination, it is "an analogue of life," in this respect fulfilling no determinate end; only the indeterminate ends of formal perfection and freedom of form, with its own distinctive arrangement of parts. Therefore for the judgment of taste a beautiful work of art has the self-forming liveliness of a living organism in nature. The gap between the formative powers of nature, with their own indeterminate purposiveness, and the free, formative powers of human beings, has been closed. Human beings can to this extent feel at home in nature, in spite of the strain of their divided selves in moral endeavor.

As the function of imaginative genius is to make the artificial appear natural, as with Shakespeare's Falstaff or Tolstoy's Pierre, so a landscape is beautiful, at least by an eighteenth-century canon, if it appears as a product of design although it is actually a product of blind causes. This is the intermediate domain, realized at Stowe and Stourhead, gardens that are representations of culture as Kant understood the term. Closing the threatened gap between moral man and natural processes from the other side, we recognize natural beauty as involving a view of natural things "after the analogy of art, and not as aimless mechanism." We see the valley and surrounding hills, with the houses and orchards fitting into the landscape, as if it were designed for the delight of any human being who abstracts from his contingent interests, and who sees it as adapted to universal human powers of synthesis in imagination. The landscape is humanized, as in the English landscape gardens developed by Repton and Capability Brown, in which symmetry and wildness are combined, the park, half art, half nature, that ends in the Ha-ha, with a wilderness beyond. The formality of the Le Nôtre garden lies on the sur-

face because, with all avenues pointing to the center, it is directed to
an end that is too visibly a determinate and statable end. Because the
concept is, as it were, visible, the effect is of something mechanical
and contrived. There cannot be aesthetic ideas behind the beauty unless the imagination is incited itself actively to create "a second nature out of the material supplied by nature."

The soul is left dull, and the arts become distasteful, if the "fine
arts are not, either proximately or remotely, brought into combination with moral ideas" (CJ §52, 5:326). Beauty induces a certain liber-
ality of thought, whether it is natural beauty or a work of genius,
alongside a feeling of the furtherance of life. How it does is a question best answered in a contrast with the sublime.

"The sublime in nature is scarcely thinkable except in association
with an attitude of mind resembling the moral" (CJ §29, 5:268). The
sublime recalls in sensuous terms the divided self of moral aspiration
and the conflict between the understanding and ideas of reason,
which extend without limit beyond experience. The sublime presents
nature in all its boundlessness, and with it nature sinking into insig-
nificance before ideas of reason. So there is the Pascalian oscillation
between fear in the face of the suggestions of infinity in the starry
heavens, and fear of the metaphysical abyss in which one can be lost,
and then the answering assertion of pride in the understanding of
nature.

By contrast, the enjoyment of beauty, natural or man-made, is a
restful enjoyment of the free play of the imagination on objects that
seem to be adapted to its exercise. The three key words that echo
through the closing pages of the *Critique of Aesthetic Judgment* are
the cultivation and the communication of feeling, which are the outcome of this free play. Repeatedly, Kant claims that human feelings
are capable of being indefinitely cultivated and refined, elevated and
ennobled, with the effect that social life becomes civilized, and bar-
barism is held back. Culture is not achieved as a triumph over nature,
and in despite of natural feeling; rather it is the natural prolongation
of a propensity of the human mind, revealed in the capacity for aesthetic enjoyment and in the natural occurrence of genius, and of genius as addressed to humanity as a whole. "Taste makes, as it were,
the transition from the charm of sense to an habitual moral interest
possible without too violent a leap" (CJ §59, 5:354). We respond with
feeling to the physiognomic and expressive properties of scenes in

nature and to works of genius with a demand for universal agreement: we presume a shared perception and a shared pleasure crossing all barriers and frontiers, and as potentially universal as reason itself.

Underlying this common sense is a judgment of the effect of forms upon the imagination and reflection upon this play of the imagination. The artist "makes the object itself speak, as it were, in a mimic language." Also "There is a language in which nature speaks to us and which has the semblance of a higher meaning." We have the idea that the apparent beauties of the phenomenal world, in themselves inexplicable, can be attributed to the supersensible substrate of the phenomenal world, and their adaptation to our imagination can also be attributed to a supersensible harmony of our faculties: a subjective supersensible substrate. But this theory of natural beauty and this theory of genius are not the explanatory theories of a natural science. They tell us only that mankind can be united not only through a shared ideal of rationality in action and shared natural science, but also through a shared freedom of imagination and a shared culture of feeling. Kant writes, in a striking Enlightenment phrase—"humanity signifies, on the one hand, the universal feeling of sympathy, and, on the other, the faculty of being able to communicate universally one's inmost self [*sich innigst und allgemein mitteilen*]—properties constituting, when taken together, the fitting social spirit of mankind [*Geselligkeit*], in contradistinction to the narrow life of the lower animals" (CJ §60, 5 : 355). Surely *Geselligkeit* is the preferred reading, rather than *Glückseligkeit* as in some editions. This is the claim that Schiller was to develop, insisting, as it seems to me rightly, that shared freedom of imagination, and a shared culture of aesthetic enjoyment, in the open museums of the world are a more plausible basis for the unification of mankind than either moral principles or natural science. But that is another story.

It is clear that the two parts of the third *Critique* do belong together for at least the following reasons. (1) The incompleteness of causal explanation, of "mechanism," in understanding natural processes, and particularly living processes, is matched by the all-important distinction between the crafts and the free or liberal arts, and in the related distinction between talent and genius. (2) The very existence of aesthetics as an independent domain of human experience could not be established without the notion of *Zweckmäßigkeit ohne Zweck,* and precisely this notion of an indeterminate end, perfection of design and form, is required for the Kantian, or critical ideal-ist, form of the principle of sufficient reason. (3) The bridge between nature and freedom has to be that common sense (*sensus communis*), and communicable culture of feeling, which see the beauties of nature as adapted to our powers of cognition and to the free play of our imaginative faculties in harmony, and, therefore, after the analogy of art; and at the same time our common sense sees in the works of imaginative genius an inexplicable naturalness that marks an affinity with that supersensible substrate of nature that is otherwise unknown to us.

At this point I claim the liberty to speculate and to go beyond the explicit statements in the text to suggest what Kant might have said, and perhaps should have said, in amplification of the doctrine of the third *Critique*.

I have been encouraged in this speculation by Eckart Förster's account of Kant's *Selbstsetzungslehre* in the *Opus postumum*, which reveals the aged Kant's insistence that the embodiment of an individual person, and his continuous awareness of it, is a necessary condition both of his affirmation of his own existence and of any perception of the phenomenal world; also Kant's realization that perception always presupposes the subject's awareness of his own bodily activity. Alongside the "*Ich denke*" of the transcendental unity of apperception, the "*Ich lebe*" of embodiment is also a condition of all possible experience.

"It is quite certain that we can never get a sufficient knowledge of organized beings, and their inner possibility, by looking merely to mechanical principles of nature . . . it is absurd to hope that maybe another Newton may some day arise, to make intelligible to us even the genesis of but a blade of grass from natural laws that no design has ordered" (CJ §75, 5:400). Mechanical cause and its distinct effect, contrasted with the inner possibility of organized beings: what is meant here by "*inner* possibility" as contrasted with causality? The answer, I think, is to be found, as usually in Kant, in the affinity between the knowing subject who is himself or herself part of nature, and the object, nature, which is to be known. Human action in the phenomenal world, the causally explicable actions of a natural creature, involves the calculation of necessary means toward naturally desired and determinate ends. The necessary means include the agent's body. So much for the phenomenal self as mechanism.

But in our "inner" awareness of the self, we are aware of another kind of purposiveness, directed to an altogether indeterminate end, and we become aware of this kind of purposiveness in preconceptual reflection. A person can experience her own movements and gestures as having their own unformulated directions and purposes, quite independent of the will and of conscious desires, and as fulfilling the need of the immediate expression of feeling. How do we become aware of the refinement of feeling, this concern for form and its perceptible expression? Here I admit to taking a jump, guided by my own philosophical beliefs. I believe that Kant, finally turning his back on Hume and on British empiricism in general, came to think that a living human body cannot be conceived, at least by the person who inhabits it, primarily as a tool for effective action, as a mechanism. It is also a complex living organism that has its own preconceptual tendencies and goals. A human body has a physiognomy of its own and has an expressive life of its own, and it is the seat of feelings, half cultivated, half natural, in this respect like a garden, when it is a living thing, and not a corpse. That is why we are driven to employ physiognomic epithets to describe by analogy the unanalyzable expressive features of a landscape or of music or of paintings, as Kant remarks, when he writes about aesthetic ideas. The liveliness of a living body saves us from being a ghost, in the form of a rational will, lodged in a mechanism, with our feelings thrust outwards into nature as a mere pathology. The directly felt organization and wholeness of our bodies, the adaptation of face and limbs to the communication of feelings, present us with the original idea of expressive form that is refined through culture into pure aesthetic categories— as in notions of rhythm, balance, symmetry, notions important to Kant in the third *Critique* alongside the more specific expressive properties.

The two levels of explanation and understanding of external processes in nature are in a sense projected from the two different levels of self-awareness, which include the direct awareness, from inside outwards, of the movements of a body as a living whole alongside the external observation of the body as a mechanical system. This awareness of the inner world of bodily feeling, with its own indeterminate goals and rhythms, is universally communicable, with its correspondences in the external world, to humanity as a whole and across all frontiers, through the cultivation of aesthetic feeling for nature and through enjoyment of the open museums of the world.

Why Must There Be a Transcendental Deduction in Kant's *Critique of Judgment*?

ROLF-PETER HORSTMANN

Philosophers have always considered Kant's third and last *Critique*, the *Critique of Judgment*, a somewhat puzzling book, although for very different reasons. Those who view Kant primarily as a descriptive metaphysician trying to establish the conceptual foundations of our knowledge of the world have found it difficult to reconcile the basic results of Kant's first *Critique* with central statements of the last *Critique*—for example, those concerning causality and mechanical explanations. Both current Kant scholars and traditional Kantians have believed that the systematic study of Kant's critical endeavor is closely linked to problems based in peculiarities of the *Critique of Judgment*. This is especially so because of the ambiguous relations between the third *Critique* and its practical and theoretical counterparts on the one hand, and the *Opus postumum* on the other. Last but not least, Kant's immediate successors, the German Idealists, found the third *Critique* rather startling in that its strong antidualistic tendency seems to contradict fundamental principles of both Kant's theory of knowledge and his moral philosophy.

Widely different conclusions have been drawn from the fact that there is no easy way of integrating the *Critique of Judgment* into the Kantian system. Modern philosophers primarily interested in Kant's theory of knowledge—especially those in the English-speaking parts of the world—simply ignored the *Critique of Judgment*. Modern

scholarly specialists in Kant's philosophy came to two mutually ex-
clusive conclusions: some claimed that the third *Critique* elaborates
ideas based on the two former *Critiques*;[1] others claimed that either
the third *Critique* as a whole or its second part, on teleology, documents a second revolution in Kant's thought.[2]

The German Idealists drew the most extravagant conclusions. Attracted by what they called the results of Kant's philosophy but uneasy about what they took to be the fundamental premises on which
these results were based, they chose to regard the three *Critiques* as
three different and in the end inconsistent versions of the conceptual
and logical basis of Kant's transcendental idealism. Of these versions,
the German Idealists took the one manifested in the *Critique of Judgment* to be the least objectionable, because in the third *Critique* Kant
concedes a restricted meaning to such ideas as teleological explanation, intuitive understanding, and a rational cause of the world. Because of the importance of those ideas for their own systematic
efforts, they tacitly decided to treat the third *Critique* as Kant's most
advanced expression of his basic convictions and ultimate philosophical intentions, although they were not satisfied with the way in
which Kant presents these convictions and intentions. This situation
led (1) to the well-known distinction between the letter and the spirit
of Kant's philosophy that became prominent in Germany during the
1790's and (2) to Fichte's, Schelling's, and Hegel's habit of regarding
Kant's first *Critique* through the bias of their appreciation for elements in the third *Critique*.

Difficulties in properly understanding the role of the third *Critique* within the Kantian system were not all that made the *Critique
of Judgment* an obscure book. The construction of the book proved
an obstacle to a comprehensible assessment of its main goals as well.
There has been much criticism of Kant's bringing together into a
comprehensive theory of reflective judgment such widely separated
disciplines as aesthetics or philosophy of the beautiful on the one
hand, and philosophical biology on the other, connecting them by
claiming a common conceptual basis in the concepts of purpose and/
or purposiveness. This criticism ranges from the suspicion of artificial-
ity via the accusation of arbitrariness to the supposition that Kant had
no guiding conception at all in conceiving the third *Critique*.

The problems mentioned so far originate in obscurities accompanying the principles by which Kant's *systematic* intentions are constructed. Yet another group of problems arises when the third *Cri-*

tique is viewed as a body of propositions concerning the mental faculty of judgment, the beautiful, and organisms. Here, complaints about difficulty in discerning exactly what Kant claims about these three topics alternate with very definite statements concerning what is wrong with Kantian faculty psychology, what is ill-conceived within his aesthetic theory, or, finally, what are the shortcomings of his views on teleology.

Given these widespread attitudes toward Kant's third *Critique*, it seems at least possible that the alleged obscurity of the *Critique of Judgment* results from a serious omission by Kant. He obviously did not succeed in giving unambiguous indications about the function and the results of the third *Critique*. In other words, his treatise on judgment lacks explicit and intelligible answers to some very elementary questions—the most elementary being the question of why the third *Critique* was ever written at all. Although I believe that this question cannot easily be dismissed as purely rhetorical, it is not the question I will discuss here. Instead, I would like to focus on one of its aspects, namely the question: Why must there be a transcendental deduction in the *Critique of Judgment*? In approaching the *Critique of Judgment* via this question, I hope to find a natural and uncontroversial connection between the theory of the faculty of judgment Kant puts forward in the third *Critique*, at least as I develop that theory here, and the main topic of this collection of essays, that is, the problem of transcendental deductions in Kant's *Critiques*.

My paper can be roughly divided into three parts. The first attempts to indicate that the very principle of the *Critique of Judgment* poses a problem concerning its relation to a doctrine put forward in the *Critique of Pure Reason*. The second outlines Kant's theory of purposiveness in the *Critique of Judgment* and in the *Critique of Pure Reason*. The third tries to show why there must be a transcendental principle for the faculty of judgment and what this means with respect to aesthetics and teleology.

When one asks what motives led Kant, after finishing the *Critique of Pure Reason* and the *Critique of Practical Reason*, to embark on the project of a third *Critique*, the most likely answer proceeds roughly along the following lines.[3] As we know from his letters of the late 1780's, Kant wanted to complete his *critical* undertaking (*kritisches Geschäft*) by elaborating a *Critique of Taste* (C 10:494). Although it is not quite clear why he was interested in integrating a theory of taste

Rolf-Peter Horstmann

into his critical enterprise, it is clear that, with the notable exception of the *Critique of Pure Reason* (cf. C 10:121–24, 129–35), the subject of taste had been part of his varying conceptions of a philosophical system since at least 1771. Immediately after submitting to the printer his *Critique of Practical Reason* in the summer of 1787, Kant started on the *Critique of Taste* (C 10:490). We do not know exactly what his intentions were in this very first stage of his inquiries. But whatever his aims might have been, there must soon have been a serious change in his conception. Kant says in a letter to K. L. Reinhold (C 10:514; written in late December 1787) that on the occasion of the preparation of the *Critique of Taste* he discovered a new kind of a priori principle. These principles, Kant claims, govern our sense of pleasure and pain (*Lust und Unlust*), which is the mental faculty (*Gemütsvermögen*) that is the subject of the *Critique of Taste*.

So not until the very end of 1787 did Kant reach a fairly definite conception of what he was going to discuss in a third *Critique*, then still called *Critique of Taste*. In the same letter to Reinhold in which he announces his discovery of new a priori principles he expresses clearly what this decision concerning the contents of the *Critique of Taste* meant for his idea of the shape of a philosophical system. He writes,

Now I recognize three parts of philosophy, each of which has its a priori principles, which can be enumerated and for which one can delimit precisely the knowledge that may be based on them: theoretical philosophy, teleology, and practical philosophy, of which the second is, to be sure, the least rich in a priori grounds of determination (C 10:514–15).

He then declares that he wants to examine the second under the title of a *Critique of Taste*.

That is almost all we know about the initial situation in which a third *Critique* was projected. The two years during which Kant wrote the book must have witnessed a remarkable process of adjusting the initial idea of a *Critique of Taste* to needs originating from sources not directly related to the theory of taste. As evidence of such a process, we may note that in 1787 there is no hint of the role the faculty of judgment will play in the theory of taste, no hint that the *Critique of Taste* will turn out to be part of a *Critique of Judgment*, and no hint that judgments of taste have a structural similarity to teleological judgments in that both must be taken as judgments of reflection.

Such information does not lead us very far, however, in the attempt to find out why Kant was interested in writing a third *Critique* in which a transcendental principle has to be deduced. Rather than investigate the details of the historical development of the *Critique of Judgment*, we might do better to rephrase the question and ask what the main achievements of the third *Critique* are in relation to the first two *Critiques*. Every answer to this question will inevitably include at least one of the following three points: (1) the theory of taste; (2) the claim that there is a transcendental principle of the faculty of judgment, that is, the principle of the purposiveness of nature; and (3) the idea that teleological judgments are unavoidable in gaining knowledge. So, if one asks what topics are dealt with in the *Critique of Judgment* but not in either the *Critique of Pure Reason* or the *Critique of Practical Reason*, one will easily detect that these topics consist in the theory of the beautiful and of aesthetic judgments of reflection; Kant claims that the basis of this theory is the transcendental principle of purposiveness, which in turn is used in our employment of teleological explanations for natural phenomena.

This answer to our rephrased question, however, although correct, is not very interesting either, for two reasons. In the first place, it does not tell us why Kant thought it necessary to get involved in questions concerning purposiveness, natural ends, and taste in pursuing his *critical* task. Second, and more important, this answer does not take into account the aspects of the third *Critique* that have some sort of counterpart in the other two *Critiques* but are treated differently in the third *Critique*. Those aspects could shed considerable light on the function of the *Critique of Judgment* if it were the case that the third *Critique* is founded on a reformulation of claims already addressed in one of the other *Critiques*.[4]

Thus looking for what is newly integrated into the third *Critique* is not enough. One must account for what is not just new but different. This is especially important for the third *Critique* because the leading idea of this part of Kant's system stands in a somewhat awkward relation to some ideas put forward in the first *Critique*. To substantiate this claim, I will first give a preliminary description of the leading idea of the *Critique of Judgment*, which we find developed paradigmatically in the two versions of the Introduction. Second, I will examine Kant's central points in the two small chapters of the Appendix to the Transcendental Dialectic of the *Critique of Pure Reason*.

Rolf-Peter Horstmann

The most important category in the third *Critique* is undoubtedly that of the purposiveness of nature.⁵ Kant introduces this concept to answer two needs, each of which has its origin in requirements arising from very different backgrounds. The first one—which I will not discuss—concerns the problem of reconciling the results of Kant's practical philosophy with the outcome of his theoretical philosophy.⁶ This problem mainly consists in accounting for the possibility of the realization of ends that we must pursue as consequences of our conception of freedom. Kant puts this problem as follows:

Albeit, then, between the realm of the natural concept, as the sensible, and the realm of the concept of freedom, as the supersensible, there is a great gulf fixed, so that it is not possible to pass from the former to the latter (by means of the theoretical employment of reason), just as if they were so many separate worlds, the first of which is powerless to exercise influence on the second: still the latter is *meant* to influence the former—that is to say, the concept of freedom is meant to actualize in the sensible world the end proposed by its laws; and nature must consequently also be capable of being regarded in such a way that in the conformity to law of its form it at least harmonizes with the possibility of the ends to be effectuated in it according to the laws of freedom (CJ 5:175–76).

The second need to which the concept of purposiveness is designed to respond has nothing to do with practical philosophy in the sense of ethical theory. On the contrary, it arises from a situation that is a consequence of Kant's theoretical philosophy. In what follows, I shall primarily be concerned with that need and that situation. Kant introduces the theoretical situation to which he has to react in the following way:

But there are such manifold forms of nature, so many modifications, as it were, of the universal transcendental concepts of nature, left undetermined by the laws furnished by pure understanding a priori as above mentioned, and for the reason that these laws only touch the general possibility of a nature (as an object of sense) that there must also be laws in this behalf. These laws, being empirical, may be contingent as far as the light of *our* understanding goes, but still, if they are to be called laws (as the concept of a nature requires) they must be regarded as necessary on a principle, unknown though it be to us, of the unity of the manifold.—Reflective judgment which is compelled to ascend from the particular in nature to the universal, stands, therefore, in need of a principle. This principle it cannot borrow from experience, because what it has to do is to establish just the unity of all empirical principles under higher, though likewise empirical, principles, and thence the possibility of the systematic subordination of higher and lower (CJ 5:179–80).

What Kant is alluding to in these remarks is clear within the boundaries of his systematic philosophy. Given the results of the Analytic of the *Critique of Pure Reason*, we must take for granted that everything in nature and nature itself (understood as the sum total of all possible objects of experience) are governed by certain highly general nonempirical laws that are the joint product of the conditions of our sensibility and those concepts without which we could not even have the idea of an object. These laws, which Kant calls principles of pure understanding, determine everything that can be an object for us in such a way that these objects and their indefinitely various relations to each other qualify as elements of a homogeneous and continuous experience that can be taken as having some sort of unity. These principles are necessary conditions of experience and its unity in that they tell us what characteristics something must have in order to be an object of experience.

These principles, however, do not account for the contingent or empirical fact that nature consists of very many individual objects that, though necessarily determined by those principles—otherwise they would not be objects for us—behave in their special ways, have their special similarities, act and react according to rules that seem to depend on the special contingent characteristics of these objects, and so forth. Though conceivably the behavior of each individual object might be utterly unlike that of other objects, so that no empirical regularities could be found to govern the behavior of objects, nature shows us that there are such regularities. These regularities have the status of empirical laws, which means that they are rules whose necessity we cannot grasp a priori.

Thus far nothing requires that Kant introduce the concept of purposiveness. This will become more intelligible when we take into account the following consideration expressed by Kant:

For it is quite conceivable that, despite all the uniformity of the things of nature according to universal laws, without which we would not have the form of general empirical knowledge at all, the specific variety of the empirical laws of nature, with their effects, might still be so great as to make it impossible for our understanding to discover in nature an intelligible order, to divide its products into genera and species so as to avail ourselves of the principles of explanation and comprehension of one for explaining and interpreting another, and out of material coming to hand in such confusion (properly speaking only infinitely multiform and ill-adapted to our power of apprehension) to make a consistent context of experience (CJ 5:185).

   This statement is meant to describe a problem whose solution can be found by means of the idea of purposiveness: if in our pursuit of knowledge of objects we could rely only on the principles of pure understanding and a virtually infinite number of empirical laws, which could not be reduced to more general though equally empirical laws, then it would be impossible for us to think of nature as an entity of which we can have a systematically organized knowledge. That means it would be impossible for us to have a connected and unified knowledge of our world of experience and by implication of ourselves. In order to avoid this situation, we must assume that "nature specifies herself with regard to her empirical laws" (CJ 5:186) in such a way that she corresponds—at least to a certain degree—to the conditions under which we can acquire knowledge. This means we must assume that nature is organized in a purposive way. However, the idea of purposiveness involved in this assumption cannot, according to Kant, be taken as an empirical concept, nor is it a concept to which a constitutive principle of the understanding corresponds. Because of this we must think of the concept of purposiveness as a transcendental principle in its own right, one guiding the faculty of reflective judgment in its attempt to come to more general empirical laws by reflecting on particular empirical laws.

   This very sketchy and superficial description of the way in which the idea of the purposiveness of nature is introduced in the *Critique of Judgment* cannot do justice to the details of Kant's arguments concerning the unavoidability of the concept of purposiveness for the unity of experience, nor does it help to address the considerable number of problems involved in the introduction of purposiveness. All this description is intended to show is that Kant in the third *Critique* wants to convince us of two points. The first is that the concept of purposiveness is a transcendental principle that, because it cannot be regarded as being a principle of either the understanding or reason, must be accepted as a transcendental principle of the mental faculty of judgment in its reflective use. The second is that it is a necessary condition for the *unity* of our knowledge of experience as a *system* of empirical laws.

   In evaluating this Kantian position, one must distinguish between the critical problem to which it attempts to respond and the systematic problem that it purports to answer. With respect to the critical problem—that is, the problem of whether and to what extent we can find a priori principles of knowledge in the respective faculties of reason, understanding, and judgment (cf. CJ, Introduction III, 5:176–79)—one may accept this position as the most convincing answer Kant has to offer, even if only for the trivial reason that it is the only one he gives. Things are different, however, with respect to the systematic problem, that is, the problem of how to account for the unity of empirical knowledge in view of the contingency of empirical laws concerning natural objects and processes for our faculty of knowledge, because the solution to this problem proposed in the third *Critique* competes with an answer Kant has already outlined in the *Critique of Pure Reason*, an answer that is largely incompatible with the theory put forward in the *Critique of Judgment*. This manifest incompatibility allows for very different options in accounting for the function of the *Critique of Judgment* in Kant's critical system overall and creates a peculiar tension for our original question about why there must be a transcendental deduction in the third *Critique*. The most extreme of these options are to claim either (a) that because of his solution of the critical problem in the third *Critique* Kant had to sacrifice an otherwise well-founded theory concerning the systematic problem as presented in the first *Critique*, or (b) that because of difficulties that Kant found in his treatment of the systematic problem in the *Critique of Pure Reason* he was led to a new solution to the critical problem, which is documented in the *Critique of Judgment*. Before I can discuss these options in detail, I must review Kant's central ideas about the systematic problem as outlined in the *Critique of Pure Reason*.

As I mentioned before, Kant deals with the problem of the unity of knowledge in the Appendix to the Transcendental Dialectic.[7] In connection with the discussion of the legitimate employment of the transcendental ideas (the ideas of soul, world, and God), Kant introduces what he calls "the hypothetical employment of reason" (A647), which is said to consist in pursuing the idea of the systematic unity of knowledge. In this context, the concept of reason is meant to designate the faculty of deducing the particular from the universal, that is, the concept of reason is used in contradistinction to that of the understanding. The employment of reason is called hypothetical in order to hint at the merely problematic status of the idea of a systematic unity of empirical knowledge, that is, to state that this idea is just a subjective rule and not an objective law. This last point is important for Kant because it shows, as he puts it,

> that the systematic unity of the manifold knowledge of understanding, as prescribed by reason, is a *logical* principle. Its function is to assist the understanding by means of ideas, in those cases in which the understanding cannot by itself establish rules, and at the same time to give to the numerous and diverse rules of the understanding unity or system under a single principle, and thus to secure coherence in every possible way (A648).

In describing the unity required by reason as a merely logical principle, Kant wants to exclude explicitly the possibility of taking that principle to be a transcendental principle of reason, that is, one that "would make the systematic unity necessary, not only subjectively and logically as method, but objectively also" (A648).

Everyone who is familiar with the first part of the Appendix to the Transcendental Dialectic knows that the sentence just quoted is the last one in that little chapter that can be given an unambiguous interpretation. As for the rest of the chapter on the Regulative Employment of the Ideas of Pure Reason, one must agree with Norman Kemp Smith, who states in his *Commentary to Kant's Critique of Pure Reason*: "The teaching of this section is extremely self-contradictory."[8] Fortunately, we do not have to deal with the problems manifest in that chapter because they have no consequences for the point that is of interest to us: namely, that the idea of the systematic unity of knowledge is not a transcendental principle of reason but rather a logical principle that we employ as a regulative one in order to bring unity into the body of our detailed knowledge.[9] I mention that there are problems with this section in order to avoid the impression that they are being suppressed for the sake of the argument.[10]

Now, the ingenious and bold move Kant makes in the *Critique of Pure Reason* in order to introduce, among other things, the concept of purposiveness in connection with the idea of the unity of empirical knowledge consists in a consideration that he expresses as follows:

> But reason cannot think this systematic unity otherwise than by giving to the idea of this unity an object; and since experience can never give an example of complete systematic unity, the object which we have to assign to the idea is not such as experience can ever supply. This object, as thus entertained by reason (*ens rationis ratiocinatae*), is a mere idea; it is not assumed as a something that is real absolutely and *in itself*, but is postulated only prob-

lematically (since we cannot reach it through any of the concepts of the understanding) in order that we may view all connection of the things of the world of sense *as if* they had their ground in such a being. In thus proceeding, our sole purpose is to secure that systematic unity which is indispensable to reason, and which while furthering in every way the empirical knowledge obtainable by the understanding can never interfere to hinder or obstruct it (A681).

With this consideration Kant wants to combine two tasks. The first is to reevaluate the transcendental ideas of soul, world, and God within his theory of empirical knowledge by assigning them a positive function within our system of knowledge without having to give them the status of constitutive principles of knowledge. The second is to specify the idea of a systematic unity of empirical knowledge in such a way that one can distinguish between different forms of that unity according to what type of object one is dealing with. How Kant realizes this twofold task can be seen in the case of the idea of the soul. Here Kant says:

If I am to investigate the properties with which a thinking being is in itself endowed, I must interrogate experience. For I cannot even apply any one of the categories to this object, except in so far as the schema of the category is given in sensible intuition. But I never thereby attain to a systematic unity of all appearances of inner sense. Instead, then, of the empirical concept (of that which the soul actually is), which cannot carry us far, reason takes the concept of the empirical unity of all thought; and by thinking this unity as unconditioned and original, it forms from it a concept of reason, that is, the idea of a simple substance, which, unchangeable in itself (personally identical), stands in association with other real things outside it; in a word, the idea of a single self-subsisting intelligence (A682).

Reason performs the same procedure with respect to the idea of God. In consequence, reason must take this idea of God as the command "that all connection in the world be viewed in accordance with the principles of a systematic unity—*as if* all such connection had its source in one single all-embracing being, as the supreme and all-sufficient cause" (A686).

This way of looking at the world is best described as a position that takes as a basic regulative principle the idea of the purposive unity of things. The purposiveness thus used is obviously meant to characterize a specific form of systematic unity.[11] This unity, however, is not a transcendental but a logical principle, and this implies that within the conception exemplified by the *Critique of Pure Reason* purposiveness, too, must be regarded as a logical, subjective principle and not as a transcendental one.

Before I can deal with some aspects of the disturbing result that one and the same concept of purposiveness is claimed to be a transcendental principle in the third *Critique* and a logical principle in the first *Critique*, I must hint at some ambiguities concerning the term "transcendental" in these contexts. Some of these ambiguous formulations may be real contradictions, as in the Appendix to the Transcendental Dialectic, where within ten pages one finds both the claim to have proved that a transcendental deduction is always impossible for (transcendental) ideas (A663–64) and the statement that in order to employ an a priori concept legitimately we first must give it a transcendental deduction by demonstrating the transcendental ideas to be regulative principles of the systematic unity of the manifold of empirical knowledge in general (A669–702). In other cases, we must face the problem that sometimes the term "transcendental" carries the connotation of objective necessity in contradistinction to subjective necessity (for example, A648), whereas in other contexts Kant speaks without hesitation of subjectively necessary transcendental principles (for example, FI 20:209). All this indicates that Kant may give the term "transcendental" more than one meaning.[12]

This observation might lead us to assume that the discrepancy in the status of the principle of purposiveness between the first and the third *Critiques* is merely a terminological problem. It might, after all, turn out that what Kant calls "logical" in the first *Critique* he calls "transcendental" in the third *Critique*. To avoid this assumption, one must find a conception of a transcendental principle according to which purposiveness as employed in the *Critique of Pure Reason* is definitely not a transcendental principle, but purposiveness as introduced in the *Critique of Judgment* is. In other words, one must find a description of a transcendental principle that allows for only subjective necessity. Such a description appears in the Introduction to the third *Critique*, where Kant defines a transcendental principle as follows: "A transcendental principle is one through which we represent a priori the universal condition under which alone things can become objects of our cognition in general" (CJ 5:181).

This description allows for subjective necessity in the weak sense that it is indefinite about the type of necessity required for an a priori condition of knowledge. I will rely on this meaning of "transcendental" in the following considerations.

We can now put our leading question in either of two ways. The first is: Why is Kant, in the third *Critique*, interested in taking the principle of purposiveness to be a transcendental principle? The second is: Why does Kant want to give up the position outlined in the first *Critique*, according to which the principle of purposiveness is not a transcendental principle? Both these questions can be transformed easily into our initial question: Why must there be a transcendental deduction in the third *Critique*?

To answer these questions, we must return to what Kant takes to be the function of the principle of purposiveness. This principle is designed, both in the *Critique of Pure Reason* and in the *Critique of Judgment*, to allow for the unity of knowledge in view of the multitude of empirical laws. Now with regard to the epistemological status of this principle, Kant has—given the conceptual apparatus employed in the *Critique of Pure Reason*—two options: he must assign it either the role of a constitutive principle or that of a regulative one. Both of these options have their problems, however. If Kant had taken the principle of purposiveness to be a constitutive principle, he would have to view it either as an empirical or as a transcendental principle. To speak of it as an empirical principle does not make much sense for Kant, because, as he says in the first version of the Introduction to the *Critique of Judgment*: "Under no circumstances can a principle like this be posted to the account of experience, because only by presupposing this principle is it possible to engage in experience in a systematic fashion" (FI 20:211; cf. CJ 5:180). But to declare it to be a transcendental principle does not make much sense either, because that would mean granting it objective necessity. Such a decision would lead to endless problems, mainly concerning the epistemological status of the principle of causality.[13] This, then, does exclude the possibility of taking purposiveness to be a constitutive principle because it cannot be taken to be a transcendental one, which leaves only the other side of the alternative; that is, purposiveness must be taken as a regulative principle.

As a purely regulative principle, however, the purposiveness of nature is just a methodological device that, though subjectively necessary, cannot be transformed into an a priori condition of our knowledge of objects in general. That purposiveness has to be treated as an

Rolf-Peter Horstmann

a priori condition seems to be an insight Kant developed in the course of writing the third *Critique*. It is in this context that Kant introduces a consideration that ties the concept of purposiveness to our manner of acquiring empirical concepts. This consideration, again, starts with the problem of the unity of knowledge: unity of knowledge with respect to empirical laws obviously presupposes the possibility of empirical laws and the means of empirical concepts. According to Kant, we acquire these empirical concepts via a process involving a number of mental faculties (cf. FI 20:220), a process whose success depends, among other factors, on the manner in which the manifold of intuition is given to us.[14] Now—and this is the crucial move in Kant's consideration—not only is this manifold of intuition organized contingently in such a way that it fits our subjective conditions of concept acquisition, but we must also assume that it is so organized even if there were to be no empirical evidence in favor of this assumption. In other words, we must presuppose that the given manifold of intuition—that is, the empirical data that we combine via comprehension into the concept of an object—are organized purposively for our concept-acquiring faculties because without (empirical) concepts there is no (empirical) knowledge at all. This presupposition, however, is not merely a subjective rule (though it is that, too) but a necessary condition under which things can be objectively known by us; that is, the presupposition of purposiveness of nature is an a priori presupposition or a transcendental principle in the sense defined above *without* being a constitutive principle.[15]

Now, it seems, we are in a somewhat embarrassing situation, because the result of our checking Kant's options with respect to the epistemological status of the principle of purposiveness seems to be that when we try to think of it as a transcendental principle there are good reasons to describe it as a regulative one, and when we think of it as a regulative principle we are forced to look on it as a transcendental one. But this impression is misleading, for the situation merely indicates that there must have been a shift in the meaning of one of the terms between the first and the third *Critiques*. As I have mentioned before, this happened with the term "transcendental," so that in the *Critique of Pure Reason* its meaning excludes the connotation of subjective necessity, but in the *Critique of Judgment* this position has been abandoned. The meaning of the term "transcendental" here no longer excludes subjective necessity, without becoming synonymous with the term "logical" as employed in the first *Critique*. So there are no problems any longer with the possibility of a transcendental status for the principle of purposiveness, given that one can agree with Kant on the doctrine of how—according to the third *Critique*—we acquire concepts.

But this does not mean that all problems are solved. Referring back to the distinction introduced above between a critical and a systematic problem, one may say that Kant has settled the systematic problem in that he has decided in favor of the transcendental status of the principle of purposiveness. But for the "critical" problem (that is, the problem of a priori principles of the faculties of knowledge) this decision leads to a new set of difficulties. Because, according to Kant, it is the very task of a *critical* inquiry to answer the question which of our respective faculties of knowledge is the basis for which a priori principle (that is, which faculty makes which a priori principle a transcendental one), the claim that purposiveness is a transcendental principle commits Kant to being very specific about which faculty purposiveness is a transcendental principle of. Here again Kant must face a dilemma originating in the results of his theoretical philosophy as documented in the *Critique of Pure Reason*, as well as his practical philosophy as formulated in the *Critique of Practical Reason*. Though important and interesting in its own right, a discussion of the question of how Kant accommodates his theory about the role our respective faculties of knowledge play in theoretical and practical contexts to his findings about the function of a priori and transcendental principles in these contexts is far beyond the scope of this paper. All I can do here is to characterize the situation Kant is in *after* having chosen to take the principle of purposiveness to be a transcendental one, being determined not to rearrange the basic elements of his faculty theory.

Kant's standard position concerning the (higher) faculties of knowledge in relation to the justification of theoretical and practical claims as outlined in the first two *Critiques* is roughly the following (cf., for example, CJ, Introduction I–III, 5:171–79). There are two types of transcendental principles: those of the understanding, which govern our conception of nature in that they make possible the very idea of an object of nature, and those of reason, on which our concept of freedom depends, which in turn provides the basis for all moral rules. Whereas there are quite a few transcendental principles of the understanding (that is, as many as there are categories), there is only one of reason (that is, the categorical imperative). Now—and this is the important point—Kant claims two things. The first is that the list of transcendental principles is exhaustive in the sense that there are no other possible transcendental principles of the understanding or of reason—at least not for creatures like us. The second is that only the principles of the understanding constitute objects objectively in the sense that they determine what an object really is for us. Kant has sensible reasons for both these claims, which I cannot elaborate here. One of the more obvious reasons is that these claims imply a very effective defense of one of Kant's major objectives with respect to natural sciences, according to which only causal-mechanical explanations of natural phenomena can be objectively valid explanations (cf., for example, CJ, Introduction VIII, §§61, 68, 5:192–94, 359–61, 381–84).

Coming back to the principle of purposiveness, it is easy to see that within this framework the introduction of purposiveness as a new *transcendental* principle poses a serious problem. From what has been sketched so far, it is clear that purposiveness cannot be taken to be a transcendental principle of the understanding because it is not a constitutive principle at all. But purposiveness cannot be a transcendental principle of reason, either, because the idea of the purposiveness of nature is not a moral law. But is there any other faculty to which we can assign a transcendental principle? The obvious answer is the faculty of judgment, which is a faculty of knowledge and which has as yet no transcendental principle.[16] Kant is not in the position to settle this question that easily, however (although such an answer perfectly corresponds to his intentions), because in the first *Critique* he treated judgment (*Urteilskraft*) as a faculty whose only task is to subsume particular cases under general rules—an activity for which no transcendental principle was required (cf. A132–36, A646; FI 20:212; CJ 5:179, et al.).

Kant resolved the dilemma arising from conflicting tendencies in the solutions to what I have called the critical and the systematic problems in his philosophical program by splitting judgment (*Urteilskraft*) into determinant and reflective judgment (*bestimmende und reflektierende Urteilskraft*). The former took over the function assigned in the *Critique of Pure Reason* to judgment in toto, that is, the function of subsuming the particular under the general. Reflective judgment was assigned a function that in the *Critique of Pure Reason* had been given to reason in its hypothetical use; that is, judgment in its reflective use is supposed to find a more general concept for a given particular.[17] The fact that this split between a determinant and a reflective function of judgment was introduced for the first time in the *Critique of Judgment* indicates that there must have been a systematic reason for doing so, though scholars have never agreed about what this reason is. My considerations so far would indicate that the systematic reason consists in the necessity of finding for a transcendental principle of purposiveness a faculty in whose activity this principle can have its foundation and which would contribute an a priori condition to our knowledge of objects.

Now we are in a position to answer our initial question of why there must be a transcendental deduction in the *Critique of Judgment*. The trivial, though nevertheless true, answer is that there must be a transcendental deduction because there is a transcendental principle, as Kant himself not surprisingly puts it in the Introduction to the *Critique of Judgment* (CJ 5:182). But to reach a systematic standpoint from which this rather obvious answer could be given without giving away too many otherwise indispensable philosophical theorems seems to have involved rearranging, redefining, and even abandoning former positions. This paper has attempted to contribute to an analysis of this process. In view of the process and its result (that is, the justification of the claim that there must be a transcendental deduction in the *Critique of Judgment*), it is not without irony that the question whether there actually *is* a transcendental deduction in the third *Critique* is a question whose answer is still highly controversial.

However that may be, in concluding it might be worth mentioning in a few sentences how the Kantian conception of purposiveness as a transcendental principle of reflective judgment leads to the respective disciplines of aesthetics and teleology. For aesthetics, or, more accurately, aesthetic judgments of reflection or judgments of taste, this connection consists in combining the idea of purposiveness, including reflective judgment as the faculty of knowledge of which it is a transcendental principle, with the mental faculty (*Gemütsvermögen*) of the feeling of pleasure and pain. Although the details of Kant's argument concerning this connection are rather complicated, the core of his consideration is contained in the following passage from the Introduction to the *Critique of Judgment*:

If pleasure is connected with the mere apprehension (*apprehensio*) of the form of an object of intuition, apart from any reference it may have to a concept for the purpose of a definite cognition, this does not make the representation referable to the object, but solely to the subject. In such a case the pleasure can express nothing but the conformity of the object to the cognitive faculties brought into play in reflective judgment, and so far as they are in play, and hence merely a subjective formal purposiveness of the object. For that apprehension of forms in the imagination can never take place without reflective judgment, even when it has no intention of so doing, comparing them at least with its faculty of referring intuitions to concepts. If, now, in this comparison, imagination (as the faculty of intuitions a priori) is unintentionally brought into accord with understanding (as the faculty of concepts), by means of a given representation, and a feeling of pleasure is thereby aroused, then the object must be regarded as purposive for reflective judgment. A judgment of this kind is an aesthetic judgment about the object's purposiveness (CJ 5:189–90).

This quotation tells us clearly that Kant, in his account of the possibility of an aesthetic judgment of reflection, relies heavily on his theory of the conditions of our acquiring empirical concepts, mentioned above. It is the very center of his argument that if, when we contemplate an object, all conditions are fulfilled that would have to be fulfilled in order to put us in the position of acquiring a concept of that object, then this object produces in us the feeling of pleasure. This feeling in turn indicates that the object is purposive for our faculty of reflective judgment, and it is because of this that we call the object beautiful. Now these conditions of concept acquisition presuppose the transcendental principle of purposiveness, and this implies that the very possibility of an aesthetic judgment of reflection is based on that principle (CJ 5:191). The fact that Kant takes the transcendental principle of purposiveness to be the material condition for the possibility of aesthetic judgments of reflection has no impact on the question of whether judgments of taste are intersubjectively valid judgments, however. It is one thing—as Paul Guyer has pointed out in his book on Kant's theory of taste—to claim that the possibility of an aesthetic judgment is grounded in the transcendental principle of purposiveness, and quite another thing to hold that such a judgment is intersubjectively valid.[18]

Kant conceives of the relation between the principle of judgment and teleology in an analogous manner. But whereas the possibility of an aesthetic judgment depends on fulfilling conditions of concept acquisition, the possibility of a teleological judgment depends on the possibility of applying to an object of nature the concept of an end understood as a concept of reason.[19] In the first Introduction to the

Critique of Judgment, Kant describes the process in which this application takes place as follows:

> If empirical concepts and laws conforming to the mechanism of nature are previously given, and judgment compares such a concept of the understanding with reason and its principle of the possibility of a system, then if this form is met with in the object the purposiveness is judged to be *objective* and the thing is called a *natural purpose*, since in the previous case things were only judged to be indeterminately purposive *natural forms*. A judgment on the objective purposiveness of nature is called *teleological*. It is a *cognitive judgment*, but belongs only to reflective and not to determinant judgment (FI 20:221; cf. 232–37, and CJ 5:192–94).

How, according to Kant, the concept of systematicity is connected with that of purposiveness is a rather complicated and obscure story that cannot be of interest to us here. We should note, however, that the passage just quoted shows clearly that in the context of teleology the reference to purposiveness has the twofold function (1) of explaining the possibility of a teleological judgment with respect to natural objects as a judgment of reflection and (2), in doing so, of restricting the validity of such judgments.

Concerning the first point, Kant insists that, because the concept of purposiveness is a principle of reflective judgment, a teleological judgment must be a judgment of reflection; with respect to the second point, he claims that because a teleological judgment is a judgment of reflection it is not an objectively valid judgment.

Following this line of reasoning, we can see why Kant always emphasizes that there is a structural difference between aesthetic and teleological judgments in relation to the faculty of judgment. Whereas, as Kant says in the first Introduction to the *Critique of Judgment* (FI 20:243–44), an aesthetic judgment is wholly based in the faculty of judgment, a teleological judgment must rely on concepts that are given by the faculties of reason and of understanding (cf. CJ 5:193–94). This assessment seems to reflect the fact that, according to Kant, an aesthetic judgment would not be possible without the principle of purposiveness understood as a transcendental principle of judgment, whereas a teleological judgment is not materially dependent on the faculty of judgment and its principle, though its validity is that of a judgment of reflection.

So, in the end, though I am not in the position to make any claims about the historical correctness of my attempt to reconcile the various motives and intentions Kant is pursuing in his third *Critique*, and though I am not even sure that my account of this story contributes to an essentially coherent reading of the basic elements of the *Critique of Judgment*, I am quite convinced that every reconstruction of the aim of this *Critique* and its realization must take into consideration most of the aspects treated in this paper. Whether they will be fully sufficient for such a reconstruction is another question.

The Deductions in the *Critique of Judgment*: Comments on Hampshire and Horstmann

REINHARD BRANDT

I propose to address the papers of Hampshire and Horstmann in reverse order. As I arrive at results substantially different from those of Horstmann, this will make it necessary, in the first part of my comment, to discuss Kant's text in some detail. In the second part, I shall try to supplement Hampshire's arguments by pointing to the two deductions of the judgment of taste as the mediating link between theoretical and practical reason.

Horstmann believes that in the *Critique of Pure Reason* Kant speaks of a general principle of the purposive unity of nature; yet he writes, "This unity, however, is not a transcendental but a logical principle, and this implies that within the conception exemplified by the *Critique of Pure Reason* purposiveness, too, must be regarded as a logical, subjective principle and not as a transcendental one" (pp. 167–68, above). This results in an incompatibility between the doctrines of the first and third *Critiques* ("this manifest incompatibility," p. 165, above). His interpretation is directed toward explaining why the logical principle is transformed into a transcendental one.

Horstmann assumes that the principles of reason Kant describes in the Appendix to the Transcendental Dialectic as merely logical are identical in substance with the transcendental principle of judgment

This paper was translated by Deborah Kerman.

in the Introduction to the *Critique of Judgment*. This view, it seems to me, is questionable.

If the principles of reason were merely logical, either the systematic organization of empirical knowledge (which, in a way, is first made possible by them) would have nothing to do with truth (that is, it would remain open whether what is known is itself systematically organized), or truth would have to be identified with a merely internal coherence. Both assumptions are completely foreign to the program of the *Critique of Pure Reason*; reason can impose the logical principles on the understanding as rules for investigation only because the principles of reason are transcendental. "It is, indeed, difficult to understand how there can be a logical principle by which reason prescribes the unity of rules, unless we also presuppose a transcendental principle whereby such a systematic unity is a priori assumed to be necessarily inherent in the objects" (A650–51). Exactly the same is true for the specification and the affinity of concepts and their objects.[1]

It is indisputable that the text of the Appendix to the Transcendental Dialectic presents peculiar difficulties, and certain expressions of Kant's could suggest Horstmann's interpretation. This interpretation urges itself the more when one reads the *Critique of Pure Reason* in light of Kant's own retrospective remarks of 1790. I will first consider certain difficulties in the Kantian exposition of the transcendental principles of pure reason, then go into Kant's own interpretation of the first *Critique* in the *Critique of Judgment* and already in the *Critique of Practical Reason*.

A significant source of the difficulty with which the doctrine of the transcendental principles of reason is afflicted lies in the tension between their systematic function on the one hand, and their location in the text on the other. As regards the former, it appears that speculative knowledge finds its inevitable conclusion in the transcendental ideas and in their associated principles. The "completion of the critical work of pure reason" (A670) is located in the deduction of the transcendental ideas. The *Critique* begins with the transcendental deduction of the concepts of space and time, continues with the deduction of the categories and the proofs of their associated principles, and culminates in the deduction of the ideas (see also A702). Intuition, concepts, and ideas are indispensable elements of the possibility of experience. Without the last, the acts of the understanding lack unity and direction; they would—if they came about at all—"grope" around and scatter in arbitrary formations. Without concepts, intuitions remain blind; without ideas, concepts are incoherent and useless.

The architectonic arrangement of the *Critique of Pure Reason* does not follow this systematic plan, however, but is built upon a different principle—thereby cramming its systematic peak into a mere "Appendix to the Transcendental Dialectic." The principle of the division of transcendental logic into Analytic and Dialectic, into a logic of truth and a logic of illusion, derives from a certain flaw of the ideas; namely, that they become dialectic through a certain use of the judgment (A643). With this basic division a central idea of the whole theory of knowledge is properly set forth. Partial knowledge of nature is possible through the understanding, without requiring knowledge of the whole and the unconditioned; but in this way the whole and unconditioned is (mis)understood as a thematizable object of knowledge itself, not as idea. As idea, the whole is indispensable for systematic experience, but that means: for human experience in general, which cannot but comprehend partial elements of it in the frame of unity and specification. The ideas and transcendental principles of reason are indispensable for a unified, self-conscious experience; but this fact is distorted past recognition under the pressure of the division of the text. The systematic completion of the transcendental philosophy appears in a mere appendix (according to the *Prolegomena*, in scholia outside the science itself; see 4:363–64) to a part of the transcendental logic, which, according to its title, describes and uncovers a certain illusion, but heralds no positive results for the knowledge possible for us. If one succumbs to the suggestion that results from the arrangement of the *Critique*, one will be unwilling to concede to the ideas and principles of reason a transcendental status, indispensable for experience, but rather will set them aside as merely logical corollaries. Automatically, one follows the devaluation that Kant himself undertook with the ideas in speculative respect—as we will see later.

The second difficulty resulting directly from the Kantian text is more complicated. There are expressions like the following: "The remarkable feature of these principles, and what in them alone concerns us, is that they seem to be transcendental" (A663)—it is not easy to add: not only to appear transcendental, but to be transcendental, an addition that nevertheless proves to be necessary. Or again, a transcendental deduction of the principles of reason is not supposed to be possible (A663); but on the other hand, it is supposed to be the case that without the principle of genus and similarity, for example, "no empirical concepts, and therefore no experience, would be possible" (A654). To give another example, if one could say, "knowledge of the understanding in all its possible modes (including empirical knowledge) has the unity required by reason, and stands under common principles," that would be "to assert a *transcendental* principle of reason, and would make the systematic unity necessary, not only subjectively and logically, as method, but objectively also" (A648). Kant formulates this sentence in such a way that the reader is inclined to say, "The principle of reason cannot be transcendental; yet we are required to affirm that it is a transcendental principle!"

The reason for this oscillation is to be found in the fact that—depending on the point from which they are viewed—the principles of reason sometimes appear as merely subjective principles (in contrast to the transcendental concepts and principles of the understanding), and at other times as objectively necessary and thus transcendental principles, that is, as "nature's own law" (A650) (in contrast to merely logical or methodological principles).

A further difficulty of the Kantian expositions, which shall lead us up to the *Critique of Judgment*, is found in the relationship between the suitability of nature for our cognitive faculties, on the one hand, and the purposiveness among the parts of nature, on the other.

The principles of reason are transcendental because they presuppose that the principles of unity, specification, and affinity, which are initially only logical or methodological, "accord with nature itself" (A653; cf. A661). This guarantees the possible truth of our systematically structured empirical knowledge. The suitability (*Angemessenheit*) means that nature is purposively organized for our cognitive faculty. To be sure, Kant initially avoids the concept of *Zweckmäßigkeit* in this connection; up until the discussion of the teleology proper (A686–87) he uses it only once, in the formulation: "Reason has, therefore, as its sole object, the understanding and its effective [*zweckmäßig*] application" (A644)—here *zweckmäßig* means only "subjective-economical" and thus neither the transcendental principle of the suitability of nature to our understanding, nor the purposive order among the parts of nature. In effect, however, the transcendental presupposition of suitability is just the assumption of a greatest systematic and purposive unity of nature. As Kant says retrospectively in connection with teleology (A699): nature is purposive in the highest degree for our knowledge, since it is adapted to the understanding and its internal systematic requirements. Thus Kant may initially avoid the expression "purposiveness of nature for our knowledge" (in contrast to the parallel passages in the Introduction to the *Critique of Judgment*)—in fact, however, suitability is nothing other than purposiveness. The concept of suitability, which Kant prefers in the formulation of the general transcendental principle, is essentially the concept of *convenientia* from §30 of the Dissertation of 1770.[2]

I would like to go into this a bit. Kant understands by *principia convenientiae* in the Dissertation "those rules of judgment to which we willingly submit and to which we cling as if they were axioms, solely for the reason that, *if we gave them up, scarcely any judgment about a given object would be possible for our understanding*" (ID §30, 2:418). The *principia* Kant mentions could signify either the merely subjective aspect of "convenience," of the understanding's own internal purposiveness (cf. A644), and so merely represent logical or methodological tools (cf. A661); or instead they could signify the (in later language, transcendental) suitability of nature for our cognitive faculty. The Dissertation seems not yet to be in command of the devices for clarifying this dichotomy, which is elementary for the *Critique* of 1781. In both cases they are principles of a maximal employment of the understanding—if one were to give them up, Kant says, "intellectui nullus plane usus esset." Furthermore, in 1781 Kant interprets the maxims of the maximal employment of our cognitive faculties in contrast to the version of 1770 in such a way that they imply the purposive organization of nature in specific parts and in the whole; whereas in the Dissertation we did not yet encounter a teleology under the *principia convenientiae*. Despite this implication, however, in the *Critique of Pure Reason* the principles of the suitability of nature for our understanding and the purposive and systematic order of nature itself remain two distinct, separate domains.

In the first Introduction to the *Critique of Judgment*, Kant says: "From this there arises the concept of a *purposiveness* of nature, as a characteristic concept of reflective judgment, rather than of reason" (FI 20:216). Here Kant partially retracts the theory of the Appendix to the Transcendental Dialectic, which he had still sanctioned in the second edition of the *Critique of Pure Reason* in 1787. This revision is essential for the genesis of the *Critique of Judgment*, as is the revision

Reinhard Brandt

of a certain part of the theory of the *Groundwork of the Metaphysics of Morals*. Both points must be addressed in order to understand the peculiar transcendental principle of the purposiveness of nature and its deduction in the Introduction to the *Critique of Judgment*.

In the Preface to the *Critique of Judgment*, the cognitive faculty is assigned to understanding, the faculty of desire to reason, and the feeling of pleasure and displeasure to judgment as their proper realms (CJ 5:168; cf. 198). The trinity of the *Critiques* results in a natural and inevitable way from this schema. From this retrospective point of view, this means for the *Critique of Pure Reason*: "Properly, therefore, it was *understanding*—which, so far as it contains constitutive a priori cognitive principles, has its special realm, and one, moreover, in our *faculty of knowledge*—that the *Critique*, called in a general way that of Pure Reason, was intended to establish in secure but particular possession against all other competitors" (CJ 5:168). The view of the first *Critique* implied here emerges as early as 1788, in the *Critique of Practical Reason*. For according to the second *Critique*, the "Doctrine of Elements" of the *Critique of Pure Reason* divides into an "Analytic" and a "Dialectic"; the former has, as the surprised reader is informed, two parts, "Transcendental Aesthetic" and "Transcendental Logic" (CJ 5:90; cf. 16). Thus the Dialectic in the *Critique of Pure Reason* is implicitly denied a transcendental status (for how can it still be a part of the transcendental logic, if transcendental logic had already been treated in the Analytic?). The Dialectic in the *Critique of Pure Reason*, therefore, has merely a negative, and, by the terminology that dominates in 1788 and 1790, no longer a transcendental function. It shows that knowledge is really not possible where no intuition can correspond to our concepts—the ideas of theoretical reason. The ideas are semantically empty concepts and can properly have not transcendental, but only logical, status. Kant himself tended *after* 1781 to hold this interpretation. In 1790, in the controversy with J. A. Eberhard, Kant says explicitly that the ideas of noumena in the *Critique of Pure Reason* have a "merely logical function" (E 8:225). The negative result of the Dialectic confirms the positive result of the Analytic, which demonstrated with the connection of intuition and concept how synthetic a priori judgments were possible in the sphere of knowledge. Corresponding to the negative result of theoretical reason, which looks for semantic contents of its ideas, we have now on the other side the positive result in the sphere of practical philosophy: the moral law and freedom prove the objective reality of the

182

ideas of reason and allow metaphysics as the science of the transcendent to rise again. In the *Critique of Judgment* the feeling of pleasure and displeasure establishes itself between the faculties of knowledge and desire; the judgment, between theoretical understanding and practical reason. Judgment has indeed no realm of objects of its own, since with nature and freedom, sensible and supersensible, the set of possible objects is already exhausted. But judgment has its own a priori principles of the exercise of its own faculty, which proves to be purposive for the mediation of nature and freedom, understanding and reason. So much for the division of philosophy, as Kant sketches it at the beginning of the last *Critique*.

If one takes Kant's description of his *Critiques* from 1790 as the sketch of the design of the *Critique* of 1781, then one gets into a structure that resembles the imaginary creations of Escher: individual pieces fit together, but the structure as a whole is distorted. The work of 1781 is conceived in a way other than that suggested by Kant's own retrospective remarks; that there should be a second or even a third *Critique* with an "Analytic" and a "Dialectic" was a completely foreign thought for Kant in 1781. That the "Transcendental Aesthetic" belongs to the Analytic, that the transcendental logic makes up the second part of this Analytic and with that divests the "Dialectic" of its transcendental function—such thoughts amount to the destruction of the architectonic design of the first *Critique*. What appears at least partially senseless from the retrospective of 1790 was for the *Critique of Pure Reason* unproblematically possible and systematically required: there were transcendental ideas of pure reason, and they and their objects were deduced according to their function with regard to experience. Thus there were transcendental principles (axioms, laws) of reason, without which the use of the understanding is practically impossible.

As was mentioned above, another structural shift must also be pointed out, which takes place in the *Critique of Judgment* in comparison with the *Groundwork*. This shift leads to the facilitation of the new concept of a "technic of nature," which in the first Introduction to the *Critique of Judgment* gets used equally for the principle of suitability and for nature's own purposive formations. (In the final version of the Introduction it is used only for the second principle.)

In the "Critical Elucidation of Pure Practical Reason" of the *Critique of Practical Reason*, Kant says unmistakably that causality under the law of natural necessity determines the appearances of outer and of inner sense; freedom, in contrast, can be attributed only to the thing in itself and is exclusively concerned with causality under the moral law (for example, CP 5:95). Nature is the domain of theoretical reason; freedom, that of practical reason. The first Introduction to the *Critique of Judgment* draws a conclusion from this dichotomy of theoretical and practical reason that contradicts the *Groundwork of the Metaphysics of Morals* and its account of the doctrine of the hypothetical and categorical imperatives as laws of practical reason. The doctrine of the hypothetical rules of action is said now to belong not to the practical, but rather to the theoretical philosophy. Since the rules concern the generation of objects of outer or inner nature (cf. FI 20:196) through the causality of our *Willkür* (not *Wille!*), they cannot be "differentiate[d] from theoretical propositions concerning things" (FI 20:197). Actions of *Willkür* in the technical realization of purposes thus belong to phenomenal nature, not to noumenal freedom. Kant writes in the *Critique of Judgment*: "Now we have in the world beings of but one kind whose causality is teleological, or directed to ends, and which at the same time [!] are beings of such a character that the law according to which they have to determine ends for themselves is represented by them themselves as unconditioned and not dependent on anything in nature, but as necessary in itself" (CJ §84, 5:435).[3] This means: with regard to teleological causality as such (whether conscious or not, is not thematized), man is not distinguished from teleologically organized nature; only the unconditional law of morality lifts him out of nature's causality.

The faculty to view nature as technic is the reflective judgment—not (as in the *Critique* of 1781) reason. This "technic of nature," which Kant introduced in the first Introduction, appears at two levels: as a fundamental principle of the suitability of nature to our cognitive faculty, and as a principle of a nature that exhibits systematic form not only for us but also in itself. These are the same two concepts of purpose we know from the Appendix to the Transcendental Dialectic as the concepts of suitability and of the purposive unity of things that provide the basic division of the *Critique of Judgment* into two parts, aesthetic and teleological judgment.

First, the principle of suitability. All knowledge of nature presupposes

that nature has observed in its empirical laws a certain economy, suitable for our judgment, and a similarity among forms that we can comprehend, and this presupposition must precede all comparison, being an a priori principle of judgment. Reflective judgment thus works with given appearances so as to bring them under empirical concepts of determinate natural things not schematically, but *technically*, not just mechanically, like a tool controlled by the understanding and the senses, but *artistically*, according to the universal but at the same time indeterminate principle of a purposive, systematic ordering of nature. Our judgment is favored, as it were, by nature in the suitability of the particular natural laws (about which the understanding is silent) to the possibility of experience as a system, which is a presupposition without which we have no hope of finding our way in the labyrinth of the multiplicity of possible special laws (FI 20:213–14).

This principle is transcendental, and the quoted sentences may be called its transcendental deduction: without assuming it, systematic knowledge of nature is not possible.

Judgment—not reason—proceeds technically with appearances in its reflection; thus it presupposes a "technic of nature." The text quoted above continues: "Thus judgment itself posits a priori the technic of nature as the principle of its reflection . . . in order to facilitate its reflection in accordance with its own subjective laws and needs while also in harmony with laws of nature in general" (*ibid.*).

In another place the concept of a technic of nature is reserved for objects that themselves exhibit the form of a system: "The *causality* of nature with respect to the form of its products as purposes, I would term the *technic* of nature" (FI 20:219). Indeed, the technic of nature in its first, wider meaning is (in contrast to the second, objective meaning) merely logical (FI 20:214, 216, etc.)—however, from a transcendental point of view, it definitely founds the second: *because* we have reason to attribute to nature in its particular laws a principle of suitability and thus of purposiveness, "we have ready in the judgment a transcendental principle of the purposiveness of nature for the purposiveness of natural forms encountered in experience" (FI 20:218).[4]

The grounding function of the—modified—*principium convenientiae* as against the principle of the purposive unity of things is familiar to us from the Appendix to the Transcendental Dialectic of the first *Critique*; at the same time a shift may be observed. "The assumption of a supreme intelligence, as the one and only cause of the universe" (A687) is in 1781 an idea given through reason's own systematicity. Thus it can and must be postulated a priori "to regard all order in the world as if it had originated in the plan of a supreme reason" (A686). If one takes the knowing person to be part of this designed world, the *principium convenientiae* follows from the idea of God—and not the other way around, as the transcendental mode of proof with its *ratio cognoscendi* would have it.

In 1788–89 God is overthrown—for a short time: the technic of nature in the sense of a purposive unity of things is not an idea of reason concerning God's intentional design, but rather a representation exclusively of judgment, founded in the transcendental principle of the suitability of nature to our cognitive faculties, and enacted only contingently. Only because we in fact come across things in the empirical world that we must interpret as in themselves purposive, does the judgment arrive at the idea of a nature organizing itself into a system. The judgment cannot and must not embark on the idea of a creator. This seemingly insignificant, yet in fact revolutionary shift (which Kant conceived only after 1787), is the reason why in the first Introduction he conceives the technic of nature as not intentional.[5] He seeks to show that the concept of final causes in nature, of an organic technic, is *not* a principle of reason and hence requires no intentionally operating cause. Rather, it is only a principle of reflection of judgment: the replacement of an idea of reason with the reflective idea of judgment implies that the conception of an intentionally operating highest intelligence becomes superfluous— the purposiveness of nature is emphatically to be shown to be nonintentional.[6]

In the final Introduction to the *Critique of Judgment* and in the work itself (with one exception: CJ §23, 5:246), Kant has abandoned the concept of a technic of nature in the principle of the suitability of nature to our cognitive faculty; it is now applied only to organic bodies, that is, where nature itself shows the form of a system (CJ 5:193, 360, 390, etc.). However, with regard to its transcendental status nothing has changed in the second Introduction: the principle of the purposiveness of nature for our cognitive faculty is a transcendental principle and can be established as such in a transcendental deduction (CJ 5:182–84). Here again it forms the basis of the assessment of real purposes through the reflecting judgment.

With the new conception of the principle of the suitability of nature to our cognitive faculty as a principle of judgment, not of reason, its relation to the concept of the maximum is stricken. The concept is never again encountered in the *Critique of Judgment*, although it was decisive for the exposition in the *Critique of Pure Reason*: con-

The Deductions in the *Critique of Judgment*

cepts of reason were employed as schemata, in order to determine
the concept of the maximum, which was thought with the transcendental principle of reason (A665). The judgment presents reason
with no goals for its maximal use, but rather supplies with the concept of purposiveness a fundamental possibility: to think as unity
something that, for the understanding, would remain only accidental
and incomprehensible.

I hope to have shown with these short remarks that the *Critique of
Pure Reason* as well as the *Critique of Judgment* grant the status of a
transcendental principle to the principle of suitability or purposiveness of nature for our cognitive faculty; thus in this there is no incompatibility of the two works calling for further interpretation.
Nevertheless, there are, as we have seen, substantial shifts in the
overall structure of the Kantian philosophy between 1781 and 1790
that lead to a far-reaching incongruence of some of its elements.

Stuart Hampshire sees the characteristic of the *Critique of Judgment* in the fact that the title of his paper denotes: the social spirit of
mankind. This idea seems to me correct and suggestive; I would
merely like to try to supplement it with a few remarks.

On the one hand, it seems to me, the aspect of the communicability of judgments can be extended beyond the *Critique of Judgment*. In
his letter to Jacob Sigismund Beck of July 1, 1794, Kant writes: "We
can only understand and share with others what we can make ourselves . . . we cannot perceive combination as given, but rather we
must make it ourselves: we must combine, if we are to represent
something as combined . . . in view of this combination, we can
communicate with each other" (C 11:515). Thus Kant relates knowledge essentially to its communicability between humans, and thus to
the social spirit of mankind. The deduction of the categories in the
second edition of the *Critique of Pure Reason* especially acknowledges
this aspect of combination and consequently communicability, when
it introduces the whole line of reasoning with the fundamental notion "of the possibility of a combination [*Verbindung*] in general"
(§15). Art and culture are media of communicability and sociability
in the third *Critique*, but the theoretical philosophy assigns to the
criterion and principle of communicability a fundamental role as
well. According to Kant, human beings have the right of public communication of their thoughts, because the assessment through others
is an empirically inalienable criterion of whether my thoughts are

actually reproducible and thus possible cognitions, or whether they are mere idiosyncracies. However rigorous and formalistic Kant's moral philosophy may seem, the intention in the *Doctrine of Right* as well as in his ethics is a conflict-free and cooperative coexistence of humankind.

Thus we will have to extend the principle of sociability beyond the phenomena of art and culture to the realm of the theoretical philosophy. On the other hand, the function of this principle in the *Critique of Judgment* seems to me to be taken too broadly by Hampshire. If my considerations in the first part of this paper are correct, sociability may form a common element of aesthetics and teleology, but the systematic justification of the unity of the two parts of the third *Critique* is already to be found in the Appendix to the Transcendental Dialectic of the *Critique of Pure Reason*, in the unity and duality of suitability and objective purposes of nature.

To Hampshire's arguments we may also add that both parts of the *Critique of Judgment* conclude with references to the practical philosophy. The *Critique of Aesthetic Judgment* culminates with the sentence: "The beautiful is the symbol of the morally good" (CJ §59, 5:353); in the *Critique of Teleological Judgment* everything conditionally good in nature and also in culture is in the end grounded in morality; teleology, too, culminates in the unconditional good of the moral will. Both parts of the book achieve what reflecting judgment is instructed to do: to bring about the transition from nature to freedom, from understanding to reason (as lawgiving faculty) (CJ 5:195–97; FI 20:246). Art and culture, which in Hampshire appear as independent components of human sociability, are for Kant only valuable, or indeed real, on the basis of morality. I would like to comment on the link between aesthetics and morals a little more closely, through an interpretation of the two deductions in the third *Critique*.

In the Analytic of the *Critique of Aesthetic Judgment* (§38), the subjective reality of the concept of the beautiful is deduced through reference to the communicable agreement of understanding and imagination as a condition of every judgment in general. The judgment of taste expresses nothing other than the suitability of something for our cognitive faculty, which manifests itself in the free play of the imagination and understanding, and a feeling of pleasure corresponding to it. With this we remain completely within the realm of theoretical philosophy; on this level neither our interest in beauty and in the disinterested pleasure evoked by it, nor the demand for universal agreement that we impose on others, can be explained. It is explained only in the Dialectic, in which Kant passes from theoretical to practical philosophy.

In the Antinomy of Taste, Kant opposes the following sentences as thesis and antithesis: "The judgment of taste is not based upon concepts; for if it were, it would be open to dispute (decision by means of proofs)" and: "The judgment of taste is based on concepts; for otherwise, despite diversity of judgment, there could be no room even for the contention in the matter (a claim to the necessary agreement of others with this judgment)" (CJ §56, 5:338–39). I shall not here examine the structure of this alleged antinomy, but rather focus on the method of its solution. In order to understand this solution correctly, it is best to go back briefly to the *Critique of Practical Reason* and *its* Dialectic (CP 5:107–48).

Again, I am not concerned with the thesis and antithesis of the antinomy found here,[7] but only with the following phenomena: in accordance with the *Critique of Pure Reason*, we expect a solution of an antinomy by means of the demonstration that an ambivalence effects the concept lying at its basis; if one distinguishes in this concept appearance and thing in itself, the contradiction is solved—thesis and antithesis must be either both false or both true. When Kant gives a deduction of the transcendental ideas in the Appendix to the Transcendental Dialectic (as we saw), this proof of the subjective reality of the ideas has nothing to do with the solution of the antinomy—yet it is precisely this that changes in the following *Critiques*! The solution of the antinomy in the concept of the highest good in the Dialectic of pure practical reason no longer follows the pattern of the *Critique of Pure Reason*. It is not shown that the contradiction of thesis and antithesis vanishes as merely apparent with the introduction of the distinction between appearance and thing in itself; rather, the real possibility of the concept of the highest good itself is required and demonstrated. In the announcement of the solution of the antinomy Kant speaks of a transcendental deduction of this concept (CP 5:113), and in the text of the solution itself he says: "Thus, in spite of this apparent conflict of a practical reason with itself, the highest good is the necessary highest end of a morally determined will and a true object thereof; for it is practically possible, and the maxims of this will, which refer to it by their material, have objective reality" (CP 5:115). For practical reason, it would not suffice that a contradiction in its dialectical concept should prove to be merely apparent. Rather, it can first make certain of the possibility of the highest good only through deducing its objective practical reality. That this conception of dialectic is completely different from that in the *Critique of Pure Reason* need not be discussed in more detail here.

In the Dialectic of the *Critique of Aesthetic Judgment* Kant follows the schema of the *Critique of Practical Reason*; he solves the antinomy not through the proof that thesis and antithesis are not contradictory once the distinction between thing in itself and appearance is introduced, but rather by giving the idea of the supersensible a positive status as the *basis* of the judgment of taste, and extends this by referring the supersensible to freedom and its law. The Antinomy of Taste is really eliminated only through the deduction of this idea ("if, however, our deduction is at least credited," CJ §57, 5:346), not by reference to the distinction of thing in itself and appearance. The demand for necessary universal agreement can only be redeemed if the judgment of taste refers to some concept. "But the mere pure rational concept of the supersensible lying at the basis of the object (and of the judging subject for that matter) as object of sense, and thus as appearance, is just such a concept" (CJ §57, 5:340). So the idea of the supersensible is the positive basis of the objective claim of beauty in the judgment of taste. Only because of that basis can it be deduced in the Dialectic and connected with the concept of the morally good. In the *Critique of Pure Reason* the situation was different: a dialectical illusion was discovered in the ideas, and it was then shown that a certain subjective reality befits them in the formation of empirical knowledge. Here, however, as in the *Critique of Practical Reason*, the deducible idea is itself used as the means of the solution of the Dialectic. The Dialectic has turned from a locus of illusion to a locus of truth.

In both parts of my interpretation, it was crucial to observe that whereas on the one hand Kant oriented himself on "the" *Critique* of 1781 as on a solid authority, on the other hand his thought underwent profound shifts. It was thus necessary to specify the remaining identities as well as the partly hidden, partly open differences, in order to be able to decipher the complicated new elements of Kant's teaching. I hope I have contributed something to the clarification of these problems, despite the shortness of my remarks.

PART IV

The *Opus postumum*

Apperception and Ether: On the Idea of a Transcendental Deduction of Matter in Kant's *Opus postumum*

BURKHARD TUSCHLING

The Prehistory of the Problem in Kant

Kant begins not as a metaphysician but as a natural philosopher with a decided interest in metaphysics. From the outset, even before declaring so in the title of the *Monadologia physica*,[1] Kant's program is to unify *geometria* (that is, mathematical science along Newtonian principles) and *metaphysica* in the sense of Leibniz and Christian Wolff. This involves breaking with Leibniz on a central point: although Kant accepts the basic principles of Leibniz's metaphysics, he rejects their core, the absolute separation of "metaphysical atoms" and infinitely divisible, dynamic matter, as well as the "preestablished harmony" that depends on this separation. Following his teacher in philosophy at the University of Königsberg, Martin Knutzen, a follower of Wolff's, Kant defends the *influxus physicus*, the causal interaction of individual substances, which is considered "physical."

In the first outline of his theoretical philosophy, Kant accordingly attempts to present "in a new light" the second principle of Leibniz's and Wolff's metaphysics, viz. that of sufficient reason. Here, as the full title of the *Nova dilucidatio*[2] indicates, Kant has already assumed an orientation that is both metaphysical and epistemological. He interprets the principle of sufficient reason, not as a logical principle (although proposition V may at first seem to suggest a logical interpretation, concerned with truth in judgments), but as a cosmological one, concerning the existence of contingently existing substances (proposition VIII). This, of course, agrees completely with Leibniz's original intentions, for example, in the *Discours de métaphysique*. Both of his "new" principles result from this cosmological interpretation of the principle of sufficient reason as applied to the representation of a world consisting of physical substances:

1. Changes in these substances are only conceivable if they are considered as actually interacting with each other, that is, if there is supposed to exist a "relation of substances in which the one contains determinations the ground of which is contained in the other," as Kant still puts it in the first *Critique* (B257–58; cf. Nd, proposition XII, 1:410).

2. This *commercium substantiarum* is not merely the result of their existence, but rather an independent, self-sufficient system of causal interaction between substances, so created by a particular act of God. Whether this interaction is to be understood primarily ontologically, metaphysically, or physically is not clear; all three meanings are apparently intended (Nd, proposition XIII, 1:412–13).

The justification for proposition XIII is most peculiar. Although he has substituted *influxus physicus* for preestablished harmony within the framework of Leibniz's theory of substance, Kant does not feel obliged to give up Leibniz's doctrine of the "absolute isolationism" of finite individual substances. On the contrary, this doctrine is the basis of Kant's conception of *influxus physicus*, and thus of his entire cosmology. Because the existence of an individual substance, considered on its own, has no relation to the existence of any other, the reality of their interaction and mutual determination is both a special *kind* of existence and a special *way* of existing. For this very reason it demands a special foundation, both in metaphysical theory and in reality, through a special act of creation by God. This conception of a world of physically interacting substances remains crucial for Kant throughout his life. The enduring basic structure of and conflict within Kant's metaphysics and natural philosophy are rooted in the ontological duality of their principles: independently existing individual substances on the one hand, community on the other. This is particularly true of the deep structure (or secret systematics) of the three Analogies of Experience, which appear as synthetic, mutually independent principles, and yet are so intimately related that their dependence can and must also be seen as logical; and of the conflict between the corpuscular, mechanical discreteness (monadology) and the dynamic continuity of matter.

For more than 30 years Kant apparently remained unaware of this conflict, resulting from his program—as exhibited in the *Monadologia physica*—to unite what Leibniz had been careful to keep apart: metaphysics and physics, or self-sufficient substances and dynamically interacting matter. The solution Kant discovered in 1756 forms, mutatis mutandis, the basis of the theory of 1786. Only with the development of the immanent difficulties in the *Metaphysical Foundations of Natural Science* did the underlying metaphysical schema become a problem, that is, in the *Opus postumum*.[3]

In 1755, the principle's proof presented the main problem. In the 1760's, it was again not the paradigm of this substance metaphysics and its contents as such, but rather its method of proof that was a problem for Kant. Perhaps it had been a problem from the outset; the "Humean problem" in its most general form certainly pushed the principle of sufficient reason to the center of Kant's efforts toward a methodologically secured metaphysics. Seen from the standpoint of the "critical" Kant—that is to say, from 1770 onwards—the assumptions underlying the proofs in the treatise of 1755 are fully dogmatic postulates, mostly borrowed from the metaphysics of Leibniz and Wolff. This is particularly true of the conception of the world as a system of individual substances, and the assumption that their existence and interdependence are subject to the law of total determination.

Hume's "reminder" made clear to Kant that progress in metaphysics, even scientific metaphysics itself, was no longer possible without examining our ability to gain nonempirical knowledge through certain concepts. But because Kant was not prepared to accept Hume's conclusions (cf. Prol 4:260), the basic contents of Kant's substance metaphysics and cosmology remained untouched by Hume's challenge. Rather, the question became "How am I to understand that, because something is, something else exists?" (NM 2:202; cf. 203; DSS 2:370). Kant is asking how the relation "reason–result" or "antecedent–consequent" can be understood as a causal rather than a logical relation. He questions, then, the meaning of *ratio* and *rationatum*, and the relation between the two expressed in the principle of sufficient reason. This question takes on its full significance only when understood in its "greatest possible extent" (Prol 4:261), that is, cosmologically. It then addresses the very problem that Kant believed he had solved with his discovery of 1755 (Nd, propositions XII and XIII): how to understand the transition from one state to another in the existence of something (of a *single* substance), and, thus, the transition from one state to another in the existence of *any* something, of *all* somethings—in a system of *omnimoda determinatio* (thoroughgoing determination) achieved by the mutual interaction of substances—and to show this transition to be necessarily determined.

This very question endures through a skeptical interlude and remains the basic problem of the Inaugural Dissertation of 1770 and of Kant's criticism after 1772. At the same time, he holds fast to the view that the world is a system of physically interdependent substances. The Inaugural Dissertation may be seen as a mere interlude, for it offered no solution to the problem in its most general form: that is, the need to provide an objective content for the idea of a thoroughgoing, necessary determination of existence and of change in everything that exists. The first *Critique* solves this problem with transcendental idealism, which must have seemed to Kant a *universal* solution because it reformulates all questions of Leibniz's and Wolff's metaphysics and, accordingly, provides a new means of answering them.

Applied to our problem this means that (i) by interpreting *things* as the objects of representations (ultimately of empirical intuitions) rather than as entities existing *an sich*, and (ii) by interpreting concepts of things (in particular, the notions of substance, of cause and effect, and of the interaction of substances) not as forms independent of knowledge, but as the structures resulting from acts of synthesis by a finite intellect, which thus gives its representations order, unity, and reference to some object (providing them with an objective content), it becomes possible to demonstrate a priori that:

(1) the objects of such empirical intuitions must exist within a single, a priori (and therefore objective and universally valid) "transcendental" time-order (the principle of the Analogies of Experience, A176–81/B218–24, esp. A177–78/B220);

(2) the concept of individual substance refers not to a thing existing of itself, but to the object of an empirical intuition, inasmuch as it is the enduring referent or substratum of the empirical determination of time (the First Analogy);

(3) the concept of the relation between cause and effect does

not refer to a relationship between substances as such, but
rather simply assigns a certain place to the existence of the
objects of our empirical intuition according to a set of rules
(the Second Analogy);

(4) the concept of a *commercium substantiarum* is not the concept of an *influxus physicus* of physically or metaphysically
conceived atoms of things existing of themselves, but only
refers to a relationship between substances as objects of
our empirical representation, and makes possible the empirical relation of simultaneity, thereby establishing an empirical *influxus physicus* of the objects of the world as it appears (the Third Analogy).

A "metaphysical" deduction is designed to show that the concept
in question (for example, the concept of a substance) is indispensable
for conceiving of something as something in particular, by showing
that the concept corresponds to one of the moments that connect
representations into a judgment, that is, an objective connection of
representations necessarily determined in various relations and thus
capable of truth. A "transcendental" deduction is designed to show
that the apprehension of the manifold of an empirical intuition can
only be an intuition of a particular something (of apparent objects)
because it is necessarily related to those concepts by which an object
is thought, and thus to the original unity of apperception of a cognizant subject. Finally, the proof of the synthetic judgments a priori
resulting from such relations (at least insofar as they concern the
conditions in apparent existence or objects of our representations) is
designed to show that every existent, which at first presents itself in
individual empirical intuitions as fully isolated from every other
existent, fits into a necessary (objective, universally valid) context.
This permits a positive inference from one existent to another (always referring to empirical intuition or representations), because all
existence, as existence of possible or actual contents of experience
and objects of a cognizant subject (and not as monads existing of
themselves), is subject to the conditions of conceptual synthesis or
unity of thought, under which alone a single experiential element
and its existence can become a part of the entire experience of one
and the same subject.

This example shows well how fruitful this "revolution" in our way
of thinking was, by interpreting concepts of things as concepts of

"thinking an object for our intuitions" (A106). Hume's critique of Wolff's purported proof of the principle of sufficient reason—that showing by means of pure logic that *rationatum* stems from *ratio* and that all *rationata* originate in *rationes* is, in fact, to show nothing at all—brought Kant to the realization that the mere analysis of the concept of the will of God into that of a cause would never bring forth the existing world (cf. NM 2:202); and that the relationship between the movement of a body (as reason) and the movement or rest of another (as result) is not a logical one, and can be explained using the words "cause and effect" and "power and action" if and only if the relation of the one as a *Realgrund* (a "real" ground, as opposed to a logical one) to the other as *Realfolge* (a "real" as opposed to a logical consequence) can be assumed as given (NM 2:202–3). The two terms remain, however, to be clarified; simply using the words in question does not explain anything.

The problems of metaphysics did not arise until Kant assumed that we have to deal not with the relations between things existing in and of themselves but with the contents of our representations, which *as such* have an a priori, necessary relation to the subject and the regularity by means of which the subject brings unity, order, and objective reference to a "something" into its representations. An existent, existing not of itself but as an object of our empirical intuition, is *for that reason* related to *all other* existents that may ever become the contents of our representations. With respect to the metaphysical assumptions of the theory of substance—no matter whether in the version of Leibniz and Wolff or that of Knutzen and Kant—Hume is simply right: there is no transition from the concept of a thing existing of itself to the concept of another such. Experience of such objects, however, does not reveal necessary relations. On the other hand, such relations become evident, understandable, and seemingly explainable when we realize that we neither have, nor can have, experience of things existing of themselves, but "only of our representations." Transcendental idealism, it seems, once and for all gives a satisfactory answer to the question posed in the essay on *Negative Magnitudes.*

Yet the sharpest and most sympathetic readers of the *Critique of Pure Reason* felt uneasy from the start. Can we really, after all, avoid returning to a "bad" idealism like that of Berkeley? Has Kant, perhaps, already done so? More specifically, with respect to the problem of comprehending the relationships of existing empirical objects: Is

not the solution of the Analogies of Experience a return to Leibnizian idealism?[4] As such, does it not abandon the *influxus physicus,*
which had been intended to unify substance metaphysics and mechanical science in such a way that the former could lay the foundation of scientific knowledge in the latter? One year after their
announcement in the Preface to the *Metaphysical Foundations* (cf.
MFNS 4:474–76n), Kant answers with corrections and additions
not only to the deduction of the categories, but also to the proofs of
the Analogies, with the Refutation of Idealism, and the reformulation of the Paralogisms. The result, as it concerns our problem, can
be summarized as follows.

"Substance," "cause and effect," and "interaction" are concepts of
relations concerning the existence not of things in themselves, but
merely of appearances, that is, of objects of our representation, intuition, and experience. Space is merely a way for us to represent objects as existing outside us. It is, however, "in us,"[5] and with it, all
things (substances and their relations) that seem outside us. Nevertheless, our experience demonstrates the existence of something enduring outside us, the perception of which is made possible "only
through a *thing* outside me and not through the mere *representation*
of a thing outside me." For this reason "the consciousness of my existence is at the same time an immediate consciousness of the existence
of other things outside me" (B275–76).

With this, the whole problem boils down to the question: How
can an existent independent of us as knowing subjects be, nevertheless, nothing but an existent only "in appearance" or "for us"? How
can such an existent, independent of us as it is, function transcendentally for our knowledge, as substratum for the empirical determination of time, duration, and the possibility of determining "*all* positions in time," making "perception of our position possible to us"
(A213/B260)? And how can such an existent with this function and
all its characteristics be the subject of a transcendental theory and still
exist "outside us"? Or, what is the same thing from the standpoint
of transcendental idealism, how can "the original apperception"
through a priori reference to the mere *form* of inner sense alone determine the *existence* of appearances in such a way that "a priori determined synthetic unity" is produced "in the time-relations of all
perceptions" (A177/B220), if the premise distinguishing transcendental from dogmatic idealism is to continue to be valid, that is, the
premise that "the matter of all appearance is given to us a posteriori"

and only "its form must lie ready for the sensations a priori in the mind" (A20/ B34)?

In the *Critique of Pure Reason*, the problem is posed objectively. Kant does not perceive it so, however. Instead, he believes that an analogy of experience can be seen as a "rule according to which a unity of experience may arise from perception" (A180/ B222). Evidently, even in 1787 Kant has no doubts about assuming that apperception can apply to given perceptions, determine them in accordance with the form of inner sense—time—and integrate them in an a priori determined, transcendental order of time. In the *Opus postumum*, Kant no longer holds this assumption. There, any perception is itself subject to the a priori rule (or rules) that all existence belongs to a single cosmic, dynamic system. This rule is, however, clearly different from the one Kant called the Analogy of Experience. The latter concerns only the a priori determined form—and not the matter—of the time-relations of all empirically given or possible perceptions that are already "objects for me" (A177/B220) and so are subject to the conditions of being objects for me, that is, to the transcendental time-order.

In the *Opus postumum*, by contrast, the very possibility a priori of being a single existent or, respectively, of being an object of empirical intuition becomes the problem. In conjunction, Kant must also explain perception and how it is possible, not only with respect to its *form*, but also with respect to its *content* (matter, existence). The single empirical existent is seen as subject to a cosmological system of forces or primordial matter. Of course, the uniformity the system enforces can also be seen as the formal unity of all empirically possible matter, but this formal unity is different from the transcendental time-order, to which the cognizant subject subjects all empirical existence of which it is aware. This formal unity is also different from the synthetic unity of the pure space of intuition created by the subject. Kant continually stresses that these unities, space and time, would remain absolutely empty if it were not for the ether or dynamic continuum. They, therefore, in themselves have no a priori demonstrable, necessary relation to a continuum of existence.

The problem or idea of the transcendental deduction of this continuum, then, is to show that apperception, by means of its relation to the forms of inner and outer sense, relates to the empirically given manifold in the following way: the unity of all empirical existence, the cosmological material system and its basic features as a dynamic continuum can, by the newly conceived relation of apperception, be in turn conceived of as a unity that is *different* from the formal structures of space and time, makes them possible, is produced by the knowing subject's acts of synthesis, and yet is independent of the subject.

This problem, produced by transcendental idealism yet insoluble within it, occupied Kant throughout the *Opus postumum*, in particular from "Übergang 1–14" on.

The problem of the transcendental deduction, or the answer to the question "What is the ground of the relation of that in us which we call 'representation' to the object?" (letter to M. Herz, February 21, 1772, C 10:130) has thus taken on the following form. In the first *Critique*, Kant assumes that, by means of the categories, apperception gives unity and a certain continuity to the manifold of empirical intuition, resulting in particular in the form of the unity of space and time and of the objects existing in them, as well as their relationships to each other. He has yet to answer, however, the question whether these transcendentally ideal, subjective formal systems are necessarily related to a third formal system: remembering the Kantian triad of the 1770's—space, time, and force—we might call that third system "force." Moreover, he must also demonstrate how this relation can be shown. Kant is understandably convinced that it *can* be shown, but again, *how* is the problem. In "Übergang 1–14," Kant still sees the problem quite objectivistically: the object or product of this transcendental unity of all existents, or the existence of an "a priori demonstrable material" is to be shown. In fascicles X and XI he then attempts to solve the problem by means of classical transcendental idealism, trying to comprehend and demonstrate the unity of all empirical existence as the product of original acts of synthesis by a cognizant subject.

The Deduction of "Primordial Matter" in "Übergang 1–14"

"Übergang 1–14" was probably written during the summer of 1799, late in Kant's life. It occupies the central period among the papers of the *Opus postumum*. Since the latter is not yet available in English, it may be useful to give some basic information on the whole, before turning to "Übergang 1–14" in particular.[6]

The earliest piece in the collection of manuscripts we call *Opus postumum* is an excerpt in Kant's own hand, taken from the *Göttingischen Anzeigen von gelehrten Sachen*, December 2, 1786. It contains a critical review of Kant's *Metaphysical Foundations of Natural Science*, aiming, in particular, at its core, the so-called construction of matter, and at the concept of an original repulsive force. Kant's early notes, mostly written on loose leaves (*Lose Blätter*), concern rather marginal problems. By 1792, however, we find him rather worried about his theory of matter as a whole. In a letter to J. S. Beck, dated October 16, 1792, he admits that, at a crucial stage of the *Metaphysical Foundations* of 1786, his argument seems to move in a circle from which he does not know how to escape (cf. C 11:377). By 1795/96 his doubts have condensed into an outline of a somewhat revised version of his theory of matter, exposed in a first comprehensive draft called "Oktaventwurf." During the following four years Kant's self-criticism becomes ever more radical. In a series of drafts, culminating in the ether proofs of "Übergang 1–14" and the *Selbstsetzungslehre* of fascicles X and XI, Kant develops radically new conceptions like that of an a priori dynamics and experiments, for example, with concepts of that same Fichte whom he, at the same time, so harshly condemns in the notorious "Declaration against Fichte." The latest drafts, dating from 1799/1800 to 1803, finally aim even at a system of transcendental idealism as such. Obviously, Kant wanted to meet the challenge of the young Schelling who is mentioned twice as the author of such a system in the latest papers written by Kant.—So much for an (admittedly) superficial survey of the *Opus postumum*.

The subject matter of "Übergang 1–14" is alternately called "matter" (Op 21:208, etc.), "universally distributed matter occupying cosmic space," "the totality of matter," "world-material" (Op 21:209–10, etc.), "what is for now (provisionally) called caloric" (Op 21:215.24), "a cosmic whole from a single material" (Op 21:217.2), "space which can be sensed" (Op 21:219.7), "primordial material [whose reality] can only be confirmed by reason" (Op 21:219.18–19), "caloric or ether" (Op 21:221.8), "hypostatized space" (Op 21:224.11; cf. 221.12), "a material space, as it were" (Op 21:223.22), "the real and objective principle of experience" (Op 21:224.4), "the basis for the unified whole of all moving forces of matter" (Op 21:224.10–11), "space itself as the universal complex of the moving forces of matter . . . , object (of the possibility) of experience" (Op 21:231.8–9), and so on. It is not the name but the function of this "material" that matters.

Kant aims at an a priori proof of this something, using a procedure he calls "proof" or "deduction." The customary label "deduction of the ether" is, therefore, justified although not quite accurate. The core of the argument is as follows. The formation of physical bodies presupposes the activity of the moving forces of matter, which are united in a universal continuum of interactive forces. It is this continuum, or material cosmic whole, that transforms space and time into an object capable of being experienced. The existence of this primordial matter and its activity, which is infinite with respect to space, time, quantity, quality, relation, and modality, can be analytically deduced from the idea of the absolute unity of experience by means of the principle of identity.

Kant elaborates this argument using more and more daring formulations, so that the various drafts make up a series culminating in the sheets designated "Übergang 12/12a/12b." Kant is well aware he is engaged in something that, seen from the viewpoint of classical criticism, is unusual, unexpected, perhaps even dubious. He tries repeatedly to convince himself and the reader that this peculiar "mode of proof," though seemingly problematic, may nevertheless be admitted because it is unique, referring to a unique object, and relating to a unique case. These doubts notwithstanding, for some time he seems to have been fairly sure of his undertaking, because among drafts bearing elaborate titles and numbered paragraphs there are copies in someone else's hand, together with Kant's originals. Obviously, Kant hoped to be able to publish his work. This did not happen, however. Instead, he became engaged in an even more profound transcendental analysis that has been handed down to us in the drafts of the Xth and XIth fascicles.[7] Why did Kant abandon the deductions of "Übergang 1–14"? How are they to be understood?

They unquestionably report the results of Kant's prior work in the *Opus postumum*. The very title of the drafts, "Transition from the Metaphysical Foundations of Natural Science to Physics," denotes the problem Kant had been struggling with for some years: clearly he wanted to improve certain shortcomings of his work of 1786. Consequently, he deals with subject matter like "On the Science of Nature in General" (Op 21:238); "On the Science of Nature in General, Founded on A Priori Principles" (Op 21:554); the "object" of physics or natural science (Op 21:563.25, 582–83); and, finally, whether the concept of an organic body belongs to science (he now answers in the affirmative: cf. Op 21:210, etc.). Understood in this way, the drafts of "Übergang 1–14" belong to a metaphysics of nature, as a supplement to the *Metaphysical Foundations*, or, perhaps, as part of a critically revised metaphysics of nature that Kant had planned to publish since the time of his intended cooperation with Johann Heinrich Lambert and that he still promised his friends to edit in the early 1790's.[8] The early drafts of the *Opus postumum* are probably meant to be preparations for such a publication. For "Übergang 1–14," however, this holds only in a restricted sense: the "transition" to physics and the questions of the theory of matter, as well as of natural philosophy in general, are dealt with only secondarily; they rank behind fundamental problems of transcendental idealism to which Kant increasingly turns in the later parts of the *Opus postumum* where he classifies his work as the "transition to transcendental philosophy" (Op 22:113.8) and, finally, even as "System of Transcendental Philosophy" (Op 21:27.3). The drafts labeled "Übergang 1–14" mark the turning point and make evident why Kant turned in that direction.

Primary matter and its deduction are, to be sure, at the root of this process. Both concern basic principles of transcendental idealism, not only of the Transcendental Analytic, but also of the Transcendental Aesthetic and Dialectic. The revision and, in the end, the reconstruction of transcendental idealism as a systematic whole are the result.

Kant diverges from classical criticism merely in attempting such a deduction of quantitative and qualitative determinations of the empirical, material content of experience. Although in 1781 he had held certain Anticipations of Perception to be both possible and necessary, at that time he seemed to rule out an a priori proof of the contents of experience.

Moreover, the basic concept of natural science or physics—matter—as outlined in the *Metaphysical Foundations* of 1786 is substantially altered. In 1786, due to his "distributive" approach to the whole of phenomena, Kant only aimed to construct the singular material entity given in an empirical intuition. The concept and theory of the ether, which had occupied him since 1755, played only a marginal role. Thus the reintroduction of this concept into the metaphysics of nature, and its elevation to the status of a basic concept, need to be justified on critical principles within the framework of a revised metaphysics of nature.

The full systematic import of this move, however, becomes apparent only if this concept of a primordial matter is seen in the context of an argument concerning space and time. The argument from the first *Critique* that empty space and empty time cannot be objects of possible experience turns out to be of crucial importance in "Übergang 1–14": primordial matter, which fills space and time continually and incessantly by its moving forces, is elevated to the rank of a first and even unique principle of possible experience (Op 21:225.25, etc.). Consequently, not merely the theory of space and time but the whole fabric of transcendental philosophy needs to be revised.

In particular, the concept of the object of possible (external) experience is substantially changed in at least two respects. First, a more consistent distinction is made between matter and body. This represents decided progress vis-à-vis the ambiguous conceptions of the first *Critique* and the *Metaphysical Foundations* ("substance," "matter," "material substance," "body"). Second, the point of reference for transcendental analysis is revised. The object given in a singular empirical intuition, the synthetic product of the schematized category and the given sensible manifold, no longer ranks as the one and only object of (possible external) experience. The concept of an object is released from the context defined by B128: "the object of all possible outer experience" now becomes the unique object of transcendental analysis (Op 21:241.2–11; 538, etc.).

This revised concept of empirical existence in space and time in turn leads to:

(1) degrading the transcendental function of space (and time). Space now is a "mere form of intuition" and it is "no object of a possible experience" (Op 21:246.12–15);

(2) blurring the distinction between space and time as forms of outer or inner sense respectively. Both are now taken primarily as determinations of cosmological existence, that is, of existence in and of the cosmic whole (Op 21:223.10–224.13);

(3) blurring the opposition between intuition and thought, between their transcendental functions, and between conceptual and intuitive determinations of existence. The classical theory of space and time is thoroughly criticized, sometimes under the label of "mathematical foundations of philosophy" (Op 21:231.8–15, 232.21–28). Space and time as mere forms of intuition, taken as nonexistent and without

any reference to something existent, are merely thought, are not objects, and are not conditions of possible experience. The doctrine of space and time as pure forms of intuition no longer establishes the possibility of experiencing space, time, and objects in space and time. Kant does, however, continue to concern himself with the further conceptual differentiation of, for example, the concept of space;

(4) blurring the boundaries between substance and force, and, moreover, between them and materialized space and existence (Op 21:233.5–14).

Taken together, all these revisions concern the relationship between primordial matter and apperception as the basis of all intellectual synthesis. Kant refers to:

[The] material [which, with] its agitating forces . . . carries with it in its concept unity of the whole of all possible experience (according to the principle of identity) (Op 21:551.15–18).

Experience of external things, however, can, as regards its material element, only be thought of as the effect of sense-objects on the intuiting subject. In view of the universality of this proposition, experience itself cannot (objectively) prove it, but, rather, it must be by the condition of the possibility of experience in general (that is, subjectively for the cognitive faculty). Thus the existence of such a universally distributed world-material can only be proved indirectly, that is, according to a priori principles. Hence, this proof is unique in its kind, since the idea of the distributive unity of all possible experience in general here coincides with its collective unity in a concept (Op 21:552.7–17).

Here, apperception and ether, the synthetic unity of the self-consciousness of the knowing subject and existence, refer to each other in a way that is completely new in Kant's transcendental idealism. I will come back to this presently.

The revisions we have observed cast serious doubt upon the consistency of the internal systematic fabric of transcendental idealism. With them, Kant tacitly (although not admittedly) revises certain principles of the Transcendental Analytic and even partially revises the principles of the Transcendental Aesthetic.

According to the newly introduced distinction between the ether (as the unique object of possible experience) on the one hand, and infinitely many individual empirical objects (as second-order objects

Apperception and Ether

of possible experience, depending in their material possibility on the ether) on the other, the classical categories apply to an object that, from the viewpoint of "Übergang 1–14" is to be considered as a second-order object only. The primary object, the collective referent of the whole of possible experience, requires a new type of concept. Kant experiments with terms like "reason" or "idea"; these terms, however, have acquired a new meaning. Thus, we have a new conceptualization that does not altogether fit into the classical dyadic scheme of concepts of the understanding versus concepts of reason.

Primordial matter combines the determinations or the functions of the classical categories of substance, causality, and interaction and at the same time absorbs the concepts of (material) space and time. By degrading the transcendental function of space and time, Kant seems to return to Leibniz's and Wolff's concept of space and time as relational determinations of things. Even if one prefers to assume that the theory of space and time as pure intuitions is still valid, the question of how to classify the a priori concept of the ether, that is, of the material continuum as "hypostatized space" (Op 21:224.11), remains open. It is neither pure nor empirical intuition, neither a pure nor an empirical concept, but combines elements originating in all these spheres.

The very concept of experience changes. Experience is now thought of as unique "all-embracing experience" (Op 21:582.22; cf. 549.20–27, 562.21–564.12, 574.21–29, 576–77, 583), that is, as a concept aiming at the "absolute totality of appearances," an idea that, according to the first *Critique*, is "a problem to which there is no solution" (A328/B384). Here, on the contrary, experience—that of singular individuals as well as that of all men past, present, and future— is conceived as being united in an absolute totality and thus in the concept of an object. It is said to be not only a, but the unique object of possible experience. Precisely here Kant departs from classical criticism, and we see more clearly than in the classical formulation of transcendental idealism that absolute idealism, first articulated in Fichte and, after 1801, in Schelling and Hegel, is inherent in Kant's transcendental idealism.

The old problem of *influxus physicus*, with which Kant as a young metaphysician had begun, becomes central once again. It is elevated to a new systematic level, as can be seen by the following statement: "What has been said of the existence of such a matter and its internal motion in time applies to cosmic space as well, namely, that by means of the coexistence of all the parts of the latter it produces a community of all bodies and, at the same time, puts the knowing subject into the condition of possible experience of even the most distant object, for example, by making the celestial bodies perceptible and, thus, an object of possible experience" (Op 21:562.21–27). In this way, Kant returns to the problem of affection. *Influxus physicus*, in particular, is now directly deduced from apperception: cf. Op 21:552.18–22,[9] 554.1–3, 560.13–22, 561.22, 574.22–575.5, 575.20, 579.24–29, 580.12–25.

The concept and systematic function of apperception become doubtful and ambiguous. Kant's reflections upon primordial matter may be read as saying that primordial matter is to be ranked as the "supreme condition of the possibility of experience of objects in general" (Op 21:554.2, 551.5, 559.10) and thus as on the same level as apperception. This reading seems evident if one chooses to assert that existence is independent of the subject. They may, however, also be read as attempts to deduce the object of all possible experience from apperception, or, to be more precise, as attempts to infer from the empirically given analytic unity of thinking empirical objects an original synthetic unity, not only of self-consciousness, but of all existence—that is, of the world of empirical objects. Here Kant finds himself confronting the same problem as Fichte, Beck, and Schelling; not surprisingly, the Refutation of Idealism becomes problematic once again.

These revisions also affect the Transcendental Dialectic. The borderline between understanding and reason and their respective concepts is blurred, for example, when Kant refers to "primordial matter, whose reality can only be confirmed by reason" (Op 21:219.18–19; cf. 220.1, 235.9–13, 241.9, 540.19, 545–46). The concept of a world-whole or the whole of world matter—and with it the corresponding notion of an absolute totality of the objects of possible experience itself—is elevated to the function of a referent of apperception. That is to say, they are to play the role of that something with reference to which a "transcendental content" (A79/ B105) or truth is supposed to apply to our knowledge.

Thus the entire systematic of the first *Critique* and, in particular, the relations between Aesthetic, Analytic, and Dialectic are put into question. Considering the delicate texture of the critical system of transcendental principles, unsurprisingly, the method of transcendental analysis changes too. The idea, the object, and the procedure of a transcendental deduction are revised, as are the task and method of transcendental philosophy in general.[10] A priori and empirical knowledge can no longer be strictly separated.

As a consequence of the new approach to the problem of idealism, of the purported deducibility of existence from apperception, of a reformulated theory of affection (not by things in themselves, but by appearances or the self), and, finally, of establishing the material whole as a referent of our representations or reason of truth, the very concept of transcendental idealism is revised. "*God*, the *world*, and the thinking being in the world (*man*)" (Op 21:32.12) are now the subject matter of this relation. Leibniz's monadology, a world of substances representing the universe from their respective points of view, is, at last, to be overcome by a version of *influxus physicus* based on critical principles. Kant thus has returned to the starting point of his metaphysics. At the same time it becomes evident that it is only one step from the so-called ether deductions of "Übergang 1–14" to the "highest standpoint of transcendental philosophy" (Op 21:32.10–11).

Conclusions

From 1755 on, there are two central questions in Kant's metaphysics. First, how can things (bodies, substances) form one world, not solely in the representations of thinking monads, but really and materially, that is, as a world constituted by universal physical interaction? Second, on what principles does our knowledge of such a world rest?

The second problem becomes urgent under the influence of Hume's criticism of Leibniz's and Wolff's metaphysics. Kant now asks: "How am I to understand that, because something is, something else exists?" (NM 2:202). Kant calls the something he seeks the relationship between "real ground" and its "real consequence," which, unlike the connection between a logical ground and its consequence, is not produced "by the rule of identity" (*ibid.*). This question, which, taken in the broadest possible sense, concerns the real link between one existent and another, involves not only the Humean problem—the question of a theoretical basis for the law of causality—but the Kantian problem as well. That is, how can one existent be thought to be related to another in such a way that things constitute a real world determined by universal causality and physical interaction?

By 1766 Kant holds these central questions, now combined into a single one, to be unanswerable (DSS 2:370). At the same time, his future approach becomes apparent. Kant thinks of philosophy as a kind of "enquiry . . . which judges its own methods and knows not only objects but also their relation to human understanding" (DSS 2:368). Does philosophy really know this? In 1772 Kant puts the same question as follows: "What is the ground of the relation of that in us which we call 'representation' to the object?" (C 10:130).

From this time on and, in particular, in the first *Critique* (in both editions), Kant conceives of the human understanding as determining the basic relationships between objects. They are nothing apart from human knowledge, and, as objects, they are merely the referents and content of representations. That is why the subjective conditions of empirical knowledge are also the objective conditions of possible objects of that knowledge; that, in turn, is why the rules for combining representations in the understanding are the basic laws of nature and of the empirical world. We cannot understand nature, the world and its objects, as absolutely independent entities but only as products of the synthesizing activity of our understanding. But empirically, that does not mean that they are not objective and independent of the experiencing subject. Moreover, their independence and objectivity can *only* be explained in the way just indicated.

Even sympathetic readers doubted this account right from the beginning: Was this really different from Berkeley's *esse est percipi*? In 1787 Kant hurries, therefore, to declare: "The mere, but empirically determined, consciousness of my own existence proves the existence of objects in space outside me" (B275). In order to leave no doubt, he adds that perception of what subsists (what determines my existence in time empirically) is "possible only through a *thing* outside me, not through the mere *representation* of a thing outside me" (*ibid.*). One is tempted to object that this "thing," which is supposed to be distinct from the mere representation of a thing, is—from the transcendental viewpoint—itself nothing but a representation. Thus, is it not true that the "*mere* representation" (my italics) is actually the mere representation of something that is itself a mere representation—in other words, that it is the representation of a representation?

Apperception and Ether

This basic ambiguity in the Refutation of Idealism is not eliminated in other sections of the second edition of the *Critique*. In the
revised Analogies of Experience Kant continues to state that the
"existence of appearances" cannot be construed a priori (A178–79/
B221–22). Although the principles regulating the "synthesis of appearances" (A181/ B224) concern only the relations between existents
and therefore are not "constitutive" but only "regulative" principles,
Kant nevertheless deduces three (if not four) well-known laws that
are constitutive for the existence of the world and of things in the
world: (1a) Whatever exists empirically as a substance is, as such, im-
mutable (unalterable, permanent); or (1b) the quantity of existence
in the empirical world of appearances remains absolutely constant.
(2) Whatever there is is integrated into a unique system of universal
causal dependence. (3) The empirically cognizable world is made up
of permanent substances that are integrated into a unique system of
reciprocal causal interaction of physical influence.

According to A158/ B197, all these statements rest upon the conditions by which the necessary reference of the empirical content of
representations to the original unity of apperception is established
and guaranteed. Particularly with respect to the rules regulating the
interrelationships of empirically existing objects, this is to say: the
conditions of a "transcendental" time-order in the possible content
of empirical representations are laws governing the temporal structure of objects in the actual world, because it is only on this condition that both (that is, empirical objects and the actual world made
up of these objects) can be "objects for us."

Such inference from conditions of knowledge to conditions of
existence appeared "strange" (*befremdlich*) to Kant in both 1781 and
1787. His doubts about it appear at A166–67/B208–9. What dissi-
pated these doubts in the end? The manifold of an empirical intuition as something given, the very "nature of our perceptions" (A175/
B216)—that is, their being gradual or intensive magnitudes—and, finally, the impossibility of perceiving space and time (A172–73/ B214)
establish for Kant the following: "All appearances . . . are continuous magnitudes, alike in their intuition, as extensive, and in their
mere perception (sensation, and with it, reality) as intensive" (A170/
B212). In other words: the general structure of singular perception
(that is, sense perception taken distributively) is transferred to the
totality of possible empirical intuitions of an individual (collective

unity of experience, first order) and to the totality of possible empirical intuition of any knowing subject (collective unity of experience, second order). This, in turn, is identified with the totality of material existence as the representational content of all subjects. The general conditions of perception are objectified as a world of appearances to which the experiencing subjects themselves necessarily belong.

"Übergang 1–14" shows that Kant is no longer content with the transcendental analysis exhibited by the first *Critique*. The concept of an "object of possible experience" now refers to both the singular empirical intuition and the "absolute totality" of "universal or all-embracing experience." The former, resulting from the application of the categories to the single empirical intuition, is conceived as a mere derivative feature of the objective whole. The argument from void space and time, already used in the first *Critique* (A173–75/ B215–16, A212/B258–59), is replaced by a more radical version, namely, that space and time as such do not refer to existent things at all; they lose, therefore, their rank as supreme conditions of empirical existents and are now seen as mere attributes of the dynamical material or primordial matter. This casts serious doubts upon Kant's claim to have shown by the deduction of the categories in the first *Critique* that the objects (not only of pure, but also of empirical intuition) are completely determined by the categories; for if space and time as such are not necessarily linked to existence, then there is no guarantee that the categories of the third class (that is, the categories of relation) do, in fact, determine the existence of empirical objects. For that reason it has become indispensable for Kant to carry out an a priori deduction of "cosmic matter."

Reversing the method of the first *Critique*—that is, inferring the collective unity of the whole of possible experience from a given distributive unity—Kant now maintains: "The object of collectively universal experience (of the synthetic unity of perceptions) is . . . *given*; the object of the distributively universal experience, of which the subject forms a concept for itself (of the analytical unity of possible experience), is merely *thought*, for it belongs merely to the form of possible experience" (Op 21:579.15–19). In this way Kant supposes the absolute totality of the synthetic unity of perception to be given a priori, that is, as "the material principle of the unity of possible experience" (Op 21:585.17–18).

Kant now thinks of the possibility of conferring unity, objectivity, or a "transcendental content" (A79/B105) upon the manifold of empirical intuitions by means of the categories. Thus, he tries to establish a priori the objective reference of our representations (that is, truth) as resting upon the material or the unique "sense-object outside us" (Op 21:582.23) as something given. Its existence, in turn, is thought to be proved "logically, according to the principle of identity, not physically, by hypothesis, in order to explain certain phenomena" (Op 21:583.12–16). Transcendental analysis is thus concerned with a subject matter that had formerly been ascribed to the Transcendental Dialectic and that had thereby been excluded from the sphere of objective knowledge, namely, the unconditioned in the existence of the appearances, their absolute totality.

These modifications blur the borderlines between intuition, concept of the understanding, and concept of reason, or, respectively, between Aesthetic, Analytic, and Dialectic. Primordial matter is set up as the supreme principle of the unity of external experience. It guarantees that what exists in space and time is connected together into one single, continually perceptible world, and that thereby it is connected with the senses of perceiving subjects, uniting both, objects and subjects, into a unique whole of possible experience. Thus apperception is linked to the dynamic continuum as its sole object, although only implicitly by means of the concepts of experience and of an experiential whole. This, however, is the basic weakness of "Übergang 1–14." *How* the totality of material existence in possible experience can be deduced from the self remains an open question and becomes the subject matter of the doctrines of *Selbstsetzung, Selbstaffektion,* and, finally, *Selbstkonstitution* of the subject as object in the later drafts of fascicles X, XI, VII, and I.

Thus the question of why Kant undertook in "Übergang 1–14" such a daring analysis (an analysis that from the point of view of the first *Critique* can only be regarded as transcendent and therefore impossible within the framework of transcendental idealism) is more or less answered: the old problem concerning what constitutes a physical world in the proper sense of the term, as well as the principles by which it can be known, required a new solution. The outcome of the transcendental deduction of the pure concepts of the understanding, which ought to have substantiated Kant's claim that *natura formaliter spectata* was due to apperception and its categories, seemed to be undermined by the fact that an important premise of the deduction—that is, the connection between space and time, on the one

hand, and the existence of things in space and time, on the other—
was itself called into question. The inference from conditions of the
synthesizing activity of the knowing subject to the absolute totality
of existence, which was to be conceived as independent of the subject
and, at the same time, as of a world of appearances transcendentally
dependent upon this subject, simply could not be accepted. The
"collective" unity of the presumably absolute whole of experience required a sufficient explanation if Leibniz and Berkeley were to be re-
futed by a coherent theory of *influxus physicus* once and for all.

Yet, the attempt to exhibit the missing link between apperception
and the ether could not but make evident that the transition from the
deduction of the form of the distributive to that of the collective content of possible experience did not solve the difficulties but only in-
creased them. Kant found himself thrown back upon the beginnings
of his undertaking—indeed, to the point of identifying synthetic and
analytic unity, the logical and the real relationship between ground
and consequence:

Once the fundamental relations have been reached, the business of philosophy is at an end. We can never know by reason alone how something can be
a cause or can possess a force; such relations must be ascertained exclusively
from experience. Our rules of reason only apply to a comparison as to identity and as to the principle of contradiction. In so far as something is regarded as a cause, something else is just being assumed; thus, there cannot
be a relation of identity between the two things. On the other hand, if we do
not wish to consider that something as a cause, there is no contradiction involved; whenever we assume something and reject something else, we are
not faced with a contradictory position. That is why the fundamental concepts of things as causes, forces and actions must be quite arbitrary, and as
such they cannot be proved or disproved, as long as they are not derived
from experience (DSS 2:370).

This pronounces the verdict on the deductions of "Übergang 1–
14," at least from the viewpoint of the *Dreams of a Spirit Seer* or the
first *Critique*. These viewpoints, in fact, are one and the same so long
as "logical" and "real" relations are taken to be absolutely distinct, or
so long as identifying them would mean returning to the principles
of Leibniz's and Wolff's metaphysics that Kant maintained in 1755.

Confronted with this dilemma, Kant does not surrender, however. The question that had occupied the center of his work in theoretical philosophy from 1772 on, namely, What is the ground of the

relation of that in us which we call "representation" to the object?
still lacked a sufficient answer. Kant must have become aware of this
while working on the deduction of primordial matter. It must have
been especially distressing because J. S. Beck, in his *Einzig möglicher
Standpunkt* of 1796, had called Kant's question completely meaningless. Kant must have felt compelled to show that transcendental
idealism is able to answer the question in accordance with the spirit
and the letter of the *Critique of Pure Reason*.

Wilhelm Dilthey thought Kant had become old unusually early
and, therefore, had not been able to view Beck's problem with a sympathetic eye.[11] If Dilthey had known the *Opus postumum*, he would
have seen that Kant, following Solomon Maimon, Fichte, and, above
all, Beck, was engaged in deducing the object from the activities of
the subject—if not, indeed, from an "original [act of] representing"
(*ursprüngliches Vorstellen*) by the subject, and this not only with respect to the intuitive and intellectual forms of space, time, and categories, but also with respect to the rational form of existence per se.
Thus Kant accepts some of the criticism of his successors. In doing
so, he modifies the basic structure of transcendental idealism in order
to preserve its substance and to answer the question of objective reference by assimilating elements taken from the various approaches of
his pupils and opponents.

He finds himself confronted with an unpleasant alternative, however. *Either* he must deny altogether the possibility that things in
themselves affect the self and, consequently, must place cosmic space
and everything in it merely "in us" (as in the first edition of the *Critique*). If so, he must conceive the knowing subject as a "windowless
monad" merely representing a "world" of empirical objects, and
must abandon the idea of *influxus physicus* once and for all, returning
to Leibniz without an ontology. He would then be following Beck
toward a viewpoint like Schelling's *System of Transcendental Idealism*.
Or he must continue the attempt, evidenced in both the first and second editions of the *Critique*,[12] to reconstruct *influxus physicus* upon
critical principles, that is, to maintain that the existence of a material
world is independent of the subject but must be proved a priori as a
condition of possible experience. In other words, he must then maintain that the empirical subject is affected by objects that are (transcendentally speaking) nothing but "modifications of our mind," but
that are really (that is, ontologically) distinct from the knowing
subject.

Kant failed to solve this dilemma. His working upon these problems shows, however, that a series of philosophical systems, published by his successors but stimulated by Kant's transcendental idealism, are not defections from classical criticism—as the orthodox view of the matter, ever since Kant's days, would have it. They are, on the contrary, attempts to save the core of transcendental idealism (whatever that may be) in face of the difficulties and contradictions that result from its own premises. Despite his official declarations to the contrary (especially the one against Fichte, cf. C 12:370–71), Kant is convinced that transcendental idealism has to be revised and further developed. He himself takes part in such an undertaking and is in the end even prepared to admit several versions of transcendental idealism (those of "Schelling, Spinoza, Lichtenberg": see Op 21:87.29–31)—at least *in foro interno*.

The elucidation of the first principles of metaphysical knowledge becomes a little brighter at the end of Kant's life. But the solution of its central problems has still not been brought into the open light of the day. Kant died aware that he must leave these problems and their eventual solution to others. This end of the story, however, is worthy of a philosopher: it is human.

Kant's *Selbstsetzungslehre*

ECKART FÖRSTER

To engage in a serious study of Kant's *Opus postumum* is a solitary task. This seems especially true of the *Selbstsetzungslehre* of the last fascicles, that is, the doctrine that the subject posits itself, or makes itself into an object of experience. Although clearly the culmination of Kant's last work—if not, as I am inclined to think, of his entire critical philosophy—this doctrine has received only the scantest attention. To my knowledge, only four dissertations have ever been devoted to it: two in the early 1920's under the banner of neo-Kantianism, and two in the early 1950's.[1]

None of them is particularly helpful. The same must be said of the treatment Kant's doctrine of self-positing received in the commentaries of Erich Adickes, Gerhard Lehmann, and Vitorio Mathieu.[2] Adickes, whose influential study predated the complete publication of the *Opus postumum* by almost two decades, failed to see in this doctrine any "real extension or fortunate development of the Kantian system,"[3] and he was "certain" that Kant's deliberate talk of "self-positing" was a mere concession to Fichte and other "extreme" idealists, indicative of Kant's desperate attempts to unify and consolidate his disintegrating school. Distinguishing between six different ways in which Kant allegedly used the term "self-positing" in the *Opus postumum*, Adickes was convinced that these subtleties were Kant's misguided attempt to outclass Fichte and all those "for whom excessive conceptual hair-splitting and a scholastic obsession with subtleties had become the mark of true philosophy."⁴ No longer at the height of his powers, Kant had succumbed to what Adickes called the general "posito-mania" (*Setzkrankheit*) of the time.⁵

I find Adickes's conjecture implausible. Kant begins to speak of self-positing at a time when he is busy completing the critical system—a time, that is, before Fichte had even turned to philosophy. Sometime between 1788 and 1790, for his discussions with J. G. C. C. Kiesewetter, Kant wrote that "I posit my own existence" in a world "for the sake of empirical consciousness and its possibility," because empirical knowledge of myself as a being determined in time can only be knowledge of "myself as a being that exists in a world" (R6313, 18:615). He added: "First we are an object of outer sense for ourselves, for otherwise we would not perceive our place in the world and could not intuit ourselves in relation to other things" (R6315, 18:619).

Clearly, Kant is drawing an important consequence from his Refutation of Idealism in the first *Critique*, namely, that if, for the temporal determination of my own consciousness, there must exist things outside me, then I must exist in space and occupy a position in space to which other things can be external. How this is to be thought of, however, especially since space itself is not something outside me but only the subjective form of outer intuition, remains unclear in this context.

There are, of course, similar passages in the first *Critique* itself, for instance: "The 'I think' expresses the act of determining my existence. Existence is already given thereby, but the mode in which I am to determine this existence, that is, how I am to posit in me the manifold belonging to it, is not thereby given" (B158a; cf. B67−68, etc.).

The question that will concern me here is: How am I to posit in me the manifold belonging to my existence, in such a way as to determine my existence? Kant's *Opus postumum* answers precisely this question, I will contend. The route I will trace to the *Selbstsetzungslehre* of Kant's last work is a long one, leading from Kant's early onto-theology, through the Dialectic of the first *Critique*, to the ether theory in the *Opus postumum*, which sets the stage for, and provides the key to, the doctrine of *Selbstsetzung*.

I

I must begin by clarifying what Kant means by "positing." In his 1763 essay *The One Possible Basis for a Demonstration of God's Existence*, Kant for the first time expresses his famous thesis that existence is not a real predicate or determination of a thing (OPB 2:72). In this context, he also explicates the term "positing": "The concept of position or positing is completely simple and identical with the concept of being in general" (OPB 2:73). Being, Kant explains, is expressed in two fundamentally different ways: either in the copula in a judgment "x is p," where the predicate is posited in relation to the subject; or in an existential proposition "x is (exists)." Kant calls the former the relative position, in which a further predicate is posited in relation to the subject. In the latter, the subject itself, with all its predicates, is posited outside the concept or the judger. This Kant calls the absolute position, or existence.

If I say: "God is an existent thing," it seems as though I am expressing the relation of a predicate to a subject. However, there is an inaccuracy in this expression. Correctly speaking, one should say: "Something existent is God," that is, "There is an existent thing to whom belong those predicates which, taken together, we signify by the expression 'God'." These predicates are posited relative to the subject, but the thing itself, together with all its predicates, is posited absolutely (OPB 2:74).

The proof Kant provides for the existence of such a being is an adaptation of an earlier argument developed in the *Nova dilucidatio* of 1755. The earlier version, in the seventh proposition of the *Nova dilucidatio,* proceeds from the notion of "the possibility of all things" and roughly goes as follows: To say that something is possible is to say that the notions or concepts that are compared or related in a judgment do not contradict each other but are compatible. We may call this the formal condition of possibility. There is also a material condition. In all comparison, what is to be compared—the material—must be given beforehand. Where there is nothing to be compared, there can be no comparison and hence no possibility. For Kant, this means that nothing can be conceived as possible unless whatever is real in every possible notion exists—and, he adds, exists with absolute necessity, because in its absence nothing would be possible and possibility itself would be abolished, which is impossible.

Furthermore, Kant argues, all these realities (*omnimoda haec realitas*), which in a sense are the material for all possible notions, can only exist necessarily if they are united in a single infinite being. For if the realities were distributed among several existing things, any of them would have its existence limited by privations that belong to the thoroughgoing determination of any existing finite thing. But absolute necessity does not belong to such privations in the way it belongs to the realities in question; the degree to which the realities were limited by privations would thus be a matter of contingency; hence, realities limited in this manner would also exist contingently. To have absolute necessity, the realities in question must exist without any limitations whatsoever, that is, must constitute a single, infinite being. This being we may call God, who is thus the absolutely necessary principle of all possibility. He is also, we may add, the ontological ground of the unity of our experience, which is single and all-embracing. This unity would be "unthinkable," Kant maintains, unless all finite substances "are maintained, in mutual relations, by their common ground [*principio*], namely, the divine intellect" (Nd 1:414, 413).

The argument just sketched leaves undetermined how the realities, the material for all possible notions, are supposed to be given to the human mind. The explication to proposition X of *Nova dilucidatio* makes clear, however, that Kant there endorses Leibniz's idea that to the soul there is always internally present, albeit only in a dark and obscure fashion, an infinite perception of the whole universe (*infinita, quae semper animae interne praesto est, quanquam obscura admodum totius universi perceptio*), which already contains within itself whatever realities must be in those thoughts that are afterwards to be illuminated with greater light, when we deliberately focus attention on them. In this way, we constantly increase our knowledge, through an ever new combination, limitation, and determination of what is present to our mind, although "the material of all representations derived from their connection with the universe remains the same" (Nd 1:408): "that there is anything at all which can be thought, from which, through combination, limitation, and determination, there subsequently results the notion of any conceivable thing—this would be unintelligible unless whatever is real in a notion existed in God, the source of all reality" (Nd 1:395–96).

Here I do not wish to examine Kant's argument critically; its basic flaw should be clear enough. Nor do I want to focus on the subtle shifts made in the argument when he recasts it in the *One Possible Basis*.[6] Rather, I want to turn directly to the first *Critique* and see how the argument appears in the light of Kant's critical position. It is in the Dialectic, in the chapter on the transcendental ideal, that we find it taken up again.

In the middle of the Dialectic, Kant presents us with a new synthetic a priori principle, namely, that of a thoroughgoing determination of all things. As we have seen, according to Kant we come to know an object by determining it, that is, by ascribing predicates to it.[7] The object is simply the bearer of certain predicates, a "something in general" that we think to ourselves through the predicates that constitute its concept. In principle, however, the object must also be *determinable* with respect to the predicates that were not asserted or denied of it. The determinateness of the object precludes the possibility that any predicate may, at one and the same time, apply and not apply to it. Or, as Kant says, "every thing, as regards its possibility, is . . . subject to the principle of thoroughgoing determination, according to which if all the possible predicates of things be taken together with their contradictory opposites, then one of each pair of contradictory opposites must belong to it" (A571–72/B599–600).

This principle rests on what Kant calls a necessary "transcendental presupposition," namely, the idea of an *omnitudo realitatis*, of a "transcendental substrate" that contains, as it were, "the whole store of material" for all possible predicates of things. His reasoning is by now familiar. We cannot think of a finite thing except in terms of some limitation or privation. But a limitation, as a determination of an object, is always derivative and presupposes the thought of the realities that it limits and that contain the data or material for the possibility and thoroughgoing determination of the thing: "All manifoldness of things is only a correspondingly varied mode of limiting the concept of the highest reality which forms their common substratum, just as all figures are only possible as so many different modes of limiting infinite space" (A578/B606).

We are thus led by reason to form the idea of an object that, although transcendent, is regarded as being thoroughly determinable in accordance with principles. In other words, we form an *ideal*, by which Kant understands an idea, "not merely *in concreto*, but *in individuo*, that is, as an individual thing" (A568/B569), determined or determinable by the idea alone.

At this point, Kant radically breaks with his earlier thought. In order to represent to ourselves the thoroughgoing determinateness of things, we need not presuppose the *existence* of a being that corresponds to this ideal, but only the *idea* of such a being. That is to say, to derive the conditioned totality, "the totality of the limited," from an unconditioned totality of thoroughgoing determination, we do not require the objective relation of an actual object to other things, but only of "an idea to concepts" (A578–79/B606–07).

Owing to a natural illusion, however, we confound what is a subjective condition of thought with an objective condition of things in general. The first step is innocent enough. For an object of sense to be thoroughly determined, it must be compared with all predicates that can be given in the field of appearances. Now whatever is real in the field of appearances is given in experience, which is inevitably "considered as single and all-embracing" (A582/B610), for there is only "one single experience in which all perceptions are represented as in thoroughgoing and orderly connection" (A110), just as there is only one space and one time in which appearances can occur. The material for the possibility of all objects of the senses must thus be presupposed as given in one *Inbegriff* or whole, upon whose limitation the determination of all things and their distinction from each other must be based (cf. A581–82/B609–10). But now, neglecting the distinction between appearances and things in themselves, we confound the unity that is merely given as a task (*aufgegeben*) with one that could be given as such:

We substitute dialectically for the distributive unity of the empirical employment of the understanding, the collective unity of experience as a whole; and then think . . . this whole [realm] of appearances as one single thing that contains all empirical reality in itself; and then again, in turn, by means of . . . [a] transcendental subreption, substitute . . . for it the concept of a thing which stands at the source of the possibility of all things, and supplies the real conditions for their complete determination (A582–83/B610–11).

If we were entitled to substitute the *collective* unity of experience as a whole for the *distributive* unity of the empirical employment of the understanding (as Kant had done in his earlier writings) and then to hypostatize what has reality only in an idea, we would indeed, Kant points out, "be able to determine the primordial being through the mere concept of the highest reality, as a being that is one, simple, all-sufficient, eternal," that is, God (A580/B608). Such an assertion can only be fallacious, however, and the aspirations of transcendental theology are curtailed once and for all. The ideal of a supreme being, according to the critical Kant, is only a regulative principle of reason that allows us to look upon all connection in the world *as if* it originated from an all-sufficient necessary cause and to base on the idea of such a cause the rule of a systematic and necessary unity explaining that connection (cf. A619/B647). But this ideal, as presented in the Dialectic, specifies no particular rule for the thoroughgoing determination of all things; it signifies the goal for our investigation and the reflective assurance that such a rule might be possible—nothing further.

II

Kant's designated title for the *Opus postumum* is "Transition from the Metaphysical Foundations of Natural Science to Physics," and the purpose and design of his last work will remain largely unintelligible unless it is related to the work from which it is supposed to take its departure, namely, the *Metaphysical Foundations of Natural Science* of 1786. I want to state two theses concerning the relation of these two works before proceeding to examine the *Opus postumum* itself.[8]

First, the *Metaphysical Foundations* attempted to lay down the principles that account for, or guarantee, the apodictic certainty reason seeks in the laws of physics, without which physics would not, according to Kant, deserve the name of a science. This work was thus to provide the a priori foundations for physics. It did not, however, account for another characteristic of physics that must be derived from a priori sources, namely, its systematic nature. When he wrote the *Metaphysical Foundations*, Kant did not fully command the conceptual devices that could provide for physics' systematicity, although, as he later put it, this work already had a tendency toward that goal. With the discovery of judgment as an autonomous faculty in 1789, however, the situation began to look different, and it is from here that the plan for a "Transition from the Metaphysical Foundations to Physics," and for an "elementary system" of the moving forces of matter derives.

Second, hand in hand with the work on this "Transition" project goes, initially at least, Kant's attempt to remedy a fundamental flaw in the Dynamics chapter of the *Metaphysical Foundations*. Kant came to realize that the explanation of the possibility of matter he had provided there—in terms of two conflicting forces, attraction and repulsion—was circular. On the one hand, attraction was said to be always proportional to the quantity of matter; on the other hand, Kant argued that only "by such an action and reaction of *both* fundamental forces, matter would be possible by a determinate degree of the filling of space," hence by a determinate quantity (MFNS 4:521, my italics).

In the early drafts of the *Opus postumum*, Kant tries to overcome this problem in his dynamical theory of matter by treating attraction and repulsion as modifications of the internal vibrations of a universally distributed, all-penetrating ether or caloric. He also tries to demonstrate that certain of the most fundamental characteristics of material bodies, such as cohesion, rigidity, and fluidity, cannot be understood except by assuming such an ether and its ceaseless internal tremblings. After years of rather fruitless attempts to develop his elementary system of the moving forces of matter from the table of categories in conjunction with the assumption of such a universally distributed world-ether, in April 1799 Kant suddenly gives his project an entirely new direction. He no longer regards the ether as a hypothesis for explaining certain physical phenomena but deduces it from the conditions of possible experience. The proof is striking in many ways; I will quote a few passages at length.

If it can be proved that the unity of the *whole* of possible experience rests upon the existence of such a material [i.e., ether] (with its stated properties), then its reality is also proved, not, indeed, *through* experience, but a priori, merely from conditions of possibility, for the sake of the possibility of experience. . . . Now the concept of the whole of outer experience . . . presupposes all possible moving forces of matter as combined in collective unity; to wit, in full space (for empty space . . . is not an object of possible experience). It further presupposes, however, a constant *motion* of all matter, by which the *subject*, as an object of sense, is affected. For without this motion, that is, without the stimulation of the sense organs, which is its effect, no perception of any object of the senses, and hence no experience, takes place (Op 22:550.18–551.7).

The principle which serves as the basis for the combination of all moving forces of matter into the whole of all possible experience is the assumption of a material which is uniformly distributed throughout cosmic space, and which penetrates all bodies internally (Op 21:540.24–27).

The object of an all-embracing experience contains within it all the subjectively moving forces of matter (that is to say, those affecting the senses and producing perceptions). Their whole is called caloric and is the basis of this universal stimulation of forces (Op 22 : 553.21–24).

[The ether] is actual, because the concept of it (with the attributes we ascribe to it) makes possible the whole of experience; it is given by reason, not as a hypothesis for perceived objects, for the purpose of *explaining* their phenomena, but rather, immediately, in order to found the possibility of experience itself (Op 22 : 554.12–17).

All so-called *experiences* are always only parts of *one* experience, in virtue of the universally distributed, unbounded caloric which sets all celestial bodies connected in one system into a community of reciprocity (Op 22 : 554.30–33).

At least three strands in this proof are important in the present context. The first concerns the nature of perception. In the first *Critique*, Kant had defined perception as appearance combined with consciousness (A120); this definition is now expanded. Any perception of an outer object is also the effect of a moving force of matter on me.

The second strand connects with the problem of the Refutation of Idealism that I mentioned earlier: for experience of outer objects to be possible, space itself must be an object of sense. Since the space we encountered in the first *Critique*, the mere form of intuition, was "neither positively empty nor positively full, [hence] not an object existing outside me at all" (Op 21:232.23–24), space now must be thought of as filled with moving forces. The ether or caloric "makes space sensible"; it is "the hypostatized space itself, as it were, in which everything moves" (Op 21:228.25, 224.11–12). Kant thus calls the realization of space the condition of the possibility of experience in general, and it is no accident that, at one point, Kant gives the ether proof in the *Opus postumum* precisely the same form that he gave to the Refutation in the first *Critique*, that is, *Grundsatz*, followed by *Beweis* and *Anmerkungen* that reflect on the method of proof (Op 21:223).

The third strand, most importantly, unites the other two and connects with our previous discussion of Kant's transcendental ideal in the first *Critique*. Perceptions of outer objects are the effects of moving forces upon us; experience, on the other hand, is the systematic connection of perceptions into a single, all-embracing whole. There must hence be a basis for combining all moving forces of matter into a whole; that is, we must presuppose a collective unity of the forces from which the distributive unity of experience can be derived: "[The ether] is actual, because the concept of it . . . makes possible the whole of experience" (Op 21:579.2–4).

I would suggest that Kant's ether is best understood as a transcendental ideal in the critical sense.[9] That is, it is the idea of an individual thing thoroughly determined or determinable by this idea alone (cf. A568/B569). Kant makes this clear in a number of passages that reflect on the peculiar nature of his ether proof: for instance, "This mode of proving the existence of an outer object of sense must strike one as unique of its kind (without example); nevertheless, this should not appear strange, since its object also has the peculiarity that it is *individual* and . . . contains in itself *collective*, not merely *distributive* universality" (Op 21:603.4–9); again, "This indirect proof is *unique* of its kind—a fact that should not appear strange, since what it concerns is an *individual* object, which carries with it real (not logical) universality" (Op 21:586.7–9); and, finally, "The object of a single, all-embracing experience is, at the same time, an individual (*individuum*)" (Op 22:611.17–18).

In calling Kant's ether an ideal I do not, of course, want to deny that Kant wavers—for a while at least—in his assessment of the status of the ether. On the contrary, I believe that Kant's ambivalence about what the proof establishes is an ambivalence about whether the ether is *only* an ideal or whether an actual object corresponds to it. At some places, for instance, Kant says that for the ether, and for it alone, "a posse ad esse valet consequentia" (Op 21:592.11; cf. 604.30–605.1). The ether thus exists "outside the idea" of it (Op 21:559.19). At other places, however, it is said to exist only "in the idea" (Op 21:553.8), and to be merely "a thought-object (*ens rationis*)" (Op 21:231.1).

After only three months, however, in August 1799, Kant abandons his ether proofs altogether. If I am not mistaken, this indicates that the critical potential of the first *Critique* had caught up with him again, and that he had become convinced that the *ideal* of an ether is all we need as a "standard for reason" (A569/B597) in the thoroughgoing determination of all things. It represents how we must think.

But I think there is also another—more external—reason why ether proof and transcendental ideal could, and should, be linked. This reason concerns the often noted (yet never explained) fact that, whereas changes in Kant's position in the *Opus postumum* usually occur gradually and over a traceable period of time, the shift in his ether theory—from hypothetical to "categorically given" material—takes place suddenly and without warning. This rather dramatic shift occurs on sheet vii of the second fascicle, which, fortunately, we can date fairly precisely. At the end of the sheet there is a reference to J. G. Herder's *Verstand und Erfahrung. Eine Metakritik zur Kritik der reinen Vernunft*, which came out in late April or early May 1799.[10] The new reflections on the ether that precede this remark are thus likely to date from the previous days or weeks (that is, March or April 1799). At that time, might an external event have caused Kant's change of mind?

In 1797, with Kant's permission, Johann Heinrich Tieftrunk, a professor at Halle and a mediator in Kant's disputes with J. S. Beck, had taken on the task of producing an edition of Kant's shorter works. Kant had offered to write a preface to this edition that "would express my approval not only of your bringing the book out but also of any commentary you might be adding" (C 12:240). He only requested that the volumes be sent to him prior to publication.

Tieftrunk complied with Kant's wish on March 12, 1799, pointing out that he had appended to Kant's works occasional commentary "for the convenience of the reader" (C 13:510). He also explained that he would need Kant's preface by the end of April for it to be included in the edition. Mail from Halle to Königsberg took about a week in those days, so Kant will have examined Tieftrunk's edition and his annotations in late March or early April 1799.

One piece of commentary by Tieftrunk seems especially important in the present context; it is almost seventeen pages long and is appended to Kant's 1763 essay *One Possible Basis for a Demonstration of God's Existence*.[11] In it, Tieftrunk discusses the relation between this work and Kant's treatment of rational theology in the first *Critique*. Again, there is an external reason for such lengthy and detailed exposition. Only five years earlier (1794), a new edition of the *One Possible Basis* had appeared—the first after the critical works. Naturally, it had invited a comparison of Kant's treatment of proofs for God's existence in the works of 1763 and 1781. There is an astonishing discrepancy between the two works that is hard to overlook.

Kant concludes the *One Possible Basis* by saying that there are four possible ways in which one might try to prove God's existence, that is (in his later terminology), the ontological, the cosmological, the physico-theological, and his own proof from the ground of all possibility. Whereas the first two are doomed to failure, the third has emotional appeal but cannot serve as a proof. This leaves his own argument as the only possible proof. In the Dialectic of the first *Critique*, however, Kant claimed that "there are only three possible ways of proving the existence of God by means of speculative reason"— the ontological, the cosmological, and the physico-theological—and concluded that none of them could in principle succeed: "There are, and there can be, no others" (A591/B619). His own proof of 1763 was not even mentioned, and it was thus natural to assume that Kant, in the first *Critique*, had not really succeeded in showing the impossibility of rational theology *as such*, and that there was still a "possible basis" for a proof of its supreme being.

Tieftrunk tried to meet this charge in his commentary on Kant's precritical essay.[12] His solution could hardly have met with Kant's approval, yet in April or May 1799 it brought to Kant's attention his discussion of the transcendental ideal, as well as his earlier argument for the existence of a being whose theoretical function was almost identical to that he now wanted to ascribe to the ether. It is easy to see why Kant could have thought that this argument might now be used more profitably. When presenting his original proof for God's existence, Kant did not yet distinguish between the unconditioned necessity of judgments and the absolute necessity of things (cf. A539/B621). That is, from the fact that we cannot think anything as possible unless the predicates to be compared are available, Kant concluded that the realities we think in these predicates must themselves exist with absolute necessity. Only in the second half of the 1760's was Kant able to penetrate the illusion involved here and realize that no contradiction can result from thinking the nonexistence of a being, no matter what that being is.[13] That, of course, was the decisive move. From that moment on, onto-theology had to become a nondiscipline, because all theoretical proofs for God's existence could now be seen as having the same chance of success as, say, constructions of a *perpetuum mobile*. An ether proof, however, would not be affected by the same problem. For it is not the absolute necessity of the ether as such that Kant wanted to establish, but only its necessity for a possible unified experience.[14] Initially, at least, the old argument must thus have seemed endowed with new and unforeseen promise. If I am not mistaken, however, Kant soon came to realize that even the existence of an ether is more than could be proven a priori.

III

These historical considerations can provide the backdrop for an appreciation of both the importance and the details of Kant's *Selbstsetzungslehre* to which I will now turn. My approach from now on will be systematic, rather than historical. Again it will be best to start from the first *Critique*, more precisely, from Kant's claim that "the synthetic unity of apperception is . . . the highest point to which we must ascribe all employment of the understanding" (B134).

Most importantly, the consciousness of myself in the representation "I" is not an intuition but the mere awareness of the spontaneity of a thinking subject. That is to say, as Kant later explicates, if I represent myself merely as subject of thought, whereby thought is taken by itself, as the pure spontaneity of the combination of the manifold of a merely possible intuition, I do not represent myself as appearance. And this is because thought as yet takes no account of the mode of intuition. "In the consciousness of myself in mere thought I am the being itself, although nothing in myself is thereby given for thought" (B429). But this self of pure apperception, this highest point of all employment of the understanding, would not exist, Kant argues, were nothing given for it to exercise its spontaneity upon. The actus "I think" would not take place if nothing empirical were given as the condition of the application, or employment, of the pure intellectual faculty. Consequently, I cannot just be the subject of thought; I am likewise aware of my existence, and the consciousness of self must be viewed as involving an intuition, although one that as yet lacks determination. As Kant says, "The proposition, 'I think,' insofar as it amounts to the assertion, '*I exist thinking*,' is no mere logical function, but determines the subject (which is then at the same time object) in respect of existence" (B429). "But the 'I think' precedes the experience which is required to determine the object of perception" (B423).

The question arises, then, how I am to proceed from the "I think" and determine the given manifold in such a way as to yield empirical knowledge of myself as an existing, corporeal being in space and time. Since existence is not a real predicate, knowledge of my own existence can only consist in the thoroughgoing determination of the given manifold, and in the positing of a certain set of representations, united under the concept of my empirical self, as outside that concept.[15]

As Kant's argument in the *Opus postumum* makes clear, the first step in the determination of my own existence must be the realization of space as an object of sense. Space must thus be represented, not merely as a form of intuition, but as something existing outside me, as something empirically given. It can be this only if it is filled with moving forces; that is to say, "There must first be a matter filling space, ceaselessly self-moving by agitating forces (attraction and repulsion), before the location in space of every particle can be determined. This is the basis for any matter as object of possible experience" (Op 21:550.28–31).

Secondly, for there to be experience of any particular object *in* space, the object's moving forces must affect the subject, in order to become known as such. As we have noticed, perceptions of outer objects are not simply "appearances combined with consciousness" (A120); they are the effects of the agitating forces of matter on the subject. Before I can refer given representations to a common object, then, I must be able to think that object as exercising the forces on me that gave rise to the perceptions. Such forces, then, have likewise to be presupposed a priori for experience to be possible.

Leaving aside for the moment the question of what forces must be thus presupposed, let us first ask how they are supposed to be known. Is there an a priori concept of force? Here Kant draws on a thought that is (to my knowledge) absent from his earlier works—a thought that gives his "Transition" project a completely new direction.

The moving forces of matter cannot be given to the subject by being passively received. They are recognized only by the subject's reaction, as forces with which we interfere: "We would not know through experience the moving forces of matter in bodies, if we were not conscious of our own activity to exercise ourselves the acts of repulsion and attraction through which we apprehend these appearances. The concept of originally moving forces is not derived from experience but must lie a priori in the activity of the mind of which we are conscious when moving" (Op 21:490.24–30; cf. 22:326.30–31).

Commentators on the *Opus postumum*—in particular Adickes and Lehmann—have here located a new transcendental deduction of the categories; I will return to this claim later. For the moment I want to point out that this idea is also prima facie a return to, or continuation of, the train of thought that was interrupted by Kant's occupation with Tieftrunk, and by his subsequent ether proofs. Immediately before the first occurrence of these proofs—on the same sheet,

"Übergang 1"—Kant had pondered the question whether in the "Transition from the Metaphysical Foundations of Natural Science to Physics" there should be an a priori division of physical bodies into organic and inorganic bodies. Although the reality of organisms, that is, bodies in which all parts are reciprocally means and ends, cannot be guaranteed a priori, Kant argued that they have to be included, albeit only problematically (cf. Op 21:212.7), in the a priori division of bodies, because we are ourselves an example of organically moving forces and spontaneous intentional action. On the sheet immediately preceding the ether proofs, Kant writes: "The principle of the spontaneity of the motion of the parts of our own bodies (as limbs), considering the latter as our own self, is a mechanism"; and, "Because man is conscious of himself as a self-moving machine, without being able to further understand such a possibility, he can, and is entitled to, introduce a priori organic-moving forces of bodies into the classification of bodies in general" (Op 21:213.10–16).

After the ether proof, in fascicles X and XI, Kant capitalizes on this idea of an a priori consciousness of our own moving forces. Only because we ourselves exercise acts of repulsion and attraction do we apprehend the appearances of moving forces upon us. But, and this is the crucial part of Kant's argument, only in the process of such apprehension can we, and do we, appear to ourselves as empirical beings. Empirical self-consciousness emerges for Kant at the point of intersection (interaction) between the moving forces of matter as they affect me, and my own motions thereon. That is to say, on the one hand, only because I am corporeal—a system of organically moving forces—can I be affected by moving forces of matter; on the other hand, only insofar as I can represent myself *as affected* do I *appear* to myself as sensuous and corporeal, that is, as an object of outer sense. Self-affection and affection through objects must thus be regarded as two sides of the same coin, or as Kant put it, "Positing and perception, spontaneity and receptivity, the objective and subjective relation, are simultaneous; because they are identical as to time, as appearances of how the subject is *affected*—thus [they are] given a priori in the same *actus*" (Op 22:466.13–16).[16]

"Given a priori in the same actus" means that from this act there originally emerges the duality of empirical self and material world surrounding it, of observer and observed. Only because I apprehend the undetermined given manifold and, in the process of apprehension, insert (*reinlegen*) into it certain fundamental forces can I represent the manifold as the appearance of an external cause of my perception, and at the same time represent myself as being affected, and hence as corporeal. "The subject affects itself and becomes an object in appearance for itself in the composition of the moving forces" (Op 22:364.24–25).

It can come as no surprise that Kant thought that after years of intensive labor he finally held in his hands the key to the problem of a "Transition from the Metaphysical Foundations of Natural Science to Physics." The moving forces I can become aware of initially will correspond to the forces I am capable of exercising. Trivially, the world we experience is a world that fits our faculties and powers of cognition. "The moving forces of matter are what the moving subject itself does with its body to [other] bodies. The reactions corresponding to these forces are contained in the simple acts by which we perceive the bodies themselves. Mechanics and dynamics are the two principles" (Op 22:326.30–327.3).

The implicit reference here to the *Metaphysical Foundations* is not gratuitous. This work plays an integral part in Kant's *Selbstsetzungslehre*. It provides the principles for the construction of the concept of matter, the fundamental forces that we must think as being constitutive of any object of outer sense. It thus provides the principles that permit a first step beyond mere thought in the determination of my existence: "What comes first (intellectually) is consciousness of oneself—an act of thought which is foundational and a priori. . . . The second is, as object of sense, to be self-affecting—not merely to be represented as object of pure intuition, but also to appear in a particular form. This is the metaphysical foundations of natural science, insofar as they contain the transition to the possibility of experience in general" (Op 22:477.29–478.5).

As the last qualification makes clear, however, the work Kant has in mind is not entirely identical with his *Metaphysical Foundations* of 1786. Apart from the circularity in the Dynamics I mentioned earlier, this text also lacked a principle that could guide the thoroughgoing determination of outer objects beyond the mere statement of their constitutive forces. Its design, of course, did not require such a principle; for a solution to the problem of *Selbstsetzung*, however, and especially for the transition to physics, such principle must be regarded as indispensable: "The transition to physics cannot lie in the *Metaphysical Foundations* (attraction and repulsion, etc.). For these furnish no specifically determined, empirical properties, and one can imagine no specific [forces], of which one could know whether they exist in nature, or whether their existence be demonstrable" (Op 22:282.12–17).

Hence there must be, in addition to the *Metaphysical Foundations*, an a priori principle that permits us to apprehend and combine the appearances of outer sense as effects of moving forces of matter on the subject, and to do so in a systematic manner. What Kant has in mind is a *schema* for combining moving forces "in conformity with the schema of the Analogies of Experience" (Op 22:377.12). This requires, as Kant says somewhat enigmatically, that the understanding "presents its own acts—being its effects on the subject—in the concepts of attraction and repulsion, etc., in a whole of experience produced formally thereby" (Op 22:377.13–16).

But what, precisely, are the acts that we exercise, and what, exactly, is supposed to yield a schema for the systematic combination of the moving forces of matter? It is not even clear in what sense there can be an a priori system of empirical forces. What is clear is that Kant's attempts in the earlier fascicles of the *Opus postumum* to provide such a system have all been unsuccessful.

Here, I believe, the importance of Kant's ether theory for the "Transition," and hence for his *Selbstsetzungslehre*, becomes apparent. The concept or *ideal* of the ether provides Kant with a "principle" or schema for coordinating—or anticipating—the moving forces of matter. To see this, recall for a moment our earlier discussion of Kant's treatment of God as the *ens realissimum*, the ground of all realities. If we were entitled to posit such a being, Kant argued, we would also be in a position to determine—analytically—the attributes that necessarily pertain to its essence. That is, such a being would have to be one (as regards quantity), simple (as regards quality), all-sufficient (as regards relation), and infinite or eternal (as regards modality) (cf. A580/B610–11; cf. also OPB 2:81–87). But, of course, we can posit these predicates only relative to the subject; we cannot also posit the subject absolutely, together with all its predicates.

Analogously, Kant argues in the *Opus postumum* that we can analytically think certain attributes as necessarily belonging to the ether—attributes it cannot lack in virtue of what it is, namely, the basis of all moving forces of matter, and hence of the sum total of all realities. These attributes can be enumerated in accordance with the table of categories. That is to say, as regards quantity, the ether must

Eckart Förster

be universally distributed in order to render space an object of sense, and to provide places for objects of experience. As regards quality, it must be all-penetrating in order to be the basis for the connection of all moving forces of matter, and hence for the unity of experience. Since it is formative of all material bodies (*körperbildend*), it must also be regarded as internally all-moving, without itself being moved (relation). Finally, since the ether is the material condition of a single, unified experience, its agitations must be necessary, that is to say, permanent (modality). The unique nature of the ether, Kant insists, allows for such unique derivation:

> The attributes of this [material] (since it is all-embracing, *individual* [*unica*] . . .) are given according to the principle of identity: namely, that it is *universally distributed*, *all-penetrating*, and *all-moving*. . . . And as such, it is necessary, that is, *permanent*. For *sempiternitas est necessitas phenomenon* (Op 21:584.22–28).

> This matter is also, as a consequence of the aforementioned attributes, negatively characterized: as imponderable, incoercible, incohesible and inexhaustible. . . . Ponderability, coercibility, cohesion and exhaustibility presuppose moving forces which act in opposition to the latter and cancel their effect (Op 22:610.9–14).[17]

For there to be an empirical object of outer sense, then, we must presuppose a priori such limitations of the original force continuum—limitations, that is, that constitute an object of experience and that the subject will have to investigate in order to proceed in its thoroughgoing determination.

It seems to me Kant thought that, since all objects of experience must depend on such limitations of the original forces of the ether, an a priori *topic* for the empirical forces, based on the analytic determination of the attributes of the ether in accordance with the system of categories, can indeed be established. That is to say: as regards quantity, all matter must be either ponderable or imponderable; as regards quality, either coercible or incoercible; as regards relation, cohesible or incohesible; and as regards modality, exhaustible or inexhaustible.

To be sure, more cannot be determined a priori. We can enlist these disjunctives analytically; thereafter we must progress synthetically and empirically. That is, the determination of the degree to which an object of outer sense exemplifies one of these attributes has to be a matter of experience. The "Transition," after all, is a transition *to* physics, not itself physics. But what is important is that the subject has been provided with an a priori guideline for the investigation of nature and a principle that permits a first step in the thoroughgoing determination of its own existence in relation to the systematic unity of experience: "In the *transition* from the metaphysical foundations of natural science to physics nothing further is required than to make clear (and to develop a priori) what [these] concept[s] contain in [themselves], and which of their consequences can be confirmed [*belegen*] with examples from experience (by means of observation and experiment)" (Op 22:566.22–27).

Selbstsetzungslehre, ether theory, and the elementary system of the moving forces of matter thus hang together inextricably. The determination of my own existence, the transition from pure self-consciousness to knowledge of myself as an empirical being, takes place for Kant within the context of the ideal of a single, all-embracing experience, itself depending on the collective unity of moving forces of matter, which the subject investigates, guided by the table of categories, progressing to a thorough determination of all phenomena—a process never completed but inevitably given as a task: "The understanding begins with the consciousness of itself (*apperceptio*) and performs thereby a logical act. To this the manifold of outer and inner intuition attaches itself serially, and the subject makes itself into an object in a limitless sequence. . . . I am an object of myself and of my representations. That there is something else outside me is my own product. I make myself. . . . We make everything ourselves" (Op. 22:82.23–26, 17–21).

Postscript

I mentioned above that both Adickes and Lehmann maintain that there is a new transcendental deduction of the categories in the fascicles I have discussed here. More precisely, they locate this new deduction in Kant's doctrine of the correspondence of our own subjective acts of motion with the moving forces of matter outside us. Thus Adickes writes that Kant's plan for a "Transition" forced him "to provide a completely new transcendental deduction of the categories," as the latter had to guarantee a "self-contained, indisputable, and complete system of the moving forces (i.e., of the most universal properties of matter based on these forces)."[18] And Lehmann, the editor of the *Opus postumum* in the *Akademie* edition of Kant's works, repeatedly argues that Kant provided a new deduction of the categories in his last work because "the 'old' transcendental deduction failed."[19] It failed, according to Lehmann, to account for the special laws of nature—for what he calls *Besondergesetzlichkeit*. According to the first *Critique*, these special laws are not derivable from the categories (cf. A127–28 and B165); according to the third *Critique* (CJ 5:180, but see already A159/B198), however, they must be seen as following "necessarily" from a principle of the unity of the manifold, if they are to be regarded as *laws*. Hence, a new deduction becomes necessary, which, according to Lehmann, must try to account for *Besondergesetzlichkeit*, and consequently has as its goal "the derivation of the 'system' of the moving forces."[20]

These claims seem to me mistaken. To argue against them in detail would require a separate paper; I will thus confine myself to two related points. First, we must recall that a deduction is an (originally juridical) justification of the use of something in someone's possession. In the case of Kant's first *Critique*, what requires justification is the use of the pure concepts of the understanding in judgments that refer to objects. Because they are nonempirical concepts, their objective reality cannot be demonstrated empirically, as their corresponding objects are not given in experience. If the use of these concepts can be justified, their relation to objects must consequently be a priori. A transcendental deduction, for Kant, is thus an explanation that these concepts (categories) relate a priori to objects. Given the nature of this project, the task of a transcendental deduction must in principle be regarded as completed when it has been shown *that* the categories relate a priori to objects.

The actual proof falls into two steps. Without going into the controversial details of the interrelation of the two steps, it will, I hope, for present purposes be sufficient to say that the first step (§20) concludes that "the manifold in a given intuition is necessarily subject to the categories" (B143), whereas the second step concludes that the "synthesis of apprehension," whereby perception becomes possible, "is subject to the categories" (B161). Neither conclusion is revised in, or superseded by, the *Opus postumum*. In fact, both results are presupposed throughout. What the "Transition" does is provide us with a theory of how experience arises from the connection of perceptions (cf. B161)—a theory that is absent from the deduction because it does not belong to it but whose temporal aspect is already developed in the three Analogies (cf. B218).

Second, in §11 of the second edition of the *Critique of Pure Reason* Kant points out that the table of categories is "extremely useful in the theoretical part of philosophy, and indeed indispensable as supplying the *complete plan* of a whole *science*, so far as that science rests on a priori concepts" (B109). He had given an example thereof, Kant adds, in the *Metaphysical Foundations*.

Such a development of a system in accordance with the table of categories is of course not a deduction of the categories but rather presupposes it. For the *Metaphysical Foundations* even to get started, it had to assume the "empirical concept of matter" (MFNS 4:470) before it could proceed to investigate the extent to which reason is capable of having a priori knowledge of this object. By contrast, a transcendental deduction must in any case proceed entirely a priori.

The "Transition" is likewise based on an empirical datum. As Kant says poignantly in "Übergang 13": "*Empirical proposition*: Matter, with its moving forces, exists. These are either primitive . . . or derivative, in community in one space. This reciprocity, however, presupposes a continuum of forces, in the form of the unity and the homogeneity of the material" (Op 21:226.25–227.1; cf. 87.5). And it is this force continuum, I suggested earlier, that provides the principle for the enumeration of the most fundamental characteristics of material objects—an enumeration that must accord with the table of categories, if it is to be systematic and scientific.

Adickes also reveals his misunderstanding of the "Transition" project by attributing to Kant the view that the motions we exercise in response to the moving forces of matter "depend on the categories."[21] Kant merely claims that we exercise acts of repulsion and attraction in apprehending a given manifold (cf. Op 21:490.24–30). From the *Metaphysical Foundations* we know that all matter is constituted by these two forces. As corporeal subjects, we can exercise these forces ourselves and insert them into the empirical phenomena. The "Transition," in addition, specifies a principle that tells us *which* acts of repulsion and attraction we must exercise in order to advance to a more specific determination of the manifold. This principle supplies us with something like a schema, Kant says, a schema "in conformity with the schema of the Analogies of Experience" (Op 22:377.12)—not, as Adickes claims, "an exhaustive a priori system of all possible . . . moving forces."[22]

Lehmann seems equally mistaken in assuming that the old deduction failed because it did not lead to the special laws of nature. This cannot be the task of the deduction, which must show that the categories relate a priori to objects. On my reading, there is no contradiction, not even a tension, between Kant's original conception of a transcendental deduction of the categories, his statement that "special laws . . . cannot in their specific character be *derived* from the categories" since we "must resort to experience" to know them, and, finally, the assertion of the third *Critique* that such empirical laws must be seen as following "necessarily" from a principle of the unity of the manifold if they are to be regarded as laws.

In the *Opus postumum*, Kant remains faithful to all three insights. If this is correct, then the old Kant, in spite of persisting rumors to the contrary, still enjoyed a much better grasp of the crucial tenets of his critical philosophy than many of his younger, "hypercritical" commentators.

Kant's "Dynamics": Comments on Tuschling and Förster

JULES VUILLEMIN

Each of my colleagues' two lectures has its own tenor, and the two lead to theses that differ from one another. Professor Tuschling sees in the *Opus postumum* a new transcendental deduction, incompatible with that of the *Critique of Pure Reason* and putting into question the content and architectonics of transcendental idealism. He relates Kant's enterprise to the criticisms and reconstructions offered by the post-Kantian philosophers.[1] Their debate focused on the dilemma between idealism and realism, which Kant never solved. Professor Tuschling then judges the deduction of the ether to be a failure, but a significant failure among the other revisions and developments of the concept of transcendental idealism.[2] Professor Förster, by contrast, interprets Kant's ether in the *Opus postumum* as a transcendental ideal and gives it a critical function.[3] He concludes that the transcendental deduction "is neither revised in, nor superseded by, the *Opus postumum*" and regards the empirical proposition that matter exists as the principle of the Transition. Thus he avoids the concerns of the post-Kantians. Through the ideal of the ether, from the self-positing of a passive self and even its apparently Fichtean unlimited sequence we can arrive at the complete determination of perceptions. This determination results in sensation as soon as we suppose an empirically given motion, or rather space filled by the interplay of the two fundamental forces. Professor Förster may appre-

ciate rather positively the moderate internal reform presented by the
Opus postumum.

I shall not try to discuss these well-argued theses.[4] I shall limit
myself to a series of questions concerning some relations they have
to Kant's architectonics, especially from the viewpoint of physics.
The first two questions are directed to Professor Tuschling and
concern the localization of the problem of the ether according to
the quoted texts, and the regulative character of the Analogies of
Experience.

Professor Tuschling defines the problem of the deduction of the
ether so generally that "the cosmological material system and its
basic features as a dynamic continuum can . . . be conceived of as a
unity which is *different* from the formal structures of space and time,
[and] makes them possible."[5] Does Kant, in the *Opus postumum*, say
that space and time presuppose the ether? Such a passage would decide the question in favor of Professor Tuschling. How then can we
reconcile the dependence of space and time with their use, recognized by Kant—besides the categories[6]—for analyzing the existence
of the ether? But does Kant speak of its existence (*Dasein*), or of
its reality (*Realität*)? All the texts explicitly quoted seem to me to
tally with a localization of the problem in what Kant calls "dynamics," that is, the theory of the filling of space (the theory that results
when to the Anticipations of Perception one adds the empirical
datum of motion). If this restrictive localization fits Kant's texts,
then the overturning of Kant's system and of all his celebrated dis-
tinctions and dichotomies would lose much of its appeal, while it
rather naturally results from an interpretation making the deduction
of the ether the new general transcendental deduction. Hence I think
it important to determine whether the words "transcendental dynamics," which unmistakably call to mind the second part of the
Metaphysical Foundations of Natural Science and which agree with the
localization I spoke of, are "only a title improvised for the occasion"
(*Verlegenheitstitel*).[7]

My second question is about the regulative character of the Analogies of Experience. Twice Professor Tuschling points out that,
being only rules, the Analogies presuppose as given an empirical existence that will itself become a rule in the *Opus postumum*.[8] Among
the reasons he adduces for not being satisfied with Kant's Refutation
of Idealism, he suggests that merely regulative principles cannot give

a sure foundation to external existence: this is why Kant still uses as constitutive the principles that he defined as regulative.

Without discussing the general problem of Kant's Refutation of Idealism, let me try to defend as empirically real his conception of the Analogies.[9] When Newton, in the third book of the *Principia*, where the question is about physical existence (*Dasein*) in astronomy, borrows the word "analogy" from Bacon, he changes the sense. For Bacon, the analogies are perceptual similarities, but Newton makes them principles ruling physical realities beyond perception. In short, they mean that induction is founded upon the identity of two equations, an identity showing that two bodies (the Moon and the Earth) obey the same force (gravitation). If by Kant the Axioms of Intuition and the Anticipations of Perception are called mathematical and are relevant to one-term categories, it is because they merely involve the possibility of the phenomenon according to its quantity or its quality.

These two principles may therefore be called constitutive. It stands quite otherwise with those principles which seek to bring the *existence* of appearances under rules a priori. For since existence cannot be constructed, the principles can apply only to the relations of existence, and can yield only *regulative* principles. We cannot, therefore, expect either axioms or anticipations. If, however, a perception is given in a time relation to some other perception, then even although this latter is indeterminate, and we consequently cannot decide *what* it is, or what its *magnitude* may be, we may none the less assert that in its existence it is necessarily connected with the former in this mode of time. . . . In philosophy the analogy is not the equality of two *quantitative* but of two *qualitative* relations; and from three given members we can obtain a priori knowledge only of the relation to a fourth, not of the fourth member itself. The relation yields, however, a rule for seeking the fourth member in experience, and a mark whereby it can be detected. An analogy of experience is, therefore, only a rule according to which a unity of experience may arise from perception. It does not tell us how mere perception or empirical intuition in general itself comes about. It is not a principle *constitutive* of the objects, that is, of the appearances, but only *regulative* (A179–80/B221–22).

Professor Tuschling has alluded to this text. My question is: from an empirically realistic standpoint, what is missing? We compute Uranus's trajectory from the system of Jupiter and the Sun. The observed trajectory does not fit with the computed one. U. J. J. Le Ver-

Jules Vuillemin

rier (and J. C. Adams) explain the perturbation away by predicting the existence of a new planet, Neptune, and its place. The computations of the astronomers stop here as the regulative rules stop, because existence is not constructed. Le Verrier writes to J. G. Galle, who observes Neptune at the place and time indicated. The observation and it alone allows an existential inference. By contrast, the theory of the solar system predicts a precession of Mercury's perihelion. Le Verrier observes a discrepancy from the theoretical prediction. He constructs existential hypotheses that no observation corroborates. His computations have been merely regulative. Here the proof constitutive of existence failed.

Professor Tuschling rightly remarks that principles are not ideas and that the three Analogies must play a constitutive role. Kant agrees, but with an argument that does not rely on the inconstructibility of existence. "In the Transcendental Analytic," he says, "we have distinguished the *dynamical* principles of the understanding, as merely regulative principles of *intuition*, from the *mathematical*, which, as regards intuition, are constitutive. None the less these dynamical laws are constitutive in respect of *experience*, since they render the *concepts*, without which there can be no experience, possible a priori" (A664/B692). Let us reword Kant's remark in Newtonian terms. Newton demonstrates the following logical implication:

Kepler's empirical laws [10] + Newton's laws of mechanics →
Newton's law of attraction.

Kepler's empirical laws correspond to Kant's mathematical principles; they are constitutive of intuition (the form of trajectories, velocities, relations between distances, and periods of revolution). Moreover, these laws are empirical insofar as they suppose as given in perception the existence of the heavenly bodies. Newton's laws of rational mechanics, by which the concept of attraction—an empirical application of the Analogies of Experience—is made possible, mention existences only hypothetically: if there is no force, any mass receives an inertial motion; if there is a force, the mass is accelerated; and so forth. Without Kepler's empirical laws Newton's law cannot constitute intuition: they must apply to a phoronomical and dynamical content. Hence the Analogies are only regulative of intuition insofar as the mathematical principles must previously determine the content to which the Analogies apply.

The Analogies are constitutive of experience. In the two-body problem, if mathematical principles make it possible to locate the bodies and determine their respective velocities, then the Analogies will make possible the complete determination of their future behavior and the measure of their masses, a measure of the matter in their substances. These determinations (masses, accelerations, general perturbations) are completely objective and constitutive. They do not, however, presuppose any construction of existence. What is constructed are its empirical permanence (mass), its changes, actions, and reactions—that is, the set of relations that given existences must have in order to become an object of possible experience. As with Le Verrier, the Analogies may even make possible the concept of the place at a given time, the mass, the diameter of a new body whose existence has not been given. That is not to say that we construct this new existence, as our failure with an alleged satellite of Mercury has proved.

The three last questions are addressed to both Professor Tuschling and Professor Förster, particularly to Professor Förster. Is the definition of attraction as a fundamental force in Kant's *Metaphysical Foundations of Natural Science* really circular? The first mention of the proportionality between quantity of matter and force occurs in the Dynamics, proposition 7, observation 2. Newton, Kant says, could not assert his law of gravitation if he did not believe that attraction is irreducible to repulsion. Kant is eager to specify that Newton's law belongs to mechanics, not dynamics—that is, that it is a law of motions that follow from attractive forces.[11] Thus one need not presuppose a given quantity of matter—a concept that will be fully defined only in Mechanics, explication 2—to introduce the fundamental force of attraction as one of the two forces by which space is filled. If Kant revised because he thought his account of the two forces was circular, he was mistaken (though the theory of the two forces is affected by other, more serious difficulties).

Another question concerns Kant's discovery of what we might call the subjective mechanisms of the faculty of aesthetic judgment. Louis Guillermit has recently shown the importance of this discovery,[12] on which Professor Förster rightly insists. Guillermit recalls how in his exposition of the self-affection of our inner sense Kant was led to explain the relation between transcendental philosophy and the motions of the mind—mental states, motions, and forces. The text of the third *Critique* that may be relevant to the development of the dynamical problem is contained in §27: "The mind feels itself *set in motion* in the representation of the sublime in nature; whereas in the aesthetic judgment upon what is beautiful therein it is in *restful* contemplation. This movement, especially in its inception, may be compared with vibrations, *i.e.* with rapidly alternating repulsion and attraction produced by one and the same object" (CJ 5:258).

It is remarkable that the *Metaphysical Foundations of Natural Science* insisted that, whereas repulsion is immediately felt in sensation, attraction is never felt but only inferred (*nicht gefühlt, sondern nur geschlossen*) (Dynamics, proposition 7, observation 1), which leads to the false assumption that it is not fundamental, but derived. Hence Kant changed his mind. But how does the internal conflict of two mentally enacted forces that explains the feeling of the sublime help us to understand the external fundamental forces? Why is it supposed in order that the affection of the subject by the moving forces become known as such?[13] Does Kant offer some explanation in his *Opus postumum?*

The difficulty, indeed, arose before Kant discovered the machinery of subjective forces. In the *Critique of Pure Reason*, we are told that reality in perception has a positive degree (there is nothing negative in intensive quantities), whereas space is filled via the conflict of two opposite forces.[14] The *Critique* borrows its examples of this from photometry as well as from proper dynamics. But when we are told that "out of 200,000 illuminations by the moon, I might compose and give a priori, that is construct, the degree of our sensations of the sunlight" (A175/B217), our construction does not rely on the same principle as it does when we are told of a "great difference in the quantity of matter of different kinds in bodies with the same volume (partly on account of the momentum of gravity or weight, partly on account of the momentum of resistance to other bodies in motion)" (A173/B214). When opposite mental forces are discovered, are we in a better situation to solve the difficulty? More generally, does the Copernican revolution require that our understanding find in itself the activities that it projects into the external world?

This leads us to another question, about the nature of Kant's ether. In the Dynamics of the *Metaphysical Foundations of Natural Science*, proposition 7, observation 2, Newton's *Principia* is approvingly quoted. The reference is to book III, prop. 6, cor. 2, attributing weight to any body, the ether included. If it were otherwise, Newton says, Aristotle or Descartes could be right when they affirm that by a simple change in material form bodies could gain or lose gravity. In other words, an imponderable ether would lead us into neglecting what is precisely the specificity of dynamics: matter as quality would be reduced to geometrical solidity.

A new attitude toward the ether is expressed in the third *Critique*, for example §14, when Kant recalls Euler's assumption "that colors are isochronous vibrations (*pulsus*) of the ether, as tones are of the air set in vibration by sound" (CJ 5:224). Though it is easy to understand the role of the ether in optics as the medium of wave transmission, its role in dynamics for coordinating the fundamental forces is not so clear. In the first *Critique*, after Kant has shown that mechanism and its hypothesis of the void involve metaphysical suppositions that are not necessary from the transcendental standpoint, he proves the possibility of dynamics, that is, of the different degrees by which space is filled with the same extensive quantity of matter.

We recognize that although two equal spaces can be completely filled with different kinds of matter, so that there is no point in either where matter is not present, nevertheless every reality has, while keeping its quality unchanged, some specific degree (of resistance or weight) which can, without diminution of its extensive magnitude or amount, become smaller and smaller *in infinitum*, before it passes into the void and vanishes. Thus an expansion which fills a space, as for instance heat, and similarly every other reality in the field of appearance, can diminish in its degree *in infinitum*, without leaving the smallest part of this space in the least empty (A174/B216).

Has Kant identified the caloric with Euler's ether? In the *Metaphysical Foundations of Natural Science*, he had used Christiaan Huyghen's spherical waves to construct the propagation of forces.[15] In this respect, the *Opus postumum* makes rather explicit a concept already used in the preceding works. The question is whether the new concept of ether solves the difficulties of Kant's dynamics and how this ideal succeeds in ensuring the collective unity of external experience. That it does is doubtful for several reasons.

First, a physical equilibrium does not necessarily require the opposition of two forces. This can be demonstrated using the molecular force between two atoms as a function of their distance of separation, shown in the accompanying figure.

With such a force "we can make up solids in which all the atoms are held together by their attractions and held apart by the repulsion that sets in when they are too close together. At a certain distance

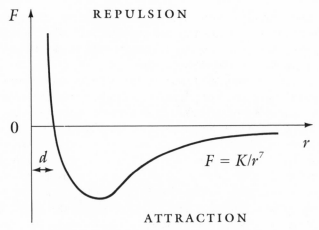

Molecular force between two atoms as a function of their distance

d . . . the forces are zero."[16] If the molecules are pushed closer, they repel each other; if they are pushed apart, they attract each other.

Second, gravitation, not repulsion, has been recognized as a fundamental force. Physicists have recognized experimentally other fundamental forces.

Third, Kant's introduction of the ether could be interpreted as an inkling of the notion of a field. Fields, however, are useful because they allow us to analyze forces into what produces the field and what it acts on. The important consequence is the principle of the superposition of fields. But this principle, which applies exactly to electrical forces, is not exact for gravity if the field is too strong.[17]

Fourth, optics shows how by interference two positive magnitudes, when added, give a magnitude equal to zero. This mechanism of interference, via the quantum-mechanical relations of uncertainty, accounts for how Kant's space is filled.

Kant is easily forgiven for his errors in physics. What finally is more questionable, however, is his move in the *Opus postumum*, be it analyzed as a new transcendental deduction or as an internal development to complete the possibility of determining perception. Does the ether belong to what we could call rational dynamics (as compared with Newton's rational mechanics)? Or is it already a step toward *Naturphilosophie*? My uneasiness about Kant's concept of the ether, even in its most limited role, concerns an obscurity in the principle of Kant's theoretical deduction. The transformations to which contemporary physics has subjected the concept of the possibility of experience warn us that it is probably the most elusive concept in transcendental philosophy. Hence it is rather ironical that the pressure of experimental evidence has been necessary to dispel our prejudices concerning the alleged completeness of this possibility, and that Kant's struggle, so well described by my colleagues, was a struggle after a chimera.

Notes

C A R L : Kant's First Drafts

I have benefited greatly from comments by Konrad Cramer, Bill Ewald, Hans Graubner, Lorenz Krüger, and Fred Lönker.

1. P. F. Strawson, *The Bounds of Sense* (London, 1966), p. 85; J. Bennett, *Kant's Analytic* (Cambridge, 1966), p. 100.

2. Cf. "How my understanding may form for itself concepts of things completely a priori, with which concepts the things (the German reads *Sachen*) must necessarily agree, and how my understanding may formulate real principles concerning the possibility of such concepts, with which principles experience must be in exact agreement and which nevertheless are independent of experience" (C 10:131). For the term *Sache*, see R4276, 17:493.13–17; R4631, 17:615; R4644, 17:623; R408, 15:165.

3. Cf. H. Cohen, *Kants Theorie der Erfahrung*, 2d ed. (Berlin, 1885), p. 77, p. 139.

4. My use of the term "subjective deduction" will be explained on page 18.

5. In a letter to Herz, written November 24, 1776, Kant reports that he is working on a final version of the *Critique*, "after I overcame the ultimate obstacles last summer" (C 10:199).

6. Cf. T. Haering, *Der Duisburg'sche Nachlaß und Kants Kritizismus um 1775* (Tübingen, 1910), p. 68.

7. *Ibid.*, p. 68; cf. H. Vaihinger, "Die transzendentale Deduktion der Kategorien in der 1. Auflage der Kr. d. r. V.," in *Philosophische Abhandlungen. Dem Andenken Rudolf Hayms gewidmet* (Halle, 1902), p. 48.

8. The interpretation of this distinction is controversial. B. Erdmann, *Kants Kriticismus in der ersten und zweiten Auflage der Kritik der reinen Vernunft* (Leipzig, 1878; rpt. Hildesheim, 1973), p. 24; and R. P. Wolff, *Kant's Theory of Mental Activity* (Cambridge, Mass., 1963), p. 85, relate the distinction in different ways to the different sections of the second chapter of the Analytic. According to H. J. Paton, *Kant's Metaphysics of Experience*, 1 (London, 1961), the subjective deduction consists in the enumeration of the "three original powers" of the soul at A94 (p. 345) which, in fact, is not a deduction at all. He freely admits that he can't make much sense of the distinction (p. 241). A Riehl, *Der philosophische Kritizismus*, 1, 2d. ed. (Leipzig, 1908), p. 504, gives the today prevailing interpretation that the subjective deduction is some kind of speculative psychology so dominant in the first edition and fortunately removed in the second edition of the first *Critique*. I follow M. Heidegger's thesis, but not his argument for it, that the subjective deduction is the most important one; cf. his *Phänomenologische Interpretationen von Kants Kritik der reinen Vernunft* (Frankfurt, 1977), p. 331.—In my opinion, the subjective deduction is based on the consideration of "the subjective sources which form the a priori foundation of the possibility of experience in their transcendental constitution" (A97) and consists essentially in the argument given in the fourth paragraph of the "Preliminary Explanation" (A111–12) and is developed, from different points of view, in the third section of the second chapter of the Analytic (A115–28). I will argue for this thesis about the "proof-structure" of the A-version of the deduction in a commentary that I intend to write on the transcendental deduction of the categories in the first edition of the *Critique*.

9. Johann Schultz, *Erläuterungen über des Herrn Prof. Kant Critik der reinen Vernunft* (Königsberg, 1785), p. 34.

10. J. A. H. Ulrich, *Institutiones logicae et metaphysicae* (Jena, 1785).

11. *Hessische Beiträge zur Gelehrsamkeit*, 1 (1785).

12. *Allgemeine Literatur-Zeitung*, 295 (1785): 299a. That Schultz is the anonymous reviewer of Ulrich's book is clear from J. G. Hamann's letter to F. H. Jacobi, April 9, 1786, in J. G. Hamann, *Briefwechsel*, 6, ed. A. Henkel (Frankfurt, 1975), p. 349.

13. *Allgemeine Literatur-Zeitung*, 178 (1785): 118.

14. C. F. von Weizsäcker, "Kants 'Erste Analogie der Erfahrung' und die Erhaltungssätze der Physik," in *Kant. Zur Deutung seiner Theorie von Erkennen und Handeln*, ed. G. Prauss (Köln, 1973), p. 157; G. Prauss, *Erscheinung bei Kant* (Berlin, 1971), p. 62.

15. Paul Guyer, "Kant on Apperception and A Priori Synthesis," *American Philosophical Quarterly* 17 (1980): 211.

16. Strawson, p. 96.

B E C K : Kant's Letter to Herz

1. Lewis White Beck, *Early German Philosophy* (Cambridge, Mass., 1969), pp. 463–67; idem, *Studies in the Philosophy of Kant* (Indianapolis, 1965), pp. 56–60.

2. H. J. Vleeschauwer, *La déduction transcendentale dans l'oeuvre de Kant*, I (1934; rpt. New York, 1976), p. 255.

3. I cannot accept Professor Carl's statement (this volume, page 6) that "The 'intellectual representations' of the *Dissertatio* are explicitly excluded." Where explicitly? Where, indeed, implicitly? They are explicitly mentioned three times in the long first paragraph and seem to me to be the central topic of the letter. When Kant denies the *usus realis* of the intellect with respect to objects of the senses, he is saying that intellectual concepts have no simple and direct relation to the objects of experience (see ID §5, 2:393).

4. This much is explicitly retained in the letter, where Kant says that concepts of magnitude (but not of quality) of sensible objects can be determined a priori (C 10:131, lines 25–26; in A. Zweig's translation, p. 72).

5. The *Reflexionen* cited in Carl's note 3 are of little help in deciding whether *Ding* and *Sache* name noumenal or phenomenal objects. R4644 suggests that *Realbegriffe* (concepts in the *usus realis* of intellect) do not refer to phenomenal objects; R4276, on the other hand, seems to require that *Sachen* be objects of experience. In his *Reflexionen* Kant tried almost everything, and therefore their evidential weight is slight except when they sustain and clarify each other.

6. In Inaugural Dissertation §24 we were told not to ascribe any sensible predicates to *intelligibilia*. *Reflexion* 4644 warns against the converse error, which I understand to mean the use of the intellectual concepts of the Dissertation as if they were categories in the sense of the *Critique:* "Wenn man von Dingen, die man nur unter der Erscheinung des Raumes kennt, allgemeine realbegriffe des Verstandes braucht (von der Art, wodurch dem Verstande die Sachen selbst gegeben werden und deren qualitaet, nicht die Grösse oder Moglichkeit), so begeht man eine *petitionem noumeni*" (17:623.6–10), which is the converse of the error warned against in the Dissertation, here called *petitio phaenomenorum.*

7. Norman Kemp Smith, *A Commentary on Kant's Critique of Pure Reason*, 2d ed. (London, 1923), p. 206.

H E N R I C H : Kant's Notion of a Deduction

1. An early example is the derivation of a notation for a scale in music from certain natural qualities of the tones: "do-re-mi-fa. . ."

2. G. Achenwall and J. S. Pütter, *Ius naturae*, appeared from 1750 on in numerous editions. The second volume is reprinted in the Academy edition

of Kant's works (vol. 19). From the third edition on, the work appeared only under Achenwall's name.

3. See Dieter Henrich, "Die Deduktion des Sittengesetzes," in *Denken im Schatten des Nihilismus*, ed. A. Schwan (Darmstadt, 1975), pp. 55–56.

4. With this remark I modify part of my "The Proof Structure of the Transcendental Deduction," *Review of Metaphysics*, 22 (1969): 640–59. When I wrote the paper, I had no idea what a deduction consists in and took for granted that it was exhaustively defined as a chain of syllogisms. But it isn't, and after finding out that this is so, I must relativize what I said in that paper. The deduction of the second edition is indeed a proof within two steps; but Kant's main reason for separating the two steps is their distinctive contribution to an understanding of the origins of knowledge. This result is compatible with the analysis of the logical relations between the conclusions of the two steps that I gave in 1969.

5. One could show that a clear connection exists between Kant's claim that philosophy is based on natural reflection and his affiliation to Rousseau, in whose work the ordinary man in a sense knows everything from the very beginning.

6. A few pages later he refers to it as "the I of reflection."

7. The deduction of the categories has still to be given for features of the "I think" that are not in focus when the general notion of reflection is discussed: its quasi-Cartesian status and its relation to truth and the form of a proposition as such.

GUYER: Psychology and the Deduction

1. Translations from the *Critique of Pure Reason* are my own, based on the text by Raymund Schmidt (Hamburg, 1926).

2. Although Locke also thinks little needs to be said about the last of these.

3. Thomas Hobbes, *De Corpore*, ch. 1, art. 2, in *Body, Man, and Citizen*, ed. R. S. Peters (New York, 1962), p. 24.

4. Thomas Hobbes, *Human Nature*, ch. 4, art. 10, in Peters, p. 194.

5. David Hume, *A Treatise of Human Nature*, ed. L. A. Selby-Bigge, 2d ed. rev. P. H. Nidditch (Oxford, 1978), I, III, vi, p. 89.

6. See generally, Hume, *Treatise*, I, III, iii, pp. 76–82, and I, III, vi, pp. 86–89.

7. *Ibid.*, I, III, iii, p. 82.

8. *Ibid.*, I, III, vi, p. 92.

9. *Ibid.*, I, III, viii, p. 98.

10. *Ibid.*, I, III, xiv, p. 156.

11. *Ibid.*, p. 165.

12. *Ibid.*, I, III, vi, p. 94.

13. *Ibid.*, I, IV, i, p. 180.

14. *Ibid.*, p. 181.

15. *Ibid.*, p. 182.

16. *Ibid.*

17. *Ibid.*, p. 183.

18. *Ibid.*, p. 185.

19. *Ibid.*, p. 183.

20. J. N. Tetens, *Philosophische Versuche* (rpt. Berlin, 1911), essay I, sec. x, p. 77.

21. Hume considers an apparent counterexample to this psychological explanation, a tendency to venture causal inferences upon single experiments, but deals with it essentially by widening the relevant likeness-classes of causes and effects to which the new case is connected so that his generalization will still hold. See Hume, *Treatise*, I, III, viii, pp. 104–5.

22. *Ibid.*, p. 108.

23. David Hume, *An Enquiry Concerning Human Understanding*, ed. L. A. Selby-Bigge, 3d ed. rev. P. H. Nidditch (Oxford, 1975), sec. IV, p. 24.

24. Hume, *Treatise*, Introduction, p. xx.

25. *Ibid.*, p. xvi.

26. J. N. Tetens, Introduction, p. iv.

27. Paul Guyer, "Kant on Apperception and A Priori Synthesis," *American Philosophical Quarterly*, 17 (1980): 205–12; idem, "Kant's Tactics in the Transcendental Deduction," *Philosophical Topics*, 12 (1981): 157–99, especially sec. IIA; and idem, *Kant and the Claims of Knowledge* (Cambridge, Eng., 1987), ch. 5.

28. P. F. Strawson, *The Bounds of Sense* (London, 1966), p. 32.

29. My grounds for this claim are spelled out in "The Failure of the B-Deduction," *Southern Journal of Philosophy*, 25, supplementary volume (1987): 67–84, and in *Kant and the Claims of Knowledge*, ch. 4.

30. Paul Guyer, "Kant's Intentions in the Refutation of Idealism," *Philosophical Review*, 92 (1983): 329–84; and idem, *Kant and the Claims of Knowledge*, part IV.

S T R A W S O N : The Doctrine of Synthesis

1. Ludwig Wittgenstein, *Tractatus Logico-Philosophicus*, trans. D. F. Pears and B. F. McGuinness (London, 1961), 5.47. I have argued the same point myself in a lengthier and more cumbersome way in "Logical Form and Logical Constants," in *Logical Form, Predication and Ontology*, ed. Pranab Kumar Sen (India, 1982), pp. 1–17.

2. In introductory lectures regularly given at Oxford University; see also P. F. Strawson, *Analyse et métaphysique* (Paris, 1985), p. 66.

3. See P. F. Strawson, "Imagination and Perception," in *Freedom and Resentment* (rpt. London, 1974), and in *Kant on Pure Reason*, ed. R. C. S. Walker (rpt. Oxford, 1982).

R A W L S : Themes in Kant

This essay draws upon three lectures circulated at Johns Hopkins University in the summer of 1983, where discussions of Kant's moral philosophy were held. The presentation here is considerably abbreviated in parts and at places much revised. In making these changes, I am especially grateful to Stephen Engstrom, Michael Friedman, Michael Hardimon, Barbara Herman, Wilfried Hinsch, and T. M. Scanlon. Discussion with them has been enormously helpful and their criticisms led to many improvements.

1. Modulo a few minor variations, my account of the CI-procedure in §1 follows closely that of Onora (Nell) O'Neill in her *Acting on Principle* (New York, 1975). See also Paul Dietrichson, "When is a Maxim Universalizable?," *Kant-Studien*, 56 (1964). I have followed Barbara Herman in supposing that when we apply the CI-procedure we are to assume that the agent's maxim is rational. See her "Morality as Rationality: A Study in Kant's Ethics," Ph.D. thesis, Harvard, 1976.

2. On this presupposition, see the instructive discussion by Barbara Herman, "The Practice of Moral Judgment," *Journal of Philosophy*, 82 (1985).

3. In describing these steps many refinements are glossed over. I am indebted to Reinhard Brandt for illuminating discussions on this score. But as I have said, the account need only be accurate enough to set the stage for the themes of moral constructivism and the authentication of the moral law, and the rest.

4. In adopting this way out we are amending, or adding to, Kant's account. It is, I think, Kantian in spirit provided that, as I believe, it doesn't compromise the essential elements of his doctrine.

5. The German is: "Will man aber dem sittlichen Gesetze zugleich Eingang verschaffen." Kant's meaning here is obscure; see below at last par. of §1.

6. I am indebted to Michael Friedman for clarification on this point.

7. John Silber, "The Copernican Revolution in Ethics: The Good Reexamined," *Kant-Studien*, 51 (1959).

8. This description is Peter Hylton's.

9. For this, see Michael Friedman, "The Metaphysical Foundations of Newtonian Science," in *Kant's Philosophy of Science*, ed. R. E. Butts (Dordrecht, 1986).

10. It should be noted that this content can never be specified completely. The moral law is an idea of reason, and since an idea of reason can never be fully realized, neither can the content of such an idea. It is always a matter of approximating thereto, and always subject to error and correction.

11. For the importance of this change I agree with much of Karl Amerik's valuable discussion in his *Kant's Theory of Mind* (Oxford, 1982), ch. VI. He discusses the views of L. W. Beck and H. J. Paton who have tried to preserve the continuity of Kant's doctrine and have denied the fundamental nature of the change.

12. For this view, and in my account of Kant's conception of the role of reason generally, I have been much indebted for some years to Susan Neiman. Now see her "The Unity of Reason: Rereading Kant," Ph.D. thesis, Harvard 1986.

13. See A644/B672: "Reason has . . . as its sole object the understanding and its effective application. Just as the understanding unifies the manifold in the object by means of concepts, so reason unifies the manifold of concepts by means of ideas, positing a certain collective unity as the goal of the activities of the understanding." Observe here that reason is *normative* in relation to the understanding and sets a goal for its activities. The understanding itself has no grasp of this goal; indeed, it cannot set goals for itself at all. Moreover, whereas the activities of the understanding are spontaneous in the sense that it operates by applying its own concepts and categories in constituting the experience of objects, and it is not, as Hume thinks, governed by natural psychological laws (for example, the laws of association of ideas), the understanding is, nevertheless, not free. It is pure reason that is free. See also A669–95/B697–723.

14. Dieter Henrich has made a study of these arguments in the *Nachlaß* and he suggests that when Kant speaks of "this vainly sought deduction" of the moral law he has his own failure in mind. See "Der Begriff der sittlichen Einsicht und Kants Lehre vom Faktum der Vernunft," in *Die Gegenwart der Griechen im neuern Denken*, ed. Dieter Henrich et al. (Tübingen, 1960), pp. 239–47. I am much indebted to this essay.

15. As Lewis White Beck says, we might expect Kant to carry out a critical regression on the presuppositions of moral experience. See *A Commentary on Kant's Critique of Practical Reason* (Chicago, 1960), p. 171.

16. This way of deducing the moral law seems to be suggested by Ernst Cassirer in *Kant's Life and Thought* (New Haven, 1981), pp. 238–47, esp. pp. 239–43, but it is not very far developed.

17. At CP 5:36–38 (in the last remark of §8), there is some critical discussion of utilitarianism but it does not, I think, affect what is said in the text.

18. There are three ideas of freedom in Kant that need to be distinguished and related in an account of the practical point of view: those of acting under the idea of freedom, of practical freedom, and of transcendental freedom. Unhappily, I cannot consider them here.

19. The third and strongest way in which the moral law might suffice to determine the will would seem to be this: we read Kant to say in the *Doctrine of Virtue* that the ends of all our actions must be ends that are also duties. The only leeway that now remains is in the weight we are allowed to give to these ends and in the choice of the most effective means to achieve them. The ordinary pleasures of life are permissible only insofar as they are required to preserve our self-respect and sense of well-being and good health, essential if we are conscientiously and intelligently to fulfill our duties. This is one interpretation of Kant's so-called rigorism, but I shall not pursue it here.

20. Kant is not everywhere consistent in his use of humanity but usually it means what is indicated in the text. Recall that, when Kant's doctor, then rector of the university, came to visit him in his last days, Kant, wasted and

enfeebled, struggled from his chair to his feet. When the rector asked him to sit down, he seemed reluctant to do so. E. A. C. Wasianski, who knew Kant's courteous way of thinking and highly proper manners, assured the rector that Kant would sit down as soon as the rector, the visitor, did. The rector seemed dubious about this reason, but was quickly convinced when Kant said with great effort after collecting his strength: "Das Gefühl für Humanität hat mich noch nicht verlassen." By which he implied: "I can still act as I should, so I must stand until my visitor sits." This well-known incident nicely illustrates the meaning of humanity. It is described in Cassirer, p. 412.

ALLISON : Justification and Freedom

1. Dieter Henrich, "Der Begriff der sittlichen Einsicht und Kants Lehre vom Faktum der Vernunft," in *Kant. Zur Deutung seiner Theorie von Erkennen und Handeln*, ed. G. Prauss (Köln, 1973), pp. 107–10.

2. I give my account of the argument of *Groundwork* III and of the reasons for its failure in "The Hidden Circle in *Groundwork* III," forthcoming.

3. A recent and forceful advocate of this line of criticism is Gerold Prauss, *Kant über Freiheit als Autonomie* (Frankfurt, 1983), esp. pp. 66–70.

4. Lewis White Beck, *A Commentary on Kant's Critique of Practical Reason* (Chicago, 1960), p. 166. See also CP 5:6, 31, 42, 43, 47, 55, 91, and 104.

5. Beck, *Commentary*, p. 166, note 10.

6. Beck notes (*ibid.*) that on pp. 6, 31, 42, and 43 Kant calls it a "fact"; and on pp. 47, 55, 91, and 104 a "fact as it were" or some equivalent expression.

7. *Ibid.*, pp. 166–67. Beck also notes that Kant cannot speak of the consciousness of freedom as a fact because he denies that we can have an immediate consciousness thereof.

8. *Ibid.*, p. 168, and idem, "The Fact of Reason: An Essay on Justification in Ethics," *Studies in the Philosophy of Kant* (Indianapolis, 1965), pp. 210–11.

9. For example, Jürgen Heinrichs, *Das Problem der Zeit in der praktischen Philosophie Kants* (Bonn, 1968), p. 45, calls it a *quasi-Anschauung*.

10. For an account of these difficulties and their relevance to Kant, see Beck, "The Fact of Reason," pp. 202–4.

11. Beck, *Commentary*, p. 169. A somewhat similar interpretation is advanced by Bernard Rousset, *La doctrine kantienne de l'objectivité* (Paris, 1967), p. 257.

12. This terminology is used by Dieter Henrich to describe the two aspects of the practicality of pure reason, "Das Problem der Grundlegung der Ethik bei Kant und im spekulativen Idealismus," in *Sein und Ethos*, ed. Paulus Engelhardt (Mainz, 1963), p. 356.

13. Kant does claim that pure reason shows itself to be practical through a fact. See CP 5:42 and 56.

14. Beck, *Commentary*, p. 169.   15. *Ibid.*

16. *Ibid.* 17. *Ibid.*

18. *Ibid.*, p. 170. See also Beck, "The Fact of Reason," p. 213.

19. Beck, "The Fact of Reason," p. 213.

20. Beck, *Commentary*, p. 170.

21. See Beck, "The Fact of Reason," p. 213.

22. Jaakko Hintikka, "Cogito, Ergo Sum: Inference or Performance?," *Descartes: A Collection of Critical Essays*, ed. Willis Doney (Garden City, 1967), pp. 108–39.

23. *Ibid.*, p. 122.

24. W. T. Jones, *Morality and Freedom in the Philosophy of Immanuel Kant* (London, 1940), p. 129.

25. Kant himself speaks of "the principle of not acknowledging any duty," which he characterizes as "rational disbelief" and as "free thinking" (*Freigeisterei*) in "What is Orientation in Thinking?" (OT 8:144).

26. Although it is probably unfair to characterize him as an amoralist, the position under consideration has obvious affinities to the view of Bernard Williams, particularly his conception of a "ground project" that cannot be appropriately subjected to an "external" moral test since it is itself the source of all meaning and rational norms for an individual. See especially the essays "Persons, Character and Morality," "Moral Luck," and "Internal and External Reasons," in Bernard Williams, *Moral Luck. Philosophical Papers 1973–1980* (Cambridge, 1981).

27. See A419/B447, A533–34/B561–62. I discuss this issue in *Kant's Transcendental Idealism* (New Haven, 1983), pp. 316–17.

28. Kant there goes on to state that "Without transcendental freedom, which is its proper meaning, and which alone is a priori practical, no moral law and no accountability to it are possible."

29. In a still unpublished paper ("Empirical and Intelligible Character in the *Critique of Pure Reason*"), I have argued that in the first *Critique* Kant provides an incompatibilist account of rational agency in general, not merely of moral agency. I also argued that, given the framework of transcendental idealism, this account is far more plausible than is generally assumed. Even if this latter claim is not accepted, however, it would still be the case that whatever metaphysical difficulties the Kantian theory of freedom is thought to involve would arise at the level of rational agency in general, not that of moral agency.

30. Kant characterizes both apperception and the ultimate ground of the selection of maxims as "acts" in this sense. See, for example, B158n and 423n, and Rel 6:21–23.

31. For Kant on moral interest, see Gr 4:449–50 and CP 5:79–80. In the latter text, he relates it specifically to moral feeling. In both texts, however, he connects it with recognition of the moral law (in the form of a categorical imperative) as binding.

32. I discuss this topic in "Empirical and Intelligible Character in the *Critique of Pure Reason*." The point is not that there cannot be any causal story about the intellectual development or concept acquisition; it is rather that such a story necessarily omits or transforms what is essential to these activities, namely the epistemic spontaneity of the subject.

33. An extremely helpful and lucid account of Kant's internalism is provided by Christine Korsgaard, "Skepticism about Practical Reason," *Journal of Philosophy*, 83 (1986): 5–25.

34. I argue for this in "Empirical and Intelligible Character in the *Critique of Pure Reason*." The main point is simply that he holds that the causal determinants of human actions at the phenomenal level are primarily psychological factors such as the beliefs and desires of the agent.

35. I am grateful to Michael Bratman for pointing out to me a significant lacuna in my original formulation of this argument.

36. See the notorious example of the malicious lie, A554–55/B582–83, and the parallel passage in CP 5:100–101.

37. For Kant's denial of scientific status to empirical psychology, see MFNS 4:468, 471. I discuss some of the problems raised by this denial for Kant's account of the causal explanation of human actions at the phenomenal level in "Empirical and Intelligible Character in the *Critique of Pure Reason*."

38. I am not here denying that respect, considered as a moral feeling, has many phenomenologically accessible features, even though, in contrast to other feelings, it is supposedly practically rather than pathologically generated. In fact, Kant provides a rich, albeit sometimes confusing account of these features in the chapter on "The Incentives of Pure Practical Reason." The point is only that respect for the law is not an introspectively accessible motive as, for example, an inclination would be.

HORSTMANN: Why a Deduction?

This paper benefited from critical comments by Manfred Baum and from stylistic and grammatical improvements kindly suggested by Thomas E. Wartenberg and, especially, by Helen Tartar.

1. See, for example, K. Düsing, *Die Teleologie in Kants Weltbegriff, Kant-Studien Ergänzungsheft*, 96, 2d ed. (Bonn, 1986), p. 38 and p. 51; H. W. Cassirer, *A Commentary on Kant's Critique of Judgment* (London, 1938), p. 176.

2. See, for example, E. Weil, *Problèmes kantiens* (Paris, 1963), p. 8.

3. Concerning the history of the genesis of the *Critique of Judgment*, see G. Tonelli, "La Formazione del testo della Kritik der Urteilskraft," *Revue international de philosophie*, 8 (1954): 423–48; and idem, "Von den verschiedenen Bedeutungen des Wortes Zweckmäßigkeit in der Kritik der Urteilskraft," *Kant-Studien*, 49 (1957–58): 154–66. For a survey of the discussion

concerning this question, see H. Mertens, *Kommentar zur Ersten Einleitung in Kants Kritik der Urteilskraft* (München, 1975), pp. 235–37.

4. M. Liedtke, "Der Begriff der reflektierenden Urteilskraft in Kants Kritik der reinen Vernunft," Ph.D. thesis, Hamburg, 1964, who proceeds on a similar assumption, comes in the end to a very different result from that I am going to argue for, because he is convinced that all the essential elements that characterize Kant's theory of reflective judgment in the first *Critique* presuppose some conception of reflective judgment such as that developed in the third *Critique*.

5. For an understanding of Kant's conception of purposiveness, K. Marc-Wogau, *Vier Studien zu Kants Kritik der Urteilskraft* (Uppsala, 1938), pp. 44–85, is still very important and informative. There is an ambiguity in the meaning of the term "purposiveness of nature," however. This term might be used (a) to claim that nature is purposive with regard to the subject of knowledge or the knowing subject, or (b) to describe nature as purposive in itself or objectively. Although Kant employs this term in both these meanings (and possibly in some others as well), the first meaning is relevant to his discussion of the purposiveness of nature in the Introduction to the third *Critique*. I use "purposiveness of nature" in this first meaning in what follows.

6. This problem is analyzed lucidly in M. Baum, "Die transzendentale Deduktion in Kants Kritiken," Ph.D. thesis, Köln, 1975, pp. 150–60. See also its discussion in Düsing, pp. 103–15, and in Marc-Wogau, pp. 28–34.

7. For a more detailed interpretation of these passages, see W. Bartuschat, *Zum systematischen Ort von Kants Kritik der Urteilskraft* (Frankfurt, 1972), pp. 39–53.

8. N. Kemp Smith, *A Commentary to Kant's Critique of Pure Reason* (London, 1923), p. 547.

9. The main problem of this chapter consists in Kant's claim that the *logical* principle of unity required by reason presupposes a *transcendental* principle of the systematic unity of nature (A651). This seems an odd claim in view of the fact that if there were such a transcendental principle, there would be no need to insist on the purely logical character and therefore merely regulative use of the principle of unity required by reason.

10. An interpretation of this chapter that opposes the "intensive reading of the text" by Kemp Smith and Jonathan Bennett and that defends the (rather un-Kantian) idea of purely regulative transcendental principles is put forward in T. Wartenberg, "Order through Reason. Kant's Transcendental Justification of Science," *Kant-Studien*, 70 (1979): 414–18.

11. Concerning the use of the term "purposiveness" in the first *Critique*, see A686–88 and especially A691.

12. That this is the case even with respect to the very definition of the term

Notes to Pages 169–73

"transcendental knowledge" in the A- and the B-edition of the *Critique of Pure Reason* is shown by T. Pinder, "Kants Begriff der transzendentalen Erkenntnis," *Kant-Studien*, 77 (1986): 1–40.

13. Concerning this point, see the accurate and well-informed analysis by J. D. McFarland, *Kant's Concept of Teleology* (Edinburgh, 1970), ch. 1.

14. An informative account of the details of Kant's view concerning concept acquisition as explained in the first Introduction to the *Critique of Judgment* can be found in Mertens, pp. 115–24. It should be mentioned that Kant addresses the problem of how to acquire empirical concepts already in the Appendix to the Transcendental Dialectic of the *Critique of Pure Reason* (cf. A654). Though he sees in this passage clearly that the possibility of concept acquisition presupposes homogeneity (*Gleichartigkeit*) of the given manifold of sensible data, he does not link the concept of homogeneity to that of purposiveness. Instead, he declares the principle of homogeneity to be a transcendental principle that has objective but indeterminate validity (cf. A663). This introduction of indeterminately valid transcendental principles indicates that Kant, in the *Critique of Pure Reason*, is not in the position to accept the idea of subjectively valid transcendental principles.

15. I take it that the same point is made by Cassirer when he emphasizes in a terminologically rather doubtful way "that the principle of judgment is subjective and objective at the same time" (p. 121).

16. Concerning the philosophical tradition and the historical sources in which Kant's conception of judgment as a mental faculty is founded, see Liedtke, pp. 33–108; and A. Baeumler, *Das Irrationalitätsproblem in der Ästhetik und Logik des 18. Jahrhunderts bis zur Kritik der Urteilskraft* (Tübingen, 1923), pp. 83–95.

17. Kant describes the distinction between determinant and reflective judgment in the Introduction to the *Critique of Judgment* (CJ 5:179). Kant explains in the first Introduction what this description is intended to mean in terms of the mental processes involved in the determination or reflection of a concept: "Judgment can be regarded either as a mere capacity for *reflecting* on a given representation according to a certain principle, to produce a possible concept, or as a capacity for *making determinate* a basic concept by means of a given empirical representation. In the first case it is the *reflective*, in the second the *determinant* judgment. To *reflect* (or to deliberate) is to compare and combine given representations either with other representations or with one's cognitive powers, with respect to a concept which is thereby made possible" (FI 20:211). A critical evaluation of Kant's distinction between two kinds of judgment is to be found in Marc-Wogau, pp. 1–15. J. Kulenkampff, *Kants Logik des ästhetischen Urteils* (Frankfurt, 1978), pp. 34–44, gives a very good analysis of what is involved in Kant's conception of reflective judgment.

18. P. Guyer, *Kant and the Claims of Taste* (Cambridge, Mass., 1979), pp. 64–65.

19. For details of this application, see Düsing, pp. 89–99.

B R A N D T : The Deductions

1. That the mentioned principles of reason are not merely logical, but rather are of a transcendental nature, is the general consensus in the recent secondary literature. See, among others, Helga Mertens, *Kommentar zur Ersten Einleitung in Kants Kritik der Urteilskraft* (München, 1975), pp. 38–45; and Thomas E. Wartenberg, "Order through Reason. Kant's Transcendental Justification of Science," *Kant-Studien*, 70 (1979): 409–23. Wartenberg shows conclusively that the transcendental principle of reason is necessary for the possibility of a systematically made experience. In his comparison of the principles with the rules of chess, however, he does not consider that the transcendental principles in the *Critique of Pure Reason* are shaped by the idea of a maximum of the knowledge of our understanding (cf. A644: "greatest [possible] unity combined with the greatest [possible] extension"; A645: "greatest possible extension"; A655: "systematic completeness"; A665: "the idea of the maximum," which is explained by what follows). Already Max Wundt wrote, following his discussion of the logical interpretation of the principles of reason: "In this sense, the common view would be correct, which wants to assign to ideas a merely methodological function for the regulation of scientific knowledge. Kant, however, is of another opinion. He expressly stresses for each of them that they have not only a logical but also a transcendental meaning." See M. Wundt, *Kant als Metaphysiker* (Stuttgart, 1924), p. 250.

2. N. Kemp Smith already mentions the connection between the principles of reason of 1781 and the *principia convenientiae* of 1770, in N. Kemp Smith, *A Commentary on Kant's Critique of Pure Reason* (London, 1918), p. 548.

3. In this context, Gerhard Lehmann, *Beiträge zur Geschichte und Interpretation der Philosophie Kants* (Berlin, 1969), p. 348 (and agreeing with him, Mertens, p. 172) speaks of an immaterial causality or causality of consciousness and thus blurs the distinction between phenomenal and noumenal determination of the *Willkür*. Lehmann completely misrepresents (pp. 342–49) the analysis of the technic of nature in §§74–78, in that he assumes an unintentional technic, of which Kant does not speak. On the quoted text, see the footnote at CJ 5:26 (with the remark that the technical imperatives belong to theoretical knowledge); see also OS 8:285n.

4. The reason for the systematic priority of aesthetic judgment over teleological judgment lies in this (transcendentally) grounding function of the principle of suitability; see, for instance, FI 20:244–45; CJ 5:194. Mertens,

p. 193, is of the erroneous opinion that the systematic priority of aesthetic judgment imposed itself on Kant "unexpectedly" (see also Wolfgang Bartuschat, *Zum systematischen Ort von Kants Kritik der Urteilskraft* (Frankfurt, 1971), pp. 230–31).

5. In his work from the end of 1787 on "The Use of Teleological Principles in Philosophy," Kant maintains that "the concept of the capacity of a being to act purposively, but without purpose and intention that lies in it or its cause . . . [is] completely fictitious and empty" (8:181). He can and must be of the same opinion in the first Introduction to the *Critique of Judgment* (contrary to Mertens, pp. 155–58), only now giving up the assumption of an intelligence creating intentionally. The work from 1787 (published in 1788) still uses this idea and, consequently, identifies purpose with intention. Georgio Tonelli, "Von den verschiedenen Bedeutungen des Wortes Zweckmäßigkeit in der Kritik der Urteilskraft," *Kant-Studien*, 49 (1957–58): 157, also interprets this passage as indicating that the theory of the *Critique of Judgment* has not yet been developed. He does so, however, in reference to the concept of a purposeless purposiveness (which is not identical with the purpose-structure without intention, that interests us here). Unless one registers this vacillation of Kant's—certainly also influenced by the Spinoza debate—the text of the first Introduction can make no sense in the context of the Kantian writings (see Mertens, pp. 155–59). Mertens is of the opinion that an unintentional purpose is a wooden iron (p. 155), but Kant wants only to use a structure, not to explain teleological causality. In this structure he can, like Aristotle before him, abstract from any intention that posits purposes.

6. Chapter IX of the first Introduction is devoted to the "proof" (FI 20: 234) of this idea. With the conception of a purpose-structure, which is to be thought without an intentionally acting subject, Kant attains to the Aristotelian *causa finalis* as a reflexive form of judgment. In Aristotle, that *causa finalis* of nature is also taken as final cause without a consciousness of purpose (see *Physics*, II 8; and Hans Wagner, *Übersetzung und Erläuterung von: Aristoteles, Physikvorlesungen* (Darmstadt, 1983), pp. 476–77). Like Kant, Aristotle could have spoken of a "technic of nature," but he avoids this paradoxical expression. I believe Kant is the first author to have used this expression.

7. A more detailed exposition is given in my article "Analytic/Dialectic," in *Arguments from Kant*, ed. E. Schaper and W. Vossenkuhl (Oxford, forthcoming).

TUSCHLING: Apperception and Ether

1. I. Kant, *Metaphysicae cum geometria iunctae usus in philosophia naturali, cuius specimen I. continet monadologiam physicam* (Königsberg, 1756).

2. I. Kant, *Principiorum primorum cognitionis metaphysicae nova dilucidatio* (Königsberg, 1755).

3. See Burkhard Tuschling, *Metaphysische und transzendentale Dynamik in Kants opus postumum* (Berlin, 1971).

4. For Kant's treatment of the Refutation of Idealism 1787 and after, see Eckart Förster, "Kant's Refutation of Idealism," in *Philosophy. Its History and Historiography*, ed. A. J. Holland (Dordrecht, 1985), pp. 295–311; and Reinhard Brandt, "Eine neu aufgefundene Reflexion Kants 'Vom inneren Sinne' (Loses Blatt Leningrad 1)," *Kant-Forschungen*, 1 (Hamburg, 1987), pp. 1–30.

5. This formulation appears in the first edition (A370); it is still assumed to be correct in the second edition.

6. For further details, see Tuschling, *Metaphysische und transzendentale Dynamik in Kants opus postumum.*—J. McCall questions some of my central points in "A Response to Burkhard Tuschling's Critique of Kant's Physics," *Kant-Studien*, 79 (1988): 57–79, published after this paper had been completed. I cannot answer his objections here, but I would like to point out: Kant himself later states that, in 1786, he had been moving "in a circle" from which he did not know how to escape (C 11:377); it is Kant who writes in the *Opus postumum* that the *Metaphysical Foundations* "contained no moving forces" (Op 21:478.11–16; cf. Tuschling, pp. 92–100); and in the *Opus postumum* Kant speaks of an absolute totality of perceptions or experience in a manner that, from the viewpoint of the first *Critique*, seems unacceptable. I agree with McCall that one must take seriously Kant's attempt to reconcile his later thoughts with classical transcendental idealism, but this cannot mean attempting to explain away revisions, contradictions, and new conceptualizations.

7. On these drafts, see Eckart Förster, this volume, pp. 217–38.

8. L. E. Borowski, "Darstellung des Lebens und Charakters Immanual Kants," in *Immanual Kant. Sein Leben in Darstellung von Zeitgenossen*, ed. Felix Gross (Darmstadt, 1968), p. 39.

9. "Thus the first beginning of the experience of the existence of such a material is the first immediate community between the sense of one subject and the senses of another; the forms of these senses, in relation to one another, contain the form of space in an a priori intuition (that is, merely within itself) and, with respect to time, they contain the representation of the successive agitation of the representation of sense. Consequently, experience is merely ideal with respect to objects; with respect to the subject, however, it is real representation but not *knowledge* of objects outside me, except with regard to their form."

10. On the "deduction," see Op 21:573.15, 586.19; cf. also the "notes" on the proof, including 216, 221, 222, 223, 226, 229–30, 230–31, 231.8–18, 233.5–14 (deduction of a "matter of experience" (*Erfahrungssache*), of the "permanent appearance of matter," the "universally distributed caloric," "from concepts, that is, according to the rule of identity, from the principle of agreement with the possibility of experience in general"); 238.22, 241.2–17, 537, 538.7–15,

539.19, 545.22–24 ("of the amphiboly of the concepts of reflection in the transition etc."); 546.6–11 (indirect a priori proof of existence); 548–49 (indirect proof from the principle of the possibility of experience, "to derive from this ground of proof its concept of *object*, and to present a priori, through reason, the conditions of the possibility of knowledge of the object, as well as its actuality"); 552.18–22 ("the thought of an elementary system of the moving forces of matter (*cogitatio*) necessarily precedes the perception of them (*perceptio*) and, as a subjective principle of the combination of these elementary parts in a whole, is given a priori by reason in the subject (*forma dat esse rei*)"); 559.6, 560.13–22, 562.3–10, 563.11–15, 564.6–12, 571.14–20, 572.16–20, 573.12, 576.2–14, 576.20–23, 577, 578–79, 580–81, 582.22, 583 and footnote, 585–86, 591–94, 595–96.

11. W. Dilthey, "Die Rostocker Kant-Handschriften," *Archiv für Geschichte der Philosophie*, II (1889): 641.

12. In the reformulation of the Principles, their proofs, the Refutation of Idealism, and the General Note on the System of the Principles.

FÖRSTER: Kant's *Selbstsetzungslehre*

1. See Focko Lüpsen, "Die systematische Bedeutung des Problems der Selbstsetzung in Kants Opus postumum," Ph.D. thesis, Marburg, 1924; Gretchen Krönig, "Das Problem der Selbstsetzung in seiner Entwicklung von Kant bis Fichte mit besonderer Berücksichtigung von J. S. Beck," Ph.D. thesis, Hamburg, 1927; Kurt Hübner, "Das transzendentale Subjekt als Teil der Natur," Ph.D. thesis, Kiel, 1951; Hermann Josef Meyer, "Das Problem der Kantischen Metaphysik unter besonderer Berücksichtigung des Opus postumum," Ph.D. thesis, Tübingen, 1952.

2. See Erich Adickes, *Kants Opus postumum dargestellt und beurteilt, Kant-Studien Ergänzungsheft*, 50 (Berlin, 1920); Gerhard Lehmann, *Beiträge zur Geschichte und Interpretation der Philosophie Kants* (Berlin, 1969), pp. 247–408; idem, *Kants Tugenden* (Berlin, 1980), pp. 1–26, pp. 96–140; Vitorio Mathieu, *La Filosofia transcendentale e l' "opus postumum" di Kant, Biblioteca di Filosofia*, 12 (Torino, 1958).

3. Adickes, p. 668.

4. *Ibid.*, p. 699.

5. Similarly H. J. de Vleeschauwer who writes with regard to self-positing: "Kant has bowed before the spirit of the time. . . . The infinite contortions of the *Opus postumum* serve to hide a conviction and basically to conceal a defeat." *The Development of Kantian Thought* (London, 1962), p. 189.

6. On this point, see esp. Dieter Henrich, *Der ontologische Gottesbeweis* (Tübingen, 1960); Tillman Pinder, "Kants Gedanke vom Grund aller Möglichkeiten," Ph.D. thesis, Berlin, 1969; Josef Schmucker, *Kants vorkritische Kritik der Gottesbeweise* (Mainz, 1983).

7. "*Determinare* est ponere praedicatum cum exclusione oppositi" (Nd, proposition IV, 5:391, cf. A598/B626).

8. For both theses, see my "Is There 'A Gap' in Kant's Critical System?," *Journal for the History of Philosophy*, 25 (1987): 533–55.

9. I thus disagree with Burkhard Tuschling's assessment of the ether in his important *Metaphysische und transzendentale Dynamik in Kants opus postumum* (Berlin, 1971), p. 175: "Was aber ist denn nun dieser Äther? . . . Ist dieser Begriff eines nichtempirischen Gegenstandes ein innerhalb der klassischen kritischen Theorie der Erkenntnis a priori überhaupt möglicher Begriff? Die Antwort ist ein klares Nein." See also Tuschling, this volume, pp. 207, 213.

10. See Adickes, p. 139.

11. See J. H. Tieftrunk, "Anhang zur Prüfung des Beweisgrundes," *Imanuel [sic] Kants vermischte Schriften*, 2 (Halle, 1799), pp. 230–46.

12. In the Preface to his edition, Tieftrunk writes: "Da ich bemerkt habe, daß manche Leser die Prüfung und Beurteilung des 'einzigmöglichen Beweisgrundes zu einer Demonstration des Daseins Gottes' in der Kritik der reinen Vernunft haben vermissen und diese deshalb für unvollständig haben erklären wollen, so habe ich in einem Anhange zu der oben gedachten Abhandlung kürzlich zu zeigen gesucht, daß der gesuchte Beweisgrund eigentlich kein anderer als der ontologische sey, jedoch nicht, wie er gewöhnlich geführt wird, sondern wie er eigentlich geführt werden sollte," p. xi. The Preface is signed January 10, 1799.

13. See Kant's *Reflexionen* 3717, 3888, 4033 (17:260, 328, 391). See also Henrich, pp. 185–88.

14. It is thus at best misleading to say, as Mathieu does, that Kant's ether proof is a new ontological proof. See Mathieu, "Äther und Organismus in Kants 'Opus postumum'," in *Studien zu Kants philosophischer Entwicklung*, ed. H. Heimsoeth, D. Henrich, and G. Tonelli (Hildesheim, 1967), p. 186.

15. "Through the concept the object is thought only as conforming to the universal conditions of *possible* empirical knowledge in general, whereas through its existence it is thought as belonging to the *context* of experience as a whole" (A600–601/B628–29; italics added).

16. It is interesting to note that Georg Christoph Lichtenberg, who had no direct knowledge of Kant's *Opus postumum*, found the doctrine developed there already implicit in Kant's earlier writings: "Eine der größten Stützen für die Kantische Philosophie ist die *gewiß wahre* Betrachtung, daß wir ja auch so gut etwas sind, als die Gegenstände außer uns. Wenn also etwas auf uns wirkt, so hängt die Wirkung nicht allein von dem wirkenden Dinge, sondern auch von dem ab, auf welches gewirkt wird. Beide sind, wie bey dem Stoß, thätig und leidend zugleich; denn es ist unmöglich, daß ein Wesen die Einwirkungen eines andern empfangen kann, ohne daß die Haupt-

wirkung gemischt erscheine. Ich sollte denken, eine bloße tabula rasa ist in dem Sinne unmöglich, denn durch jede Einwirkung wird das einwirkende Ding modifizirt, und das, was ihm abgeht, geht dem andern zu, und umgekehrt." *Georg Christoph Lichtenberg's vermischte Schriften*, 2, ed. Ludwig Christian Lichtenberg and Friedrich Kries (Göttingen, 1801), pp. 92–93.

17. "The properties of this world-material are (1) that it is *imponderable*. For ponderability presupposes the capacity of a machine—that is, the moving forces of a body as instrument of motion; this itself presupposes, in turn, the internally moving forces of a penetrating material, able to produce, by means of the inner motion of the constituent parts of the lifting device, the capacity to move. (2) *incoercible*. For any body coercing this matter (a container) could have such a force only in virtue of a property which must be presupposed in order to resist the expansion of the material. (3) *incohesible* in regard to all its parts, neither fluid nor solid matter, but repulsive. (4) *inexhaustible* with respect to even the smallest quantity. All this regarded in a whole" (Op 21:231.28–232.12).

18. Adickes, pp. 237, 236.

19. Lehmann, *Kants Tugenden*, p. 273.   20. *Ibid.*, p. 121.

21. Adickes, p. 241.   22. *Ibid.*

V U I L L E M I N : Kant's "Dynamics"

1. Burkhard Tuschling, this volume, pp. 208, 215.

2. *Ibid.*, p. 216.

3. Eckart Förster, this volume, p. 226, and his note 8.

4. When invited by Professor Förster to participate in this section, I answered that I was not an expert on the *Opus postumum*, and we agreed that I should not have to examine whether the proposed interpretations of this text were historically sound.

5. Tuschling, this volume, pp. 200–201.

6. *Ibid.*, p. 203.

7. As Professor Tuschling put it in the original version of his paper. For the notion "transcendental dynamics," see also his *Metaphysische und transzendentale Dynamik in Kants opus postumum* (Berlin, 1971).

8. Tuschling, this volume, pp. 200, 211.

9. See J. Vuillemin, *Physique et métaphysique kantiennes* (Paris, 1955), pp. 335–37.

10. More exactly, Kepler's law of areas and the third law.

11. The mention of the proportionality of attraction to quantity of matter in Dynamics, proposition 8, note 1, anticipates Mechanics and is not presupposed in the definition of dynamical attraction.

12. Louis Guillermit, *L'élucidation critique du jugement de goût selon Kant* (Paris, 1986), p. 82, pp. 143–47.

13. Förster, this volume, p. 231.

14. Vuillemin, pp. 129–94.

15. *Ibid.*, p. 167.

16. Richard P. Feynman, Robert B. Leighton, Matthew Sands, *The Feynman Lectures on Physics* I (Reading, Mass., 1970), pp. 12–13.

17. *Ibid.*, pp. 12–19.

Index of Persons

Index of Persons

Haering, T., 17, 249
Hamann, J. G., 250
Hampshire, S., 176, 187, 188
Hayms, R., 249
Hegel, G. W. F., 30, 158, 207
Heidegger, M., 250
Heimsoeth, H., 265
Heinrichs, J., 256
Henkel, A., 250
Henrich, D., 69–70, 104, 115, 252,
    255f, 264f
Herder, J. G., 227
Herman, B., 254
Herz, M., 4–11 *passim*, 16f, 21ff, 201, 249
Hintikka, J., 120, 133, 257
Hobbes, T., 49f, 55, 95, 140, 252
Holland, A. J., 263
Horstmann, R.-P., 177–78
Hübner, K., 264
Hume, D., 25–26, 50–57 *passim*, 61,
    65–68 *passim*, 74–77 *passim*, 93–97
    passim, 156, 195, 198, 209, 253, 255
Huygens, C., 245
Hylton, P., 254

Jacobi, F. H., 250
Jones, W. T., 121, 257

Kepler, J., 242, 266
Kiesewetter, J. G. C. C., 218
Knutzen, M., 193, 198
Korsgaard, C., 258
Kries, F., 266
Krönig, G., 264
Kulenkampf, J., 260

Lambert, J. H., 204
Lehmann, G., 217, 230, 235–37, 261,
    264, 266
Leibniz, G. W., 25, 36, 41, 61, 66, 93–97
    passim, 146ff, 193–99 *passim*, 207, 209,
    214f, 220
Leighton, R. B., 267
Le Verrier, U. J. J., 241–43
Lichtenberg, G. C., 216, 265–66
Lichtenberg, L. C., 266
Liedtke, M., 259f
Locke, J., 36, 48–49, 55, 252
Lüpsen, F., 264

Maimon, S., 215
Marc-Wogau, K., 259f
Mathieu, V., 217, 264f

McCall, J., 263
McFarland, J. D., 260
McGuinnes, B. F., 253
Meier, G. F., 4
Mertens, H., 259–62 *passim*
Meyer, H. J., 264
Moore, G. E., 95–98 *passim*

Napoleon I, 33
Neiman, S., 254
Newton, I., 98, 155, 193, 241–46 *passim*
Nidditch, P. H., 252f

Ockham, W. of, 129
O'Neill, O., 254

Pascal, B., 153
Paton, H. J., 18, 96, 250, 254
Pears, D. F., 253
Peters, R. S., 252
Pinder, T., 260, 264
Plato, 21, 95, 97
Prauss, G., 250, 256
Price, R., 95
Pütter, J. S., 33–38 *passim*, 251
Pyrrho, 115

Rawls, J., 136–41 *passim*
Reinhold, K. L., 160
Repton, H., 152
Riehl, A., 18, 250
Ross, W. D., 95–98 *passim*
Rousseau, J.-J., 252
Rousset, B., 256
Rüdiger, A., 41

Sands, M., 267
Schaper, E., 262
Schwan, A., 252
Schelling, F. W. J., 158, 202, 207f, 215f
Schiller, F., 145
Schmidt, R., 252
Schmucker, J., 264
Schultz, J., 18, 250
Schütz, C. G., 18
Selby-Bigge, L. A., 252f
Sen, P. K., 253
Shakespeare, W., 152
Sidgwick, H., 95–98 *passim*
Silber, J., 254
Smith, N. K., 25, 166, 251, 259, 261
Spinoza, B., 216, 262
Strawson, P. F., 20, 56, 249f, 253

Library of Congress Cataloging-in-Publication Data

Kant's transcendental deductions.

(Stanford series in philosophy. Studies in Kant and German
idealism)
    Includes index.
    I. Kant, Immanuel, 1724–1804. I. Förster, Eckart.
II. Series.
B2798.K227   1989   193   88-34920
ISBN 0-8047-1583-1 (alk. paper)
ISBN 0-8047-1717-6 (pbk. : alk. paper)